RECOLLECTIONS OF
LOGAN PEARSALL SMITH

By the same Author

———

THREE ACRES AND A MILL
(Dent)

WILD FLOWERS IN BRITAIN
(Batsford)

ROBERT GATHORNE-HARDY

RECOLLECTIONS
OF
LOGAN PEARSALL
SMITH

The Story of a Friendship

CONSTABLE · LONDON

LONDON

PUBLISHED BY

Constable and Company Ltd.

10–12 ORANGE STREET, W.C.2

INDIA *and* PAKISTAN

Orient Longmans Ltd.

BOMBAY   CALCUTTA   MADRAS

CANADA

Longmans, Green and Company

TORONTO

First published 1949

Printed in Great Britain by the Shenval Press
London and Hertford

DEDICATED
WITH AFFECTION AND GRATITUDE
TO
ALYS RUSSELL

INTRODUCTION

I feel it a privilege to endorse this book about my brother, Logan Pearsall Smith, by my friend Robert Gathorne-Hardy, 'the passionate apprentice', as I often think of him. I shall always feel grateful for the great happiness he gave to my brother's later middle years, and now I am additionally grateful for this glowing picture of his work and personality.

That their friendship ended under the sad cloud of my brother's last long illness was a tragedy indeed, but one that needs to be told in any faithful biography. My brother would be the first to wish the whole truth to be told, as a partial portrait can never be a faithful nor a lasting one.

From time to time younger friends would ask for his opinion when they were at work on memoirs or recollections. His advice was always firmly given, 'Tell the truth'. But I cannot do better in this respect than to quote the words of our old friend who, as my brother has written, had so profound an influence upon him, 'Do not prettify me,' said Walt Whitman to Horace Traubel; 'Be sure to write about me honest: whatever you do do not prettify me: include all the hells and damns.'

ALYS RUSSELL

AUTHOR'S PROLOGUE

I first got to know Logan Pearsall Smith towards the end of 1928. Our acquaintance very soon deepened into a close and intimate friendship, which endured up to a week or so of his death. The qualification is a painful one, and it might be said that a death-bed estrangement needs no mentioning.

'I find,' he wrote to me in 1943, 'that people are really afraid of their dead, and have that primitive notion that the dead are malicious and dangerous—the *nil nisi bonum,* and the widow's weeds and mourning wives put on are really disguises.'

'I hope,' he would often say to me in talk, 'that you won't kill me all over again after I'm dead.'

All the truth doesn't always have to be told; some revelations indeed, however exact, are in themselves a wounding of essential truth. But that once during our acquaintance Logan Pearsall Smith became insane, and that his last years went by in a state of growing craziness—these are facts of prime concern in understanding, not only the man, but what he would have looked upon as far more important, the artist as well.

Prehistoric beasts have sometimes been reconstructed in their entirety from no more than a handful of bone. Every now and then, however, as with the ichthyosaurus, a whole skeleton turns up, with impressions of its perishable parts outlined upon the rock, to confirm or confound the conjectures of palaeontologists, and to illustrate other, unreconstructed fragments. So have men done in the study of an artist's mind, working often from guesswork, and from half-correlated facts. In Logan Pearsall Smith we have, as it were, the entire bodily structure, and a chance of reconstructing those parts which would, in the usual course of time and oblivion, perish and be lost.

Few other writers can have left behind them material for so complete a portrait, or so deep an analysis, as he did. Huge bundles of rough drafts, hundreds of letters, innumerable anecdotes in the memories of friends—these are all available; in addition to this he carried out a large part of his work in company. I was present and assisting when most of his books and essays were being written from 1929 onwards. During the seventeen years and more of our friendship I do not think a greater period than twelve weeks ever went by without our meeting, and so long as that on but two or three occasions. As a rule I saw him once a week, or at least once a fortnight; frequently I was in his company for days on end.

From a huge store of memories, I have presented, as best I could, the portrait of my friend, illustrating his character with anecdotes, many of which, in themselves, are trivial, and some distressing. Others I have added when it seemed to me that they might aid those best qualified to elucidate the darker recesses of his spirit. If I may seem to have obtruded too much of my own person and my own work—well, the verity and value of a narration can the better be estimated, when the character and temper of the narrator is ascertainable. We can judge best the truth of an anecdote by knowing the teller of it.

'Still,' as he himself once wrote in a letter to me, 'all this inner argument and self-defence are obvious proofs of a sense of guilt, and a kind of self-contempt.'

It will for long be a matter of ascertainable fact that my old friend, after I had been at his side for many years, turned, in the very gates of death, to cut me off from his friendship. It will be equally evident that I must have written down these recollections with that fact painfully and evidently in my mind. To be despised and rejected has a more than honourable precedent; nevertheless philosophers allow a man, without loss of dignity, to defend his reputation and good name. I cannot say that there is nothing of self-defence in the following pages. This, however, I can say, I have never willingly or knowingly perverted the truth in my record, nor have I at any time consciously attempted to distort the narrative into an apologia. I have written down no conjectures without first making clear that I was doing so.

Another source of prejudice might be imputed to me. It will easily be deduced that, on account of this last sad gesture, I was exposed to another loss, and one that could be measured by material standards. No one, until he has experienced such a loss, can tell by what feelings he may, in consequence, become possessed. It is incumbent upon me to explain why there was no particular danger of my story being perverted by such feelings.

The only man to whom a remedy was possible became my friend, and so adjusted things, that I could not feel a sense of grosser loss. Few men would·have done this; of those who had thought of it, most would have carried out their plan on the scheme of high intentions and low accomplishment laid down by Jane Austen at the beginning of *Sense and Sensibility*. My friend, however, not only made over to me certain rights of personal value, but gave me as well so much of material worth as largely removed the loss which, it might be held, could otherwise have warped and perverted my backward vision.

Therefore, in acknowledging the permission kindly given to print in this book many extracts and letters from my correspondence with Logan Pearsall Smith, I must also record a gratitude, too large to be easily measured or expressed, for the benefits and generosity towards me of Mr John Russell.

I must also express my deeply felt gratitude, for their help and advice in the writing and shaping of this book, to Mrs Alys Russell, the sister of Logan Pearsall Smith: to Mr Bernard Berenson, his brother-in-law: and to his niece, Miss Julia Strachey.

Finally, I must record my deep regret that the death of Miss Hilda Trevelyan has made it impossible to acknowledge publicly to her my gratitude for allowing me to use in this book her charming and truthful little portrait of Logan Pearsall Smith.

R.G–H.

xi

1928

As a relationship survives most pervadingly its nightfall in the death of a friend, so may its dawn sometimes follow a propitious lark-light, a happily foreboding crepuscule.

While I was growing into a man, I loved the poems of John Donne with a passion which, I sometimes feel, can have beset in its full intensity only young men of the 1920's, and of the early seventeenth century. To satisfy our insatiable affection Logan Pearsall Smith produced, in 1920, his *Selected Passages from the Sermons of John Donne*. In the summer of 1921 I spent part of the long vacation at Oxford, working for an exam. Although I had begun to study medicine, literature, my true love, was already laying siege to my heart. I had discovered Sir Thomas Browne, and wondering what other marvels of prose that dark and starry period of our literature might reveal, I took notice of some names mentioned by Pearsall Smith in his introductory essay on Donne; among these was Jeremy Taylor's. The next time I was in Blackwell's I searched among the alphabetically ranged books and, coming on a small seventeenth-century volume called *B. Taylor's Opuscula*, I took it out and turned the pages idly over. Suddenly—it was like some bright, gay, physical apparition, of stars, or flowers, or coloured lights—I came on a noticeable passage and read this—

'For thus the Sun is the eye of the World; and he is indifferent to the Negro, or the Cold Russian, to them that dwell under the line, and them that stand near the Tropicks, the scalded Indian, or the poor boy that shakes at the foot of the Riphean hills . . . and some have only a dark day and a long night from him, snows and white cattel, a miserable life, and a perpetual harvest of Catarrhes and Consumptions, apoplexies and dead palsies; but some have splendid fires, and aromatick spices, rich wines, and well-digested fruits, great wit and great courage; because they dwell in his eye, and look in his face, and are the Courtiers of the Sun, and wait upon him in his Chambers of the East.'

Seven years or so later I was working in an antiquarian bookshop. I was 26 years of age. Medicine had gone by the board, and after it a lawyer's profession. I had worked on the staff of a monthly magazine:

idled a year or two: and here I was, if not living fully a life of letters, at least earning an income from the sale of literature. I had started work, in spare time, on my first novel. I still read Jeremy Taylor, and was collecting material for a bibliography of his writings.

My brother Eddie was a partner, senior to me, in the same business. We worked, at separate desks, in a large book-walled room on the first floor. My own desk was in a well-lit alcove; behind were modern first editions, and in front of me books mainly of the seventeenth century, including a nice little stock of Jeremy Taylors.

One day I heard a slow shuffling step, as a customer came upstairs into the room. Then, in a quiet, rather shy voice he asked Eddie, 'Have you got any first editions of Jeremy Taylor?'

'You'd better see my brother,' said Eddie, 'he knows more about Jeremy Taylor than I do,' and he called me over.

I saw a largish man with a stoop that disguised his height; it wasn't so much that he appeared fat, as that his weight seemed too much for his strength. His back and shoulders and legs were curved; his neck appeared crushed down by his head against his shoulders. His spectacles rested on a long and pointed nose (the nose so faithfully exaggerated in Max's caricature); his hat was straight on his head, with grey hair showing behind it; his clothes were nondescript and expensively respectable. It might have been a well-to-do elderly clergyman who chose not to wear his clerical collar.

Almost at once we were talking passionately about Jeremy Taylor.

'I'm making a book of selections from his works,' said the customer. 'I've already done one from Donne, and I think Taylor needs it too.'

'You're Mr Pearsall Smith,' I said.

'Yes,' he breathed rather than uttered this assent, hiding, with blank features, an exultation far larger than I could possibly have dreamed of at the time.

'You ought to include a bibliography,' I suggested.

'I'm doing one,' he answered, and pulled out of his pocket part of what was no more than a meagre check-list.

'I've been working on a more detailed one,' I said, and took my notes out of a drawer in my desk. 'You can have my notes, if you like.'

'This is far beyond me,' he said, as he looked at them with gratifying admiration. 'You must do the job. I'm sure the Oxford Press would like to print it with my selections. Come to lunch with me and we'll talk it over.'

He bought a copy of Taylor's *Doctrine and Practice of Repentance*, fixed a day for lunch, and left the shop.

If my narrative is to be honest I shall have plenty of curious abuse to record; the picture would be false without it. To leave out the sometimes intemperate praise I often received would equally deface the truth. I had no idea at the time that I was leaving any particular personal impression. Absolute Taylorians make up a very small society, and they will forgive all social and moral offences among themselves in order to talk over their bright particular saint. It was natural, I felt, that we should have fallen thus upon one another's intellectual bosoms.

More than 17 years later, during the last of all my painful visits to him, and when his crazed spirit had turned against me, he said, in a moment of calm, 'That time when I first saw you in the shop, I said to myself, "This is one of the finest flowers of English civilization, Eton and Christchurch". It has been suggested to me,' he went on, quite in his old manner, 'that there's another flower equally fine. Can you guess what it's supposed to be? Harrow and Magdalen! Don't you feel that that's altogether a shocking idea?'

As I said, I wasn't in the least aware then of the personal illumination he imputed to me. We met as 'milvers'[1] to use a fill-gap word, which Pearsall Smith had invented for an unappreciative world.

1929

His selection from Jeremy Taylor was complete by this time; only a critical introduction needed finishing off, and the first letter I ever had from him was in answer to a suggestion of mine that he should include in this introduction a pleasant anecdote about the young Jeremy Taylor. This he did, as a footnote; 'I must look up those anecdotes of Jeremy,' he wrote (15.1.29). 'But I am not, of course, pretending to write his life.'

I now began to see him regularly; sometimes I got leave to absent

---

[1] This word he deliberately made up as filling with wanted meaning a vacant sound; he introduced it publicly to the world in *Afterthoughts*: 'But what festivals of unanimity we celebrate when we meet what I call a "Milver"—a fellow-fanatic whose thoughts chime in a sweet ecstasy of execration with our own!' Before this, it had actually made independently a little quiet progress. A favourite boast of his was that a stranger had once asked him the etymological origin of this word.

myself from work and we would make short expeditions. Among the first of these was a visit to Mr Geoffrey Keynes.

'I think you would like to see his books,' he wrote to me (23.2.29), 'though to me, when I went before, it was rather heart-breaking—I felt that I had wasted my life, and been walking all these years in a vain show. Still, it is something to have a glimpse of the ideal, even if one knows one will never attain it. You, however, being young; and with your life before you, need not be afflicted by these melancholy reflections.

'Have you, by the way, any pins you can stick into Geoffrey Keynes, any Donne or Sir Thomas Browne items he hasn't mentioned, or has described inaccurately? If so do bring them along. He had stuck a pin into me, by calling my book a book of *Beauties* (which it is) though he swears that he did not mean to be offensive. But offence was taken; and being as I am—or hope I am—of a violent and vindictive nature, I should like to avenge myself upon him. Anyhow modern psychology tells us that we ought to avenge injuries at once, because otherwise our suppressed feelings may come out in boils and pimples.

'By the way, Keynes writes "Three of my sons have whooping cough" . . . I hope this won't deter you—he is a surgeon, and ought to know if there is any danger. But imagine writing "Three of my sons"! What procreative fervour—I am glad that such a phrase will never drop from my chaste pen.'

The visit, as I remember, was a success. Pearsall Smith had thought of mentioning, as a pin-prick, that he once owned a superb painting by Blake (a special author and artist of Mr Keynes's predilection), and had been swindled in the sale of it. I, it seems to me now, must have been possessed by a fiercer jealousy than I realized, for I recollect few separate treasures but only an enormous envy and an undefined agglomeration of bibliographical marvels.

A few days later he wrote (6.3.29) telling me that the Oxford Press would like to print my bibliography as an appendix to the *Golden Grove;* he went on to say that they were reluctant, for financial reasons, to reproduce Jeremy Taylor's portrait in the book;

'but I shall insist on this, for I am sure, as I tell them, that his ghost will like it. Don't you think it will? I am sure you will agree with me.

'I long to go over your bibliography, and if I could find a mistake in it I should indeed be happy.[1] But I have no hope of this. A good

---

[1] There were errors in it, of course; but he never had the satisfaction of discovering any of them.

4

bibliography is to me above the price of rubies, although these jewels have I believe gone up of late immensely in value . . .

'I so much enjoyed our trip to St John's Wood [that is, to Mr Keynes], and your company added greatly to my enjoyment. I felt for one thing that you appreciated the moral beauty of my refusal to use my stiletto when Geoffrey Keynes, by talking of Blake's drawings, bared, so to speak, his bosom to the blow.

'I really believe that my New Year's resolution to be a nicer person and lead a better life is beginning to bear its fruit. I cannot honestly say however that any of my friends have remarked the change. It will burst on them, and blind them, I hope with its sudden effulgence.

'I sent Keynes a rare little volume of Henry James, and have had a most friendly letter in return. So I hope our warfare is accomplished, though I feel—didn't you feel it the other day?—that he has a pin-sticking nature. I cannot condemn him for this, for I am myself not exempt from this failing, and have just stuck a whole pincushion full into Robert Bridges, who however asked for it, as it were, when he sent me some proofs and asked for my comments. This was more than human flesh—even redeemed human flesh like mine—could resist. But he is well-equipped with weapons of retaliation, and I dare say I shall get the worst of it in the end.'

I have the pleasure of no more than the most casual acquaintance with Mr Keynes, and I don't know of any reason for imputing a 'pin-sticking nature' to him. But of this I am quite certain; he would have been vastly surprised had he known then that Logan Pearsall Smith supposed a state of warfare between them.

At other times I would go out with him, to look around other London bookshops. After one of these sorties, he wrote me the following letter. The binding he alludes to was on a copy of Jeremy Taylor's *Golden Grove*; it is a beautiful object—I possess it now—made by Mearne, or one of his contemporary imitators.

'I find myself haunted now and then,' he wrote to me from Hampshire (26.3.29), 'by that binding we saw at Pickering's—it glimmers and atracts me, and when I return to London I shall steal guiltily back and have another look at it, if it isn't sold. But my better self hopes that it will be sold, for my better self views these lusts of the eye with disapprobation.

'At present I am out of temptation, as I have come to my house down here to recuperate after two attacks of influenza, and breathe, like the King, the sea air and the south-west wind. Already, like the King, I am much recuperated—but no bulletins are issued. Desmond MacCarthy is with me, and we spend much time denouncing this generation of vipers as we walk by the sad sea shore.'

Mr Desmond MacCarthy was publishing, in *Life and Letters* (April 1929), the essay on Jeremy Taylor, and he goes on to say

'When I read the proofs I hated the article and thought it wretched and worthless; but it may be better than I think. There is no blacker moment than when one first sees a piece of one's own prose in print. Later on it may shimmer and gleam again, but the first sight of it is awful.

'There is another awful meditation that visits me sometimes when I lie awake at night—the fearful thought namely that when *The Golden Grove* is published, you will point out to me lovely passages that I have overlooked and omitted. That nightingale you quoted sings in my ears a dolorous song—I haven't dared to look up the passage.'[1]

A little after this he wrote to me, still from Hampshire (11.4.29):

'I very much liked your bibliography in *Life and Letters*—.[2] I thought it exactly what was pleasant and appropriate. I begin to suspect that you know more about J. T. than I do; whether I like you or hate you for this is another question—probably the two ingredients are not unpleasantly mingled in my breast.

'. . . ominous to my mind is the fact that the BBC is taking up the subject [of sermons as literature] and will begin next month to bellow through space fine passages from old sermons. They offered me some nice money—which I am glad to say I refused—to write in the *Radio Times* a popular introduction to the series. I am by nature a lover of unfrequented shrines, and when the crowds arrive with their litter I am tempted to turn to other altars. Am I to blame for leading on the crowd? My author's vanity—and his vanity is the canker and curse of an author's life—flatters me by saying that I am to blame, but my common sense answers this with the melancholy reflection that we are all Time's children and simply discover what is already in the air. We keep at the most but a few days ahead of the crowd, which would arrive anyhow without our leading. So if a Jeremy Taylor boom is upon us, you and I cannot be blamed, and can console ourselves with the rise in value of our volumes.

[1] This was the sentence I'd shown him 'to be filling the roomes of the understanding with aery and ineffective notions is just such an excellency, as it is in a man to imitate the voice of birds; at his very best, the Nightingale shall excel him'. Wrongly, as I must think, he had not included this among his selected passages.

[2] A check-list, with short comments, which was printed in the same number as his essay.

'I am returning to London and will come to see you at Conduit Street. I want some time to have a serious talk with you about a certain old Bishop of Norwich whose works in an immense folio of 1,400 pages I bought the other day in Southampton, and am now busy in reading.

' "God and his Angels sit upon the scaffolds of Heaven and regard us—"

' "If there be any sons of Thunder amongst you; if you ever rattled the terrible judgement of God upon sinners——"

' "I am a stranger even at home; therefore if the dogs of the world bark at me, I neither care nor wonder——"

'that's how he writes, but I dare say you know all about him—though I am sure the BBC doesn't.

'I am happily situated between two old book-shops, one at Southampton and one at Portsmouth, where London prices are not yet heard of. I am told these places are also ports of importance, but their importance to me is the old folios I find in them.'

I did know about that old bishop, Joseph Hall, and wrote saying that I had a faint vague germ of a plan for writing about him (alas, after 17 years, that plan still survives but still, alas, it is no more than a germ; as Coleridge quoted, in print, at the end of his unfinished poem *The Three Graves*, 'Tomorrow and tomorrow and tomorrow').

I was also able to take his fancy with this passage from a sermon of Hall's:

'I have read a book of one *Haitonus* a monk . . . written some 340 Years ago . . . wherein with much confidence he affirms that in the Country of Georgia there was a certain province called Hamsen, of three daies journey about, so palpably dark continually, as that no man could see his hand in it, that the inhabitants of the borders might hear many times in the woods, the noise of men crying, of horses neighing, of cocks crowing, but no man durst venture to go unto it, because he could not find the way out again; which he says with much ernestnesse that he saw.'

He answered (20.4.29):

'Here is the sentence I tried to quote from Hall, "Shall he go for a freeman that is a slave to his Curtizan; that is at the command of her eyes and hangs upon the doom of her variable lips" (*Olive Tree*, p. 30).

'I have never been a wild enthusiast for copulation, but a sentence like this is a great incentive to profligacy. I am so glad that you contemplate a book on "Jos. Norvic." as he signs himself. As I told you I feel that he is beginning to shake his old bones at Norwich and ask why

7

he too can't see his names in the paper. The craving among these old ghosts for publicity may become a nuisance, but after all the dusty years it is a kindly thing to do something to gratify this amiable weakness.'

About the beginning of May, Edmund Gosse's books were to be sold at Sotheby's. We were both anxious to buy some of these.

A month or two before this we had in the shop a particular copy of the first edition of Boswell's *Life of Johnson*. It had a page which was cancelled in almost every other copy known. In the original state this page carried a not altogether proper conversation on conjugal fidelity. On our little printing press, I and my friend Kyrle Leng printed a few copies of this suppressed conversation as a small tract in an edition of 30 copies; we called it *Conjugal Fidelity*.

About the Gosse sale, Pearsall Smith wrote (3.5.29):

'I feel this of the Jeremy Taylors. I must have the *Golden Grove*; I once had it in my possession for some time, and would now like to possess it until I join the former owner on the further side of the grave. As I think I have told you, I miss Gosse much more than I expected to, for I didn't know him intimately, wasn't very fond of him, and wouldn't have trusted him around the corner. But we had tastes in common, and that, for people with tastes, is one of the strongest of bonds. I find that among those who have played that vanishing trick called dying on me, it is to the ones who shared my thoughts that my thoughts keep most constantly turning; and Gosse has taken his place in this company. So if you bid on my behalf for the *Golden Grove* (as you kindly said you would) don't let any reasonable price deter you. But I should like very much to go over the catalogue with you—could you by any chance lunch with me next Wednesday or Thursday? If it is fine we might visit Bolingbroke's tomb at Battersea Church which is not far off, and is a little island of the early eighteenth century still existing in a rather rare perfection.

'I suppose all the Johnson Tracts on Conjugal Fidelity are sold? If not, I should like to buy a copy to give to Birrell, who is much excited about it.'

We had a copy to spare, and he wrote acknowledging it (7.5.29):

'It is really most kind of you to let me have another copy of that unedifying page. I saw the pessimistic gleam of greed in old Birrell's eyes when I showed him my copy, and I know how pleased he will be to have it. . . .

'I have just had a rather pessimistic affair with a clock, which has left me, as these affairs do leave one, somewhat exhausted.'

The visit to Bolingbroke's tomb was the first of the many literary pilgrimages that I was to make with him; it was a beginning, a test—though we neither of us knew it—which was to bring about and justify that large part of our lives which during the succeeding years we spent together. I remember it only faintly; but I have the picture of a shadowy church, with dusty windows that hinted of sunlight outside, and the rather terrifying, dimly glowing alabaster face of Bolingbroke's wife (or is it his mother?).

The Gosse sale went off successfully. He got his *Golden Grove*, and I, among other things, at a huge cost, which emptied some of my shelves to meet it, a Latin Grammar of extraordinary rarity, compiled by Jeremy Taylor when he was keeping a school in Wales during the late 1640's. On the subject of these books, Pearsall Smith had remarked that he could never altogether satisfy the sense and gust of possession.

'I always put new things that I've bought beside my bed,' I told him.

'I took great delight in the long-desired book'; he wrote to me (13.5.29) 'it slept beside me (not with me); I woke up to read the description on p. 42 of the joys of Heaven—joys which I shall taste before you do, as I am so much nearer that golden threshold.

'And yet how difficult it is to possess one's possessions! Mine elude me and still keep aloof. I cannot really appropriate them and make them mine, save in the rarest and briefest moments. Perhaps your method of going to bed with them is the best. I hope you had a happy night with the Grammar—you deserve it after your audacity in making it your own.

'I think you said you were reading Hall—do look out for aphorisms and pithy sentences with which he enriches his pages. Those that I have collected from him make me want to find some more. Also out-of-the-way iniquities—the two I discovered "polluting the house of God with abominable altars" and "Singing with Nero while the city burns" have been a great delight to my criminal imagination, though neither of them quite equals the giant sin that so took Donne's giant fancy.[1]

[1] A description of this enormity would not be permissible in modern language; but for those who like searching out dark corners in books for the record of darker sins, I may say that he was alluding to a passage in *Ignatius his Conclave*. In the edition most easily come by, that of 1653 (which is part of a volume usually referred to as *Paradoxes and Problems*, 1652), the giant sin begins to be recorded on p. 149. He used to say that he had tried to include this passage in his Selections from Donne, but that the delegates of the Oxford Press had refused to accept it: a wise and natural decision. If his story was true, the irresponsible gaieties of euphoria, to which I shall soon be alluding, must have beset him so far back, at least, as 1920.

'My soul is at present feeding on a strangely beautiful and purple patch I found in *The Times* last Thursday, where its Manilla correspondent, after an arid description of the sun's eclipse, suddenly cabled: "The weather was cloudless, the conditions were perfect. Acacia trees closed their leaves as for the night; dew fell, chickens roosted, and the peasants in the outlying villages, terrified by the awful phenomenon, supplicated the Saints".

'Could this sentence, which Flaubert might have written with the help of Gibbon, be the chance product of a journalist's pen? I cannot think so.'

As I said, the little afternoon excursion to the Bolingbrokes in Battersea church was, all unintentionally, an experiment; that it entirely succeeded is evident from the suggestion which he now put forward, that we should make a pilgrimage to the scenes of Jeremy Taylor's loveliest work. Accordingly, on June 7th, we went down to South Wales, and stayed at the Ivy Bush hotel in Carmarthen. 'How about June 7th or 8th,' he had written to me (17.5.29), 'for our visit to J. T. and the Carberys[1] at Golden Grove? The date will suit them, they say, and will suit me.'

Among the qualities of his character which had most impressed and bewitched me, was an unparalleled aesthetic sensibility. Words outworn and over-worked must be reduced to their primitive meaning in order to express it. His enjoyment of any beauty—of countryside or picture or building or a concatenation of words—was like a delphic inspiration; to enjoy such things with him was to be possessed by a sort of maenad enthusiasm.

Between the fortunately named estate of Golden Grove and that poetical eminence Grongar Hill, meanders, gracefully serpentine, the River Towy. Romantic painters have made many landscapes romantic. But this landscape—I feel I should be using the name in its original form of landskip—had already, unpainted, the quality implied by that word about which Pearsall Smith had composed a learned study. Down in that lovely valley is the little railway station where you can see placarded up, unbelievably, the name 'Golden Grove'. We drove up to the modern house and the modern church. No building appears to remain that Taylor knew; but Taylor had walked here, and here he had collected, like rare flowers, the images which glitter and tremble and

[1] The noble couple who rescued Taylor during the Civil War, and for whom he composed the greater part of his most splendid writings.

blossom in his writings; here 'He who stilleth the raging of the Sea, and the noise of the Waves, and the madness of the people, had provided a plank' for him; here, to further paraphrase his words, he gathered a few sticks to warm him, a few books to entertain his thoughts, and here he brought forth, as easily, it seems, as a thrush sings, the loveliest prose in all our lovely language. Mysterious and sacred the place was, with those spirit echoes of a music three centuries old; and the mystery and holiness and beauty of it all became doubly quickened by the evident and passionate relish of my companion. But can I do better than quote from his own allusion to this particular pilgrimage, and to another which we made in the following year?

'Strange, as another sentimental pilgrim, Henry James, has expressed it, strange and special the effect of the empty places we stand and wonder in today for the sake of these vanished people; "the irresistible reconstruction, to the all but baffled vision, of irrevocable presences and aspects, the conscious, shining, mocking void, sad somehow with excess of serenity". Something of the effect he describes I have experienced at the Golden Grove in Wales, in which Jeremy Taylor preached his golden sermons; in the rectory garden at Bemerton, where George Herbert butterfly-netted his butterfly conceits, and in the nearby soil of Sidney's Arcadia out of which, like a blue flower, the word *romantic* grew.'[1]

Leaving Golden Grove, we travelled in our hired car, up a muddy lane, almost to the top of Grongar Hill, on the other side of the valley. Here the exquisitely endowed poet of the eighteenth century, John Dyer—to be called 'minor' only for the smallness of his output—was inspired to write the freshest poem between the times of Milton and of Blake.

It will be evident from the letters which I've already quoted that Pearsall Smith's outlook on life was an ironic one. But in his feelings at the presence of beauty there were no trammels to his unabashed and serious response. Beauty and art were, I believe, the only matters about which he was wholly serious. The personal affections that stirred him so deeply had their streaks of pain and inconvenience; these he resented, as he never resented the toils and troubles and exasperations of composition. I had seen already the delicious fluttering of the spirit in him at the turn and flow and fall of a beautiful phrase; I had seen the actual tears paying homage in his eyes; but it was at Golden Grove, I think,

[1] *Reperusals and Re-collections*, 1936, p. 24.

that I first had an inkling of the overbearing importance to him of such feelings.

On the Sunday of that week-end he insisted on going to the evening service in Carmarthen church. As we came out he murmured ' "For the means of grace, and the hope of glory", what phrases! You don't know how lucky you are to have been brought up in the Church of England.' (He, of course, was born and bred a Quaker.)

After we got back he wrote to me, using for the first time my Christian name (27.6.29):

'My Dear Bob', he wrote, '(If I may call you so—I hope you will call me Logan—as I am not a don it won't be compromising)'

I had taken some photographs on our pilgrimage, and sent him prints, copying out on the backs, where it was appropriate, lines from Dyer's *Grongar Hill*.

'Grongar Hill', he wrote (15.7.29), 'appears with its eighteenth century magic (and that century has a magic of its own) and the views and verses are in pretty accord. The view of the railway station [Golden Grove], combining the magic of words with the safe, prosaic but potent charm of the Great Western railway, makes a strong appeal to my feelings, and forms a good subject for meditation. My mind is still full of South Wales, and our enchanting trip. We must make another pilgrimage sometime.'

I was young at this time; and in spite of the bravery and, as I would like to claim, the scholarship of my literary passions, I was, I think, young in intellect. Inward ripeness was not very evident. I had outlived Keats—a saddening reflection—and all my published writings were to be found in those bibliographical notes which Mr Desmond MacCarthy had printed as a pendant to Logan's essay.

On this hopeful yet rather callow young man, a little frustrated, and with better taste than judgment, Logan turned the glittering and intellectual light of his affectionate approval. His presence and conversation and flattering attentions worked upon me as those drugs are said to work that can elevate the senses and sharpen the wit. I seemed to see powers in myself; my artistic sensations, wild and rambling, revealed themselves as something that could be ranged and cultivated and comprehended. We had known each other for about nine months, and the wine of his talk, and his liking for me, had become delights that I felt I couldn't very happily do without. And then a curious thing happened.

The light of welcome no longer beaconed in his eyes when I met him. Did I bore him? I wondered; up to the present my conversation whether frivolous or solemn had seemed to give him pleasure. Did he resent after all the familiarity, as from a contemporary, which he had so definitely invited? I didn't know—how should I, since Logan himself didn't seem properly aware of it yet—that I was witnessing one of the cyclical depressions which so troubled his later years. He suffered from a mild form of that madness known as manic-depression. I find in the letters of these early years various allusions to post-influenzal lassitude, to unnamed and unknown germs, to some undefined chronic little illness.[1] Gradually the changes became more apparent and were recognized—exuberant periods of euphoria or gaiety, when he wrote and talked unceasingly, and perpetrated the most preposterous practical jokes: and long, dark, sullen months of dullness when he sat almost silent, perpetually reading, and receiving only very short visits even from the most intimate of his old friends.

1930

In the spring of 1930 appeared at last *The Golden Grove*, his book of selections from Jeremy Taylor. I wrote my appreciation of it.

'It was kind of you to write,' he answered (3.5.30). 'I was wretchedly ill all the autumn when I was doing the proofs of *The Golden Grove*, and the book became almost a nightmare to me—I felt nothing but weariness and disgust, and would have been glad to suppress it altogether. But it begins to shine a little now and recover its lustre—I dare say it is all right. I have worked on it a good deal at various times—and then put it by, as I like to put by my books to mellow. It is a great pleasure to me that you like both the selections and the introduction—you are the person most worth pleasing, as you know more than anyone else about the subject. I find it pleasant to see our names on the same title-page, I hope that this means that our friendship is established on a good basis—if indeed you care for the friendship of such an old relic as I often feel myself.

[1] In older letters of his (written to other people, and long before I knew him), I have come across allusions to attacks of a mild, listless invalidism. Although he recognized these, he did not, it appears, look upon their return as something regular and altogether inescapable. During one such period, in 1919, he imbibed thirty-six volumes of Hazlitt.

'I am glad that the little obscenities in my introduction didn't escape you—writers who take their vocation seriously owe it to themselves, in my opinion, and to their readers, to sprinkle a few gay obscenities over their pages; though this isn't always easy, especially when one writes on sacred subjects. I am afraid I omitted Jeremy Taylor's adjective "fat"[1] before the eunuchs—this may have added to the temptation. But one does what one can——

'Have you noticed the marvellous blossoming of the blackthorn this spring? The hedges in Hampshire were like drifts of moonlight, and there were little trees, luminous, like rustic brides, with this pale adornment. Have the poets ever done justice to the blackthorn? I cannot remember that they have. Robert Bridges might have done it—I cannot write to him now, alas, to ask him why he never did.'

Robert Bridges had just died. At the time we were printing privately a poem which many years before he had sent to Logan, *On receiving Trivia from the Author*. In acknowledging a proof Logan had added (1.4.30):

'I am nourishing by the way rather a grievance against you—I felt the other day—or was I wrong?—that you didn't appreciate the sentence that I read you about the Mediterranean waters, "The radiance streaming towards him from the *luminous and unfading azure at his feet*".[2]

'But you are young, so I forgive you, and hope that when you are older you will realize that a beautiful phrase is the most important thing in the world—that nothing else really matters.

'Do come to luncheon . . . I have some books I hope you haven't.'

Miraculously, in this same spring, we came on another copy of the Jeremy Taylor Grammar. I asked Logan if he wanted it.

'I called on Friday,' he answered (15.4.30), 'and was sorry to hear that you were away and not well . . . I wanted to ask you whether I really want that Grammar of J. T's. My trouble is that I am so seldom able, as I have told you, to possess my possessions—if they have intrinsic beauty I can sometimes catch a gleam from them, but if their value is

---

[1] He had collected in one paragraph some of the curious enormities, derived from classical writings, against which Taylor had warned his readers; these, Logan wrote, 'could hardly have caused much disquiet in the breasts of his hearers in South Wales. Whatever mundane temptations the rural solitudes of that locality might have afforded, it was hardly necessary, moreover, to warn them against corrupt longings for garments stained with the blood of the Tyrian fish, for oysters of Lucrinus, for the tender lard of Apulian swine, or condited bellies of the Scarus; for Galatian mules, or eunuchs for their slaves from Tunis.' The last two luxuries were taken from a sentence in *Holy Living*, where the eunuchs are qualified as 'fat'.

[2] From Scott Moncrieff's translation of Proust.

only the value of rarity, I only feel that they are mine when others envy them; and as no one envies my Jeremy Taylors but you, and as you possess the Grammar, what satisfaction holy or unholy can it give me? I must either invent in imagination other green-eyed collectors, or save all my money to buy something immensely expensive which you do not possess.'

Meantime he had started on my education. Not infrequently, during professional forays into country bookshops, I had noticed a beautifully produced work of the early eighteenth century, in three volumes, and illustrated with lovely engravings by Gribelin; this was *The Characteristics* of the third Earl of Shaftesbury. I had been told, and had accepted the opinion, that this work was unreadable, and had often regretted that so enticing a vesture had been put upon so apparently dusty a composition. One day Logan asked me, to my surprsie, 'Do you ever read Shaftesbury?'

'No,' I said, 'I always understood he was quite unreadable.'

'Look at this,' he said, and showed me a passage. The author, writing about toleration, playfully imagines an English law being passed against the writing of poetry, and in particular love poetry:

'We might perhaps', the passage concludes, 'see a new *Arcadia* arising out of this heavy Prosecution: Old People and Young wou'd be seiz'd with a versifying Spirit: We should have Field-Conventicles of Lovers and Poets: Forests wou'd be fill'd with romantick Shepherds and Shepherdesses: and Rocks resound with Echoes of Hymns and Praises offer'd to the Powers of Love: We might indeed have a fair Chance, by this Management, to bring back the whole Train of Heathen Gods, and set our cold Northern Island burning with as many Altars to VENUS and APOLLO, as were formerly in *Cyprus, Delos,* or any of those warmer *Grecian* Climates.'

I was bewitched, as he intended I should be; but the ultimate consequences were not altogether fortunate. Urged to it by Logan, I planned to write a book about Shaftesbury, and I read up all I could on the subject. It eventually became apparent to me that to bring off such a work, I should need a full acquaintance with intellectual life in late seventeenth century Holland, together with a specialized knowledge of such writers as Descartes, Spinoza and Leibnitz. Unless I was ready to bungle it, the task was beyond me. Logan forgot my plans about Joseph Hall, but, like that Malay in the *Opium Eater,* this unwritten book on Shaftesbury became a ghost which was sometimes to trouble my relations with him, as the Malay made terrible the later poppy dreams of de Quincey.

But with the other great writer that Logan, in his words, 'put on me' there was no unfortunate sequel. Bernard Berenson, his brother-in-law, once said over-modestly to Logan, or so the latter affirmed, 'If either of us is remembered after we're dead, it will only be because we knew Santayana'. Logan made the introduction with a present of his own selection, *Little Essays from the works of George Santayana*. Acknowledging my first letter on the subject, in which I had made a professional offer for some of his own first editions, he wrote (8.6.30):

'You are corrupting me, but that is not unpleasant, especially when (which must be unique at my age) the process is lucrative as well. First editions of my books have a certain value, I believe, in America, where I have many readers;—whether this fact does more credit to that continent than it does discredit to me is a point for nice discrimination, but a query perhaps, in Sir Thomas Browne's phrase, "too sad to insist on".

'I am glad you like Santayana and hope you will go on liking him. His thought is serene and severe—much too severe and serene for most people, but it has the purity of a mountain spring, "The ice-brook's temper", and there is nothing, to my mind, that can so refresh the spirit. He faces the truth without illusions; sees the universe as it is and our humble status in it; but though truth is cruel, as he says, it can be loved, and it makes free those who have loved it. The freedom of spirit one can learn from him is in itself a kind of mastery of life, and eliminates from it almost all its sadness. That at least has been my experience, and I can imagine no greater blessing. But I am afraid I will bore you with my preaching.

'Does your press ever undertake printing little books for authors, and if so, on what terms? I have been amusing myself by writing a little collection of thoughts and meditations on growing old—the odd process to which we are all subjected, and which is full of curious interest —I have polished and polished my phrases till I have made them as lucid and luminous as I can, and I should rather like to see them in print, but would rather print them at my own expense, as I don't want to publish them at present. I will show them to you one of these days.'

(These reflections were, of course, the aphorisms which he soon decided to publish as *Afterthoughts*.)

This summer we went for another literary pilgrimage. At my suggestion, George Herbert was the saint of our particular homage. Sun and clouds lit up the cathedral at Salisbury. I had felt its beauty before; with Logan, I suddenly realized the truth, which he gave to me as the opinion of Sir Kenneth Clark, that this was the most perfect building in Northern Europe.

'I once told Roger Fry that,' said Logan, 'and he got very angry, because, as you probably know, he *hates* English art and didn't like to allow that any English building was supreme. But when I asked him what building in Northern Europe he preferred, all he could do was to get very angry, and blurt out "St Paul's". I felt that I'd scored off him. Don't you think I had?'

At Carmarthen we had paid a little homage to Richard Steele, who died in that town; and after reverently visiting Golden Grove we had driven over to Cardigan for lunch, to pay a formal call, as Logan put it, on Katherine Philips, the 'Matchless Orinda', a not unattractive seventeenth-century poetess and an acquaintance of Jeremy Taylor. (I remember, after we had lunched at Cardigan, going into a plentifully-autographed public urinal. 'Shall we write up "Robert Bridges"?' suggested Logan).

Near Salisbury, likewise, we paid two formal calls. Rather timidly, among the palladian splendours of Wilton, we burnt a little spiritual incense to the chivalrous ghost of Sir Philip Sidney. Logan mentioned him, and our guide assured us that the particular tree existed still, under which he had written his colossal and all but unreadable *Arcadia*—a feat, if that was the sole place of its composition, worthy, for physical endurance, of St Simon Stylites, or some assiduous American pole-squatter.

Our other lesser saint was Hazlitt. After inspecting as good tourists (and Logan was nothing if not a tourist) Old Sarum and Stonehenge, we visited Hazlitt's inn, The Pheasant, at Winterslow.

'We shall have to go in,' said Logan. 'Though I'm always frightened of pubs. Now you, I suppose, are quite at home in them. You order our drinks; I shouldn't know what to ask for.'

A companion's timidity always make me brave. I hadn't yet become, as I am now, an addict of that most English of all English institutions; but I was quite ready to order our drinks.

'Can you lean with one elbow on the bar and talk to barmaids?' he mumured as we went in. However the landlord, and not a barmaid, served us. Logan asked about Hazlitt. The name, I think, was quite strange to him; but with the air of a man who is anxious to please all of his public, he affected some knowledge of this immortal customer.

'But that,' he said, when he had evidently gathered from Logan something about Hazlitt's profession, 'was a long time ago.' He was more taken up with an incident, shown in a crude print on the wall, when, close to The Pheasant, early in the last century, a tiger had escaped from a travelling menagerie, and attacked the mail coach.

The cult which took us to Golden Grove was more separate and obscure than that whose shrine we venerated at Bemerton. To suck the essence out of a holy place, it is wise to make use of every serviceable feeling; but that little private pride which was so potent in Wales had less of power in Wiltshire. Nevertheless we were able to discover at Bemerton, amid the sunlight and leaves and shining of the river, a sweet and Waltonian calm. I remember the darkness of the little church where, at his induction Herbert had stayed so long alone that a friend, wondering what kept him, had looked in through the window, and seen him lying prostrate in front of the altar. I don't know what alterations have been made to the parsonage; we were wise enough not to inquire. Courteously, in the absence of the rector, we were shown into the garden by his housekeeper. There, to one side of the hot lawn, she pointed out the medlar tree which Herbert himself is supposed to have planted. And ahead, over the river, framed in clouds and leaves and rushes—standing up as Constable so marvellously painted it—we could see the sky-braving and incomparable spire. And so, with a last obeisance of the spirit to that 'sweet singer of the temple', we left, not altogether unmindful of another rector of Bemerton, John Norris, one of the Cambridge Platonists, who foreshadowed in his thought the metaphysical discoveries of Bishop Berkeley.

For tangible mementoes of this little trip I have the one photograph which Logan ever allowed me to take of him (I have one other, taken some years later, without his knowing); he is standing in the garden at Bemerton, looking at his copy of George Herbert's *Temple;* as well, in token of our drink at The Pheasant, Logan gave me a copy of Hazlitt's book of essays called *Winterslow*. Neither then nor later did I quite fall for Hazlitt as Logan wished; but he never made much of a grievance out of this.

That summer he spent some time in Sussex, trying, I think, to stave off a cyclical depression, which he put down to physical ill-health. He wrote (1.8.30) mentioning an American Donne enthusiast, who, he suggested, might like to visit our shop.

'Don't let him be a bore—he seemed, a few years ago, a most charming youth; but a few years can change charming youths, alas, into crashing bores, as perhaps you know;—and Americans, when they take to teaching literature, are apt to become the most desiccating bores in all the wide world. If the youth . . . does call on you, you must tell me whether he has undergone this dismal transformation, or whether you think I would like him still. If he has kept his extraordinarily charming appearance, that would be something; but not, to me one considers things wisely, enough.

'I have transferred my old bones, my MSS. and microbes and re-pinings, to a wooded nook on one of the high hills in Sussex for the benefit of the air, as Chilling [his house near Southampton] is supposed to be so relaxing. The air is certainly good; and the house, an old, but modernized farm-house, is not uncomfortable. I have a splendid view to far horizons from my bed, which to me is a great felicity, and to be preferred to any companion in it. At Chilling I could see the sea and ships—here, I look far over the Sussex weald to the South Downs and Chanctonbury Ring—a view slightly tarnished by the thought of Belloc, and yet beautified to my memory by the fact that at the bottom of this hill I lived for years alone, after I left Oxford, poor, unsuccessful, happy, improving my mind and trying to learn to write English prose. It was a dream, but an enchanting one, and I have never really re-covered from it—I still feel myself young, full of promise, and just on the verge of the great discovery—

'I am still under the enchantment of our pilgrimage to Salisbury.'

A fortnight later he wrote (14.8.30):

'The American . . . has been staying in the neighbourhood and came to see me the other day—disglorified, of course, donnish, married, rather dull, and shorn of his beams. Well, "dreams fade", as an author has informed us, who, to prove his point, is himself, I am told, under-going that process.

'However this Donne-enthusiast seemed to regard me as a distin-guished author . . . but his deference, though pleasant, was not enough I found to fill a whole afternoon with bliss. But I am not writing to ask for your sympathy, but to say that I am going to Frome for this week . . .

'I hope in Frome to see the house and visit the haunts of the young lady of Frome who met there, according to the limerick, with so rich an adventure . . .

'My American, by the way, told me that he was going to buy a copy of the *Golden Grove*, which will mean some pennies for me. Dis-enchantments are often expensive, but by this one I shall actually profit, so I need not complain.'

He wrote again, from the same place (26.8.30):

'The high air and high society—the unancestral seats of four Labour Peers surround us—are doing me good, and my mind is full of sky-blue meditations—the purity of my thoughts will astonish, and, I hope, abash you.'

'How', he wrote a week later (3.9.30), 'do you manage to lead a pure life—if you do lead a pure life—in a world so full of perils and temptations?'

Early in September, he wrote to say that he was going to Italy. He suggested that I should travel as far as Paris with him. This wasn't possible at the time, and eventually we arranged that I should meet him there for a day or two on his way home. 'I have had a book sent me from Dobell's,' he wrote in the same letter (11.9.30),

'which is to me a priceless possession, though it did not cost me much. The little quarto edition of Bridges' poems printed by Daniel in 1884. I nourish a hope—but only a faint one—that you do not possess a copy; for, as Thomas à Kempis says in the *Imitatio Christi*, "Until we are sure that our friend has failed to find a rare edition we have purchased, the ultimate ecstasy of possession cannot—so God decrees—occur."

'However, I saw Oliver Brett (or Esher, as they now call him) on Tuesday; and by telling him of this quarto which he does not possess, though he collects Bridges, I made him grind his newly-ennobled teeth. This, like the sound of Triton's blast to Wordsworth, or the sight of Proteus, has made me considerably less forlorn.'

I was able to counter this challenge by telling Logan that I already possessed that exquisite little quarto. I sent him at the same time a copy of my first novel. His acknowledgment was full of generous enthusiasm which modesty forbids my transcribing; but the same modesty convinces me that his praise was more for the promise than the performance. Let it suffice—and so much is essential for this narrative—that at least this promise was up to Logan's hopes; the consequences to me were prodigious.

A few days before he left England he wrote to me (22.9.30):

'In Weymouth where I have been staying, I found a charming little wizened old bookseller with an odd passion (not felt, I believe, in Conduit Street) for selling rare first editions below their prices on publication. I made a number of guilty purchases, and my next night was disturbed by pains and pangs of conscience, and a feeling that I ought to return and tell him that he must really charge more. My hostess, however, forbade this; and being an accomplished Freudian, declared that I must be suffering from an anal complex. To this imputation I replied that if in consequence I had to undergo an operation, the surgeon's bill would be sent to her;—such is the merry and elegant tone of wit which prevails in psychoanalytic circles.

'I still feel this pang of conscience; and although it is not localized yet in the spot my hostess so elegantly suggested, I fear it may yet produce distressing consequences there, and I thought that these might be mitigated or indeed averted—and perhaps handed on to you—if you would take off my hands in your business capacity seven first editions of Tennyson at the price I paid for them, which was eighteen shillings. If the whole staff at Conduit Street is in consequence afflicted with emerods—as God afflicted the Canaanites who stole the Ark—I shall bear it with equanimity—however great may be the consternation among the young men of St Giles. I reck not of them.'

He wrote next from the Berensons' home near Florence (8.10.30):

'I find it very pleasant here, in the luxury and splendour of this great Italian villa. Mrs Wharton is here, and Santayana nearby;—we are a little group of not unsuccessful people, old and ill and gay and disenchanted; and our tongues wag as freely I think as any tongues in Europe. The long perspectives of elderly people, their wealth of ironic reflections and observations and improper anecdotes, does much to compensate them—does indeed, I believe, more than compensate them—for the loss of youth and all the injuries of time.'

He wrote (17.10.30) about arrangements for meeting him in Paris; I was coming by the Golden Arrow.

'Unfortunately,' he said, 'the special snobbish sensation of travelling by this *train des snobs* is no longer to be tasted; one used to arrive at the boat before the common ruck of first-class passengers; and at Calais one stepped at once into the golden train, while one's inferiors were harried and hurried into the *douane*. You still escape this ignominy, but the common ruck come by another boat, and there is no opportunity of spitting in their faces.'

He spoke of my book in the same letter, and mentioned the presence of

'A gift which may come to . . . richer fruition. You must nurse and mature it well, and not force it into hurried production.'

In this last sentence I was first hearing that severe but inspiring voice, familiar to so many young writers whom Logan took an interest in.

We met in Paris, and did all that respectable tourists ought to do— sightseeing and sitting in cafés and eating. Back in England, having our dinner in the boat-train, he talked about my book. 'You'll never write well enough,' he went on, 'while you're living your present life. You must have leisure.'

Then he said, 'Do you think your job in the shop will last?'

'I think so,' I answered.

'These amateur businesses never do last,' he said. Logan, as I afterwards discovered, was the slave of a word or a phrase; if it took his fancy, it possessed him, so that he uttered and followed it with no thought as to its truth or its wisdom. In his last words was the germ of an aphorism. That his prophecy became justified, was in no way due to his perspicuity and insight. Our shop was not an amateur mushroom, and that it did indeed fail in the end as a London firm was due only to the world slump which swept away many a competent and seemingly established business.

'Would you like to work for me?' he added.

I think that I answered nothing articulate. I was entirely surprised, and such a rearrangement of my life, with all its consequences, was difficult to imagine.

'Don't answer now,' he said. 'Think it over. I'm a decent, trustworthy sort of person. Ask one of my friends, if you like—Desmond MacCarthy; he knows me well; he'd tell you that I can be trusted.'

To satisfy questions of a more sordid interest which, as he knew well enough, must then, or at a later time, creep out for my consideration, he gave me on the spot such an undertaking as would lay them, not only for that occasion, but for all that might remain to me—and my expectations were long—of mortal life.

Then he changed the conversation. 'I don't sleep well at present', he said, taking out his little note-book, 'and lately, when I'm lying awake, I've been trying to compose aphorisms.' (He was not actually mentioning these aphorisms for the first time, having indeed, as I have already recorded, made a suggestion that I should print them for him.) 'Here's one I can't get right. "We have to water our souls with the dew of poesy, or they will become parched, and die." It's a great truth, but it sounds mawkish. What does it need?'

I didn't answer at once; but this time my hesitation wasn't due to embarrassment. I seemed to have an inkling of what was wanted.

'Couldn't you,' I said at last, 'put in something about manuring them?'

'That's it!' he said beaming, and put his hand in his pocket. 'I'll pay you a shilling for that,' and he handed me the coin. The aphorism ended as 'We must water our souls with the dew of poesy, and manure them as well.'

Before we parted in London, he mentioned again his suggestion of my working with him. 'Perhaps,' he added, 'you'd be willing to come abroad with me sometimes. I'd pay your expenses, and you would act as a sort of courier—order meals and rooms, and pay tips and hotel bills and buy tickets and all that sort of thing, which bores me so much.'

His restrictive conditions were two, and rather curious; I was not to get married; and I must not attempt to write best-selling novels. His explanation of the first was that young authors who get married are bound to ruin their talents by writing for money; indeed it fell under much the same head as his second condition, for, as he put it in *Afterthoughts*, 'Writers who write for money, don't write for me'.

His offer was a very enticing one; however, either through timidity, or from an exaggerated feeling for security, I hesitated. But at last, after consulting wise friends, and getting reassured that my presence was not essential to the shop, I accepted. Logan told me that the first work he'd got on hand was to edit a selection from the critical writings of Mr Desmond MacCarthy. These were scattered among numberless periodicals of all kinds, and the first job was to sort out and arrange what looked like innumerable newspaper cuttings.

Just at this time Kyrle Leng, the friend that I share my home with, became desperately ill; for two or three days his life was quite uncertain; and then, mercifully, he began to recover. Logan wrote in answer to my news (21.11.30):

'I am very much distressed by the news in your letter. I had hoped that Kyrle had practically got over his trouble and now this recurrence must be very sad (I think I know how sad) for you. I wish that there was anything I could do to help you—you must let me know if there is anything, but I am afraid there isn't.

'In other circumstances your letter would have given me the greatest pleasure, as I can think of no more delightful (and to me more valuable) prospect than the prospect of collaboration with you. I will, as you suggest, send you a tiny section of the mountain of papers which have to be sifted—and it is a mountain. I have dug but a little way into it so far, but far enough to find what seem to me pockets of real gold— some enchanting writing, and behind it an enchanting literary figure and personality, very individual and distinct and charming. I am greatly encouraged, and think the volumes we produce will be a real addition to literature.'

Logan's practical contribution to Kyrle's well-being was the gift of the 1902, privately printed, edition of *Trivia*.

Apart from all matters of health, Kyrle's illness very nearly had other unfortunate consequences. To explain this I must go a little into our domestic arrangements.

We were looked after then by an elderly housekeeper, whose maternal feelings beamed full in all their devotion and jealousy on the two young men she was 'doing for'. It very quickly became obvious that a nurse must be called in; this news engendered such jealousy as, for the moment, swamped even the affection and anxiety of our loving old domestic. To make things possible, I was driven, as the saying goes, to 'words'. I later got, as is customary with such people, an oblique apology; after the nurse had turned up, the housekeeper whispered to me, 'She's really a very nice girl' (I'd had time to give a warning of difficulties). But in spite of this, my 'words', somewhere deep down, were still rankling; jealousy, though smothered, was unassuaged. Following, without knowing it, Logan's principles, she felt a sort of hygienic necessity for revenge.

When Kyrle was first taken ill, I'd moved my mattress on to the floor of his room; on my denuded bed I'd begun sorting out the MacCarthy cuttings according to Logan's plan, each group being marked by a large piece of paper.

After relieving the nurse for a spell at Kyrle's bed-side, I went back to find that all the arranged papers had disappeared. To my anguished questions the housekeeper replied, sulkily defiant, 'I thought they was rubbish. I gave them to Ivy [the "help"] to take them home to light the fires with.' Since old newspapers for kindling always accumulated in large heaps, and never before had Ivy received so gracious a present, the malice in this action can have lurked only a little way beneath her conscious mind. I thought of the masterpieces of literature and all the irreplaceable MSS. which from time to time have been lost through the hidden malice of servants; had I become the victim of a slighter instance? Ivy was in the house at the time, and rushing gaily home she rescued—to my immeasurable and inexpressible relief—the precious papers.

Since everything turned out all right, I later told Logan about it; he shuddered a little at the danger escaped, but in no way blamed me for so unpredictable a happening. Sixteen years later, however, there was a crazy and rather disastrous repercussion.

Logan wrote to me a little later (6.12.30):

'I sent you another slice of Desmond on Thursday, and hope it arrived safely. The more slices I eat from this great cake, the more the taste grows on me . . . his style reflects his candid, delightful mind, which in its turn reflects in a candid and charming way all sorts of things and people. (This metaphor is a little shaky perhaps but luminous enough, I hope, to convey my meaning.) I think the articles printed in a book will have the cumulative effect of presenting an ingenious and frank and genuine literary personality.

'Desmond sends you his love, and says he hopes that you are not bored with the job. His complex[1] seems to have faded away, or dissolved or whatever complexes do—he comes in almost every day, and is always delicious company. If we can only bottle some of his charm in a book, we shall be doing the world a real service. Courage! therefore, and dig away—I hope the digging doesn't bore you. I have, as I hope you have, another job on hand; I am writing what I have been brooding over for several years—an essay on Shakespear of all things —an attempt, that is, to say what have been my real experiences in the great, difficult wild adventure of reading and re-reading and reading over again all his plays, and baskets full of books about him. Almost everybody who writes about Shakespear goes mad before he has finished—one cannot face that enigmatic figure and keep one's reason. I have no sonnet theory, I haven't tried to explore the ominous cavern of the third Dark Period, nor am I tempted to join the Gadarene herd of porcine believers. My madness takes the form of believing that I have written a damned good essay—you will have to listen to it some time—that shall be a part of the sad and sombre task which you have so recklessly undertaken.

'I do hope that Kyrle is progressing all right, and that you will be able to come to London next week. I am lunching out—let me see— Tuesday, Wednesday and Thursday, but so far am not engaged for Monday and Friday. Why do I lunch out? Again I ask you. As other people always understand one better than one understands oneself, perhaps you will explain this to me. Am I worldly; or is it the vanity of shining—or thinking that one shines—in conversation?

[1] He had mentioned this 'complex' in a previous letter (28.11.30). 'A curious situation has arisen out of this undertaking of mine. Desmond's conscious self is delighted that I should take it in hand, and is most grateful; but the unconscious self is stubbornly against it, being aware perhaps that one can have a much greater reputation by not publishing, than by putting all one's cards on the table. Jackson of Cambridge has just been given the O.M. for not publishing anything. I like these complex, Henry Jamesean situations, and should be enjoying this, if it did not deprive me of his company—his unconscious self, regarding me as an enemy, keeps him from ever coming to see me—he drops parcels of MS. at the door, but never comes in.'

'Well, I hope I don't bore you with my letters—I always feel a slight misgiving when I drop them in the postbox.'

As will be seen, I must later on have reproached him, pleasantly and gently, on account of his respect for what he called 'the Great World'; such a preoccupation struck me as undignified, and unworthy of one with so fine a mind and talent. The catalogue of engagements reminds me of his encounter with a lady who wanted him at her luncheon table when he had little inclination to show himself there. 'Can you come to lunch on Monday?' she asked him over the telephone; he couldn't. 'Tuesday then?' No. 'Wednesday?' No. 'Thursday?' 'Make it Monday,' said Logan.

1931

And so I started to work with Logan. This occupation took up a great part of my life until 1939; and it lasted, even after that, intermittently, between the ties and obligations of my war work, until a few months from the end of his life. The work gradually became more and more intermittent, for, with increasing years, the periods of gloom, his 'interlunaries' as he used to call them, became more and more pronounced and of longer duration. During these periods he did no creative work, but would sit silent and still, reading endlessly. He was easily tired then, and saw very few of his friends. I would visit him fairly regularly; but often a stay of more than twenty minutes seemed to tire him. He wasn't, I think, as unhappy as he made himself out to be; indeed I think he was rather proud of his condition; and, although his intellect didn't, in such times, work creatively, he absorbed vast quantities of knowledge—mainly historical—and filled the ends of his books with intelligent annotations. If proofs of a book came in at such times, I would correct them for him; and I might write unavoidable letters to strangers. Otherwise, during these gloomy seasons, my life was my own.

All the time that I knew him he was suffering from a mild, chronic cystitis of the bladder—the after effects of prostate trouble. Such a continual poisoning will, I believe, affect the brain, but in his case it can have done no more than aggravate a mental condition which was, without doubt, hereditary. His father, who had a very odd religious career, gave more than once occasion to fear for his sanity; but the family complaint came out more pronouncedly in an uncle. He, so Logan told me, used, in his periods of elation, to demonstrate his belief in the fellowship of man by inviting stray negroes in to meals. His wife was vexed at this, and remonstrated in vain. At last, knowing another weakness of his, she cunningly pretended to fall in with his ideals, and, as each negro left, she gave him, to prove her enthusiasm, the equivalent of £10. Her husband being very stingy, this expenditure was too much even for his intoxicating sense of joy and brotherhood.

The first communication I had from Logan in 1931 was a postcard. On it he had stuck a newspaper heading. 'Swindler poses as Bishop. Wears clerical dress and gaiters. Asking for money.' Across the top of this he had written, 'So you are at it again, I see.' Such communications became familiar to his friends, and betokened the zenith of his euphoria. At the time I hadn't yet discovered the cyclical nature of his moods, and took this for no more than a spontaneous, if rather startling, outburst of high-spirits.

The next thing I had from him was more decorous, namely the limited edition of *Afterthoughts*. I had seen many of them in MS, and had helped him out with the proofs. Over these he had taken immense care, correcting the maxims, and altering the arrangements of pages in a way that brought in a large bill from the printers. I read the book through, and wrote enthusiastically, saying, I remember, that these were obviously the best English aphorisms to appear since those of Halifax. This I still believe; Logan's aphorisms betray that characteristic vertiginous avoidance of deep feeling, which alone kept him from actual greatness; but they also show the crystal polish of which only the most exquisite of artists is capable.

Kyrle proposed one emendation; in the maxim 'Solvency is entirely a matter of temperament, and not of income', the last words, he suggested, were unnecessary. Logan resisted, and the maxim remained unaltered when, in 1933, *Afterthoughts* became a part of *All Trivia*. At last, in 1945, when he extensively revised that book, he succumbed, attributing the suggestion, curiously enough, to Edith Wharton.

'Though I shall see you to-morrow,' he wrote in answer to my letter (24.2.31), 'I feel I must write and thank you to-day for one of the kindliest letters I ever received. Praise for my writing from you is a delicious draught, for we both love the same kind of perfection—I have pursued

27

it all my life with patience and passion, and there is no one I think—at least I have never found anyone—whose thoughts chime with mine in a pleasanter harmony. When you like what I write I begin to like it myself;—my little book seemed to me a little heap of ashes when I saw it in print, but now I find gleams of beauty in it, after reading your letter. That you should like the essay[1] also makes the cup overbrim. . . I am afraid the little book is going to be too fashionable and make me too fashionable also—I have been floating since I saw you in this world of glitter and pomp and iced champagne—a world that I like all the more because I have no illusions about it and forget it at once when I emerge from its portals. I have been really living, however, in that book of Conway[2] letters; in that group of beautiful seventeenth century souls which flowered around Lady Conway with her high thoughts and her eternal headache. The beauty and remoteness of the setting—the rare—and rarified passion—that touched their souls in common—their subtle and exquisite friendships—all enchant me and give me as much pleasure as I can bear. Only I have no one but you to whom I can describe my ravishment. With poor old Gosse I could have talked it over, but he has hid his head underground where I can't get at him— a tiresome trick of the old which I shall play on you one of these days, by the way.

'My jealous friend is in the right, I am sure, about that dark region,[3] though my bosom-jesuit is trying to convince me that I found it in Hall myself . . .

'Can you out of kindness (though no part of our bargain) give me the name tomorrow of some book which has been both fashionable and first-rate? Circumstances may arise when the thought of some such Phoenix—if such Phoenix there be—may be a comfort to me.'

'You can't be both fashionable and first-rate'; Logan had just published this aphorism, and he was troubled, or professed to be troubled, by the approbation of 'fashionable' people, to use a detestable and vulgar adjective.

[1] Probably his essay, *On Reading Shakespeare*, which I must have read in typescript.

[2] 'Conway Letters, The Correspondence of Anne, *Viscountess Conway, Henry More*, and their Friends, 1642–1684'. A most excellent book, edited by Miss Marjorie Hope Nicolson, and published in England by the Oxford University Press. Lady Conway was famous for her learning, and almost more so for her perpetual headache, which became renowned throughout intellectual circles in England and Holland; she composed a book on philosophy which impressed Leibnitz; and she was a friend of Jeremy Taylor's who examined, in her presence, a man troubled by a ghost.

[3] The strange country of darkness which I had discovered in Joseph Hall's Works (see p. 7). Logan had used it in his Shakespearian essay.

'But it's an excellent little book; what's the harm in having a success?' I said, when I saw him.

'But I find that fashionable ladies are carrying the book round with them, and reading out extracts wherever they go.'

Now it's true that Logan was enjoying just then what he called a 'swim-gloat'; *Afterthoughts* had gone down well. He was, as we've seen, lunching out, and he was being asked to week-end parties which were liable to be photographed for the Press (Logan escaped what he would probably have called that last ignominy); but his evidence for the approval of 'fashionable ladies' betrayed a curiously simple view of worldly affairs.

He'd been giving away copies of *Afterthoughts*; however second-rate the smart recipient might have been—and many, I suspected, were worse than second-rate—they had that particular talent of those who live on the social light of other people's eyes—they knew, that is, how to pay relishable compliments; Logan digested happily their skilfully composed flatteries; their praise was evidently as sweet to him as the praise of wise, fastidious men. I was surprised, and I think a little shocked; but I didn't say anything to smother his joy.

In answer to his request, I called his attention to the success of Mr Sassoon's *Memoirs of a Fox Hunting Man*, which I knew he had admired. This, he declared, perfectly satisfied him.

He paid us a short visit about this time. We had just bought a pair of wrought-iron eighteenth century Italian gates. When he saw them, he insisted on paying for them, pressing this retrospective gift upon us so so gaily, so hopefully, and so sincerely, that it was impossible to resist him. (When, after his death, I showed these gates to his sister, Mrs Russell, and told her the story of them, 'Ah,' she responded, 'there was the real Logan!')

'I haven't had the bill yet for the gate,' he wrote (28.3.31), 'but will pay it at once and with pleasure when it arrives. I do think it kind of you to let me add this adornment to your garden and river-encircled promontory—I regard it partly as a votive-offering to the Pang—the young river-god who gives you so friendly and more than friendly an embrace as he passes down his pleasant valley. These Berkshire streams are fine striplings and altogether enchanting creatures—if I were a poet I should write the young life of one of them—all the experience he goes through till he dives into the Thames—how he falls in love and lingers at this place or that—how he is gleefully raped, and hurries on to each

29

new adventure, sometimes made to work his way in a mill and sometimes to show his fine form in a gentleman's park—a fine subject for a fine young poet!

'I am still speechless but am free otherwise from my cold. It is odd being cut off from human intercourse in this way—I rather enjoy it, for too much of my life is spent in talking, considering all the books there are to read.'

The poetical advice came, it seemed to me, somewhat late in time. Excellent as it would have been in the 1730's, the subject was not one to be happily dealt with two hundred years later.

Enclosed in this letter was a typed out request from a Primitive Methodist lecturer to quote some passages from *Afterthoughts*. 'Is *this* Fame?' Logan had written across it.

A postcard followed this letter (6.4.31):

' "Ye cannot drink of the cup of the Lord and the cup of Devils; ye cannot be partakers of the Lord's Table and of the Table of Devils." (I *Cor.*, x. 21.)

'So Paul says and Cudworth[1] repeats it—rather disconcerting, don't you think? Perhaps they are wrong—anyhow I hope to see you Friday.'

In the spring of 1931 he went for a short time to Italy. He wrote to me from the Berensons' villa, near Florence (8.5.31):

'I am living happily enough in a corner of this great villa—indoors, most of the time, as it rains almost every day.[2] But there are 40,000 books in the house, and so many of them that I want and ought to read, that I am as it were paralysed in front of the shelves and don't know where to begin.

'I have been coming here every year for many years, and hitherto the house has been full—too full—of tongues and talk, art-students, pilgrims, people of fashion, the ticking of typewriters, arguments on aesthetics, and echoes of gossip; but silence has fallen on all that, and the corridors and libraries only echo to my footsteps, as I wander about in the twilight; for all the shutters are closed, the doors barred and locked, and I can't even step into the garden without summonsing (*sic*) a grim porter to let me out. I enjoy the leisure and silence of the long wet days,

---

[1] Ralph Cudworth (1617–1688), one of the Cambridge Platonists. His most famous work, which I have never read, is *The True Intellectual System of the Universe*; experts declare it to be unreadable. In a sermon preached before the House of Commons in 1647, he nearly achieved greatness as a prose-writer.

[2] This had been corrected from 'most of the time'. Of some letters he made careful preliminary drafts, which he kept. Most, if not all, that he wrote to me were impromptu, showing no more forethought or strict care than such slight and obvious corrections.

and feel that I could live happily like this for ever, but I have to be back in London this month sometime.'

After he was back in England, we planned another literary pilgrimage, this time to the homes and countryside and grave of Edward FitzGerald; the excursion was easily arranged, for we were able to stay with my mother, near Aldeburgh.

'I have always,' he wrote (16.6.31), 'wanted to make a pilgrimage to the scenes of FitzGerald's leisure and loves, and pay my tribute to the memory of Posh; and besides I shall be glad to get away from London for a bit, as I have got myself into hot water by sitting at home and ·reading Dante instead of going to see my friends.'

My parents had gone to live in Suffolk when I was eleven years old; I must have been twenty-two when I ceased to make my home in that county. Its beauty was bred into me and I knew it well enough to love entirely the half-toned loveliness of its landscapes, those gentle slow rivers and unspectacular hills, those gradually pendant woods, the skies that seem to be always bright with clouds, and where few prospects fail to reveal the gracefulness and greying splendour of an ancient church tower; a land that is the lovely and altogether appropriate mother of such artists as Crome, Cotman, Gainsborough, Crabbe and FitzGerald. Its deep and quiet and unobtrusive beauty is one that not many people can feel at their first sight of it.

In Wales and Wiltshire we had explored and worshipped together at shrines unfamiliar to both of us; here I was the guide and I looked jealously for Logan's opinion of my engrafted home. There was no need for fear; he took in, with all its purity and delicacy, the aquatinted colours and forms of the sea-neighbouring countryside. We visited Aldeburgh, Crabbe's borough, with its grey sea and grey shining estuary that evades the sea, and its steeply shelving beach of grey shingle (and there are the waste salt marshes which Crabbe so bleakly and beautifully described); we went to Orford, with its rose-red eighteenth-century houses (shattered, alas, now, and wrecked by bombs), and the ancient keep, and the church where a Norman colonnade strides roofless into the graveyard; we showed him the great church at Blythburgh, where through the walls, made up almost entirely of glass, the low sky shines from beyond; and near Blythburgh we showed him where wave covers the ghostly city of Dunwich. One buttress of a fallen tower is all that remains; the old graveyard flows down in landslides to the beach. I picked up some bones and showed them to Logan.

'Take them away, Bob,' he said. 'You're young; but I don't like to be reminded of my mortality.'

There are no ecstasies in the letters of FitzGerald; it was the quiet, almost the dull appropriateness of his residences that charmed us in Lowestoft and Woodbridge; in the latter town we bought picture post-cards, and the old-fashioned look of the centenary pilgrims at Fitz-Gerald's grave made a pleasant subject for irony; more so did the view of his street lodgings where, at road level were represented, to Logan's delight, in a shop window, three shining white water-closet fittings.

'Ah, there's the Bull,' he said, when we were walking in Wood-bridge. 'When Tennyson stayed with him he had to sleep there; Fitz-Gerald told him some gossip, and then said rather nervously, "Don't let this get to the Bull".'

Tennyson ran in his mind that day—perhaps from the association with FitzGerald, and that evening, not over subtly, Logan dragged into the conversation an anecdote about him.

'People have curious ideas,' he said irrelevantly, 'about what is the matter with the world. Tennyson used to trace all evil to people who asked for signed photographs. My sisters[1] once went to visit him in the Isle of Wight, and he spent almost the whole time denouncing hunters of his autographed pictures. When they were leaving, Hallam Tennyson said to my sisters, "Did you ask my father for a signed photograph?" "No, indeed," they said, "we shouldn't dream of doing such a thing." "I think you'd better," said Hallam.'

Four years later, as I shall tell, Logan collected what sayings he could of a lady who was famous for the occasional oddity of her talk. Among them was this incident: A. C. Benson was once present with her at a sticky dinner party; he talked restlessly and continuously, trying to make things go. Afterwards she came up to him. 'What a pity,' she said, 'that you're only a *tête-à-tête* talker.' Logan could be unsurpassable as a *tête-à-tête* talker; I often wish I had made a record of his best remarks. If he put his mind on a subject, and wished to say what he felt and be-

---

[1] His two sisters (later Mrs Berenson and Mrs Russell) had gone to visit Tennyson, armed with a letter of introduction from Walt Whitman, who had said of them 'Smith has two admirable daughters—I have a real affection for them—for their unusual qualities. When they went to London I broke an iron rule of my life, not to give letters of intro-duction to foreigners. I wrote to Tennyson on their behalf, they went and delivered the letter and spent a precious afternoon with Tennyson as a result'. Horace Traubel, *With Walt Whitman in Camden.*
Mrs Russell confirms the story.

lieved, he talked like an angel; the artist, the ironic or uproarious wit, and the writer would be talking. On such occasions, he would face deeper feelings than he dared consider in his writings; he would also make use of a robust wit too unrefined (I don't mean improper, though he liked improprieties) for his delicate pen.

I once mentioned a book of American scholarship I'd heard of. Books of American scholarship, as many readers know, can be worthy of a new renaissance; some, on the other hand, appear to have been composed expressly for the book-shelves of hell. The work I asked about was evidently of the latter class.

'It's an interesting subject,' I said.

'Yes; it's an interesting subject, and he knows all about it,' said Logan, with pregnant reticence.

'What *is* it like?' I asked.

'It's like—it's like—' he paused— 'It's like an enthusiastic negro writing about Horace.'

But it was in private conversation that I first noticed the dichotomy of character which was to become later on so strangely evident in him. There was the wise friend, the enchanting man of letters—and there was also the diner out who blew his trumpet at dinner tables. He had a large collection of stories; some were short, and entertaining like the one he has just told in my mother's house, some however were very, very long, with always this same 'business' of pauses and asides, and every time the same variously pitched tones of voice. (I should emphasize that it was only his innumerable repetitions which, like a succession of blows, stunned the life out of these stories; at first hearing they were often the finest of entertainment.) A multitude of contexts might set him off, and once he was started, nothing, simply nothing, could be done; the story was bound to run on like an old gramophone record to its long-known, far off and altogether inevitable end. 'You've heard this before,' he would say to me. 'But you're paid to listen.' My only resource—I don't know if anyone else ever thought of it—was, when a twenty-times repeated story got too much for me, to get up and go to the lavatory. At a party among old friends he could add as well or better than any both to serious and humorous talk; but on more formal occasions he might be less successful.

One morning in London he said to me, 'I've got an unpleasant job for you today.'

I knew that a distinguished artist was bringing his wife to lunch.

'I know what it is,' I said. 'I'm to talk to Mrs —— to prevent her from interrupting her husband.'

That was the plan; but there was no question of —— saying anything for his wife to interrupt; Logan dominated the table, allowing no one else a single word, until, when we were having coffee, ——, quietly as befitted his exquisite manners, raised his gentle voice, and broke, at last, into Logan's talk.

Once, when Logan had been good-naturedly telling some ridiculous story against me in public, I retorted that I knew one which could make him look still more ridiculous. He asked to hear it, but I spared him. Later on, when we were alone together, and after great pressure, I reminded him of this luncheon party.

'Good gracious me,' he said. 'What on earth made you think I should mind hearing you tell that story? I like being made fun of. Besides,' he added gaily, 'it's always interesting to learn about oneself and one's weaknesses.'

Years after, acting on this precept, as I had often done to his amusement, I was to vex him gravely by telling a story far less to his discredit.

Returning from Suffolk and from this digression—in August we arranged another trip to Paris, after which, when I'd left him, he was to visit Mrs Wharton, and other friends of his in France.

'I shall expect you,' he wrote (1.8.31), 'to pick me up in Chelsea sometime after ten o'clock . . . I go to London on Thursday, and as the universe is so unstable and full of change and trepidation, if this aspect of it disconcerts me, as it sometimes does, I will ring you up on Thursday at about seven to try to get a reassurance through the intervening space that you are really likely to appear out of that mystery the following morning. Time-tables and dated railway tickets all confidently assume the stable course of things, but grave misgivings are suggested by metaphysics——.

'My sister has landed me here in a dreary little house—high up, but otherwise with no attractions—the home of a couple of invalidish vegetarians, beslimed with dreadful arty pictures and framed quotations inculcating the higher life, "As you make your thought so you must lie on it" adorns my bedroom. I find more solace (when rightly used) in another motto,

> "Bid Friendship with its holy rites
> Consecrate our days and nights."

'The books are books of the Higher Thought and the works of

Alfred Noyes, Arthur Machen and Stephen Phillips. I shan't spend many days in this atmosphere, but prolong my stay in France.'

In Paris, I remember most vividly his buying plaster busts of French writers, which, stained to resemble terra-cotta, afterwards stood along the tops of his bookshelves.

He wrote from France saying that his health was not very good; he was evidently entering a phase of depression. When he got back, I heard from him again; I had written saying that I had found myself writing a number of poems, adding, I remember, that I had never been so fruitfully impelled since, as a schoolboy, I had poured out pages full of enthusiastic slush. I must have invited him to stay with me.

'Your letter,' he wrote (27.8.31), 'has followed me from France to this idealistic and "aim-higher" hill-top, whither I moved my old bones a few days ago. I am moving the said bones to Chelsea on Sunday next, and there they must repose for a while—I hardly feel up to any journeys at present. But if you feel like coming up . . . for a little work, I shall be delighted to see you—you might bring my essays if you have finished them and show me your catch of fleas. But if the Muse is importunate, and you don't want to interrupt this happy flow of inspiration, you must postpone your journey. Such visitations are sacred, and must be made the most of when they felicitously happen to us. In any case, send me a line to London.

'I should love to pick fleas from your Garments of Narcissus,[1] and hope you are flinging them about in the freest and frankest manner—to reveal oneself is to reveal others to themselves, for we are all made of the same stuff, though that stuff makes but a scanty appearance in literature.'

In my answer I admitted a limit to my powers of self-revelation.

'Delighted to see you Wednesday,' he answered on a postcard (31.8.31). 'But am sorry you are troubled by this importunate sprouting and exfoliation of fig-leaves. It must be the wet weather.'

At this time Kyrle became ill and had a sudden operation in a Reading nursing home.

'I am so glad,' Logan wrote (3.9.31), 'to hear that the operation was successful and that Kyrle is comfortable. I have been anxious and unhappy about you both. You mustn't think of coming up to London while Kyrle needs you—there is not the least hurry about our work. Desmond has two volumes ready for publication, and I have just got a third from the typist . . . He has also promised me two unpublished

[1] The name I intended for my group of poems.

35

chapters of autobiography—one on "the beginnings of Bloomsbury" —which will add interest to our Vol. IV.

'I am living here alone in London—my sister is abroad, and there is not a soul I know in town. I read and read; or wander about the streets, gazing into shop-windows, or looking for charming faces—an inexhaustible pursuit.

'I suppose you are staying at Reading while Kyrle is in the nursing home. If so, do send me your Reading address; and if you have vacant hours, and would ever care for vacant company in them, I should like nothing better than to transfer my books and old bones to some Reading hotel for a few days, and go on with my reading there (the pun is inadvertent), seeing you at odd moments, and perhaps Kyrle, when he is well enough to see visitors. I can't remember whether I have ever mentioned it, but I have become fantastically fond of both of you—one forgets sometimes to speak of such things—and to be in your company is ever to me a delight . . .

'If . . . I could be of use to you in any way, engage rooms with bath at the best hotel (where I hope you will come as my guest), telephone or wire in the morning, and I will arrive by the train that reaches Reading at 5.45—the nice Midgham train. Honestly, I should love this, —I make the proposition from no spirit of kindness, and you mustn't fall in with it in any such spirit either. You have enough trouble as it is so don't let this suggestion bother you, or even trouble to answer it. We each suspect each other enough of being unselfish and kind; but there is no occasion now for such a misgiving. I have nothing to do in London, and should like to come to Reading, but only on the clear condition that you would like me to come.'

I rang up to say that I had ordered rooms in a quiet pleasant hotel on the outskirts of Reading; the diffidence, however, which had glowed so delicately through his letter, persisted, and he said that a threatening cold would prevent his coming. But almost immediately he wrote (5.9.31):

'I am wishing now that I was in Reading—the threat of a cold was apparently a false alarm, and it would be so pleasant to see you . . .

'I have plunged into a tremendous debauch of reading—another gigantic reperusal—Carlyle this time—40 vols. of his life and works, and 14 of his letters. A craving for Carlyle comes over me every now and then—a desire for the special kind of intoxication which the spirit in that great bottle produces. It has come on me now, and I am yielding myself recklessly to it. But this time I shall try to keep a record of the experience, note its effects, and try to see exactly what it is that produces the intoxication—there is an essay then to be added to my book; if I can keep my head clear enough to write it. I will bore you with the subject when we meet.'

The essays and the book which he alludes to were to become *Reperusals and Re-collections*, which was eventually published in 1936.

The ghosts to be called on in our neighbourhood are not very eminent; all I could introduce Logan to were Charles Kingsley and Miss Mitford, respectable people, both of them, but not to be deeply reverenced. Vistas more exciting are opened up through an indifferent portrait in the Reading museum, by Haydon, of Miss Mitford—a link, even at third remove, with Keats, was something for more solemn approaches. But when we went to the museum we found only an exhibition of indifferent locally-wrought water-colours. I never, somehow, was able to show that portrait to Logan, who always professed to deny its existence, affirming it to be a delusion of mine.

On this occasion, I dared the experiment of taking him to the cinema. Once before I had been with him, in Paris, when we saw the Surrealist film *Un Chien Andalou*. Of this film, I regret to say, Logan was no more worthy than I; so unworthy indeed, were both of us, that we at first mistook a pretty enough 'short' of abstract designs for the masterpiece we had come to visit; and concerning that we had nothing more gratifying to say than that we could now, we felt, claim to be thoroughly in the swim. In Reading, Logan responded a little more sympathetically to *Animal Crackers* by the Marx Brothers; it possessed, he declared, a certain pathetic humour.

Shortly after this, in attempting to combat his periodic depressions, he decided to avoid cinemas, for fear of the germs which, he was afraid, might bring on, or exasperate, his condition of listless gloom.

One of the things which struck him in Reading was the adjective in the advertisement for a 'commodious' residence.

He went on to stay near Frome. He wrote from there (14.9.31):

'As I was your spiritual guest, so to speak, at Reading, I feel that I ought to send you an acceptable Collins, to thank you for your hospitality and kindness, for both of which I am infinitely grateful. Only one drawback—I was so happy at Reading that my subsequent visits are rather tarnished in comparison. I do strive so hard to be worldly, and you make it so difficult for me! Worldliness provides the illusions, which are pleasant, but they do wear thin at times. However, I am enjoying myself here, and not repining—it is a perfect place and the company is amusing, and I shine, or at least I think I shine (which comes to the same thing) in conversation.

'I stopped at Trowbridge and dropped a tepid tear on the tomb of Crabbe. It is a fine church, and the old rectory a picturesque and commodious old house (I am haunted by the word "commodious", which I picked up in that avenue of Reading, and shan't be happy till I can insert it in some piece of perfect prose). "Jewel-coloured words" is another phrase (borrowed from Swinburne's prose) which I itch to steal, but I will be generous and let you have it for 6d., if you want it— you might use "jewel-coloured" for your mosaics.[1]

'I realized at Trowbridge that my visit was not spontaneous—it was the Time-spirit that wafted me there—Crabbe died there in 1832, and his centenary comes next year—I was simply the first of the pilgrims who in a few months will be flocking thither. Thus we are led by the nose when we think we are doing things of our own volition, and what we think we have discovered for ourselves today, we shall find in the *Daily Mail* tomorrow.'

This was followed up by a postcard (18.9.31). 'Did I say "jewel-coloured" in my letter? It should be "jewel-tinted".'

I spent the Christmas of 1931 with my mother; as there was no one else for it at the time, she asked me to go to the early service with her. Although I had for very long been indifferent in matters of religion, I didn't in the least mind going. I wrote to Logan, mentioning this, adding that I had not in consequence been the subject of a miraculous conversion.

'I am glad,' he answered (30.12.31), 'you weren't thunderstruck by a clap of Salvation, though you were certainly asking for it. It would be most awkward for your followers to be led to Jesus in this manner, and might cause a scandal in the courts of heaven.

'I am enjoying a real old-fashioned pre-war cold, and as I am speechless and woolly-headed I think you had better postpone coming up till next week. . . . Then, if I am all right, and the weather is propitious, we might pay our call on the Bertrams at Mansfield Park.'

When I next saw him, he said, 'I don't know that I like to speak to you. Do you know what you've been doing? You've been eating your God. It's the most shocking thing I've ever heard of.'

I thought at the time he was making a gay blasphemous joke as he would often as gaily crack an improper one. And he was, of course, joking. But I have realized since then that he really was a little shocked

---

[1] A poem I had showed him.

—not as an orthodox Churchman might be shocked at a renegade taking the Sacrament; but he was shocked at the Sacrament itself. It was the voice, all right, of the ironic elderly writer, but mixed with it was the voice of that Quaker child who was 'brought to Jesus' at the age of four.

Very strange to me now is the inward observation I made at about this time. 'Logan,' I more or less said to myself, 'is as gifted and complete a writer as I've ever known; and yet there's a greater lack of strangeness in him than I've ever noticed in any other artist.' (My comment on that now could be only a wordless exclamation mark.) He used to say that anyone could become a fine prose-writer, by hard work. His own character, as I first knew it, was, I think, to a large extent, his own deliberately wrought creation; although he had rejected half the ethics and all the doctrines of his natal faith, he had, as isn't unusual in such cases, retained the dead framework of his beliefs, and the mechanic structure of his old morality. What he had lost with the assurance of actual salvation, and what he had missed by the too-late results of his unconversion, were things, as I learnt afterwards to believe, which warped, troubled, and eventually tortured his spirit almost beyond endurance.

But sometimes, as in the case of my Christmas communion, his vestigial prejudices emerged entire. His distaste for the theatre, too, though in part aesthetic, was, so many of his friends believed, largely an undischarged residue of his Quaker upbringing. This upbringing bequeathed, as well, golden legacies, generosities and goodnesses, which spirits, far less worldly than Logan's, often fall short of.

I did some work once, collecting signatures on behalf of an excellent but financially unsuccessul writer, in order that he might get a Civil List pension. While I was engaged on this, Logan gave me a cheque for about thirty pounds (I forget the exact sum). 'Pay this into your account,' he said, 'and send him a cheque for the amount, saying it's from an anonymous admirer. You needn't tell anyone about it.'

The allusion, in this last letter, to Mansfield Park, was the result of a communication to *The Times Literary Supplement* by Dr R. W. Chapman; in this he had almost certainly identified that fabulous mansion with an actual building, Cottesbrooke Hall, not far from Northampton. Our excursion, if I remember right, did not come off until the following winter. We went down, and hiring a car in Northampton, drove out to the sacred estate and were, perhaps overwillingly, convinced. I vividly recall the distant large red eighteenth-century house as we saw it from the churchyard, and, in the foreground, broad withy beds, golden-red in the winter sunshine. A year or two later, Logan was able to enter the house, which we could not then do. Instead, feeling that it was the correct thing, he insisted that we should call on the rector. We introduced ourselves; to Logan's name he listened blankly, but on hearing mine, he said, 'Oh, I've heard of you; you write books, don't you?' I had by that time published three books; but I am afraid that he was most probably thinking of a great-uncle of mine, who wrote a number of books on sport. (People are ignorant over such matters; I have even been asked if I was the author of *Under the Greenwood Tree*.)

When we had left, Logan said nothing about this, and after a while —it was irresistible—I brought it up, saying, of course, nothing about my great-uncle. Logan was unresponsive. An hour or two after he said, 'You know, now I come to think of it, I believe that I'm rather annoyed at that clergyman knowing about you, and never having heard of me.'

1932

A cyclical gloom seems to have pervaded the first half of 1932. The stage hadn't come yet when he was to take for granted these strange immersions. He tried remedies; he gave up, so far as he could, going into public places, for fear of microbes; he took medicines; he sampled the effects of 'high air', which varied from a few hundred feet in Sussex to a few thousand in the Alps.

'The world doesn't look quite so black as it did,' he wrote (13.3.32), 'thanks I suppose to the arsenic. It's odd that one's view of the world should be a chemical one, but since this seems to be so, one must bless the chemistry which can brighten it a little.'

The arsenic didn't have much effect, and in May (7.5.32), he wrote from the Berensons' in Italy:

'Yes, I came to Italy—to my sister's house in the mountains near Florence which has been for many years a sort of second home for me . . . I am very lazy here, and have hardly been outside the garden. But it is a big garden, with woody walks and streams and nightingales—

all lovely with the exquisite and brief beauty of the Tuscan spring.'
He ended, 'this is a dull letter, I am afraid, but I am going through a
dull time—from which, however, I hope I shall soon emerge'.

About a month later (5.6.32) he wrote rather more cheerfully from
Switzerland. My second novel had just been published and he had read,
in some advertisements, quotations from kindly phrased reviews.

'I am perched here, and have been perched for the last two weeks, on
an alp hanging over the Lake of Geneva, which spreads out blue below
my window. The air is splendid and revives my spirits . . . Desmond was
here for a while, but has now departed—we had much chess and went
on many expeditions among the mountains. It is rather dull now he is
gone, but I have lots of books to read . . .

'I hope your head won't be turned by success—or rather I ought
perhaps to hope that it will be turned, as that sensation is among the
pleasantest that one can experience.'

But neither arsenic, nor high air, nor Tuscany, nor the Alps, had any
lasting effect on his condition; early in July (8.7.32) he wrote to me
from London:

'My collapse seems to be more of a collapse than ever—it is a kind
of tiresome eclipse that I have been through before, and I must wait
and read novels and be perfectly lazy till it is over.'

In September I sent him the poems I had been writing. He answered
(4.9.32):

'I like the poems a good deal, but have not the mental bite at present
to criticize. I am sorry you have found the summer otherwise barren.
You can't always be writing of course, but it is dangerous to let the
mind lie fallow for long, it is apt to run to seed, and the fallow field produces in the end nothing but weeds. When the impulse to write fails,
the remedy is to peg away at the delightful task of improving one's
mind—to give three or four hours a day to study and serious reading
and the mastery of some subject in which one is interested. If one forms
a regular routine of work, and is able to carry out self-imposed tasks,
one is all right. But very few people seem capable of this—almost no
one in fact. But I have confidence that you are an exception to the rule.
—— told Desmond the other day that he found himself so idle at
All Souls that he had had to go to the Bar to keep himself in regular
employment . . .

'I have found a new form of self-torture—chess problems—I spend
hours of agony over them every day.'

D   41

You can hear in this letter the whistle of the lash, the crack of the whip. While talking over Logan, after his death, another intimate friend of his said to me, 'Logan always had an ugly streak of cruelty in him.' Our virtues take care of themselves; the trouble is to find a use for our faults. In that carefully-wrought edifice, which was his character, Logan, during his golden days, made his vices benevolently profitable. His love of power appeared in the guise of good actions and generosity; his streak of cruelty took on the form of a ruthless and implacable tyranny in the art of letters, a tyranny in no way troublesome to his affections.

That autumn I published in *The Times Literary Supplement* some additions and corrections to my bibliography of Jeremy Taylor.

'I have returned to London,' he wrote (2.10.32), 'and am beginning to emerge a little, I hope, from the interlunar cave in which I have been hidden. I'm not yet up to work, but should like to see you, if you are up in London any of these days. Propose yourself to luncheon.

'I was much impressed by your bibliographical notes in the *Lit. Sup.* —a display of pedantry I greatly envied.'

His emergence from the cavern of gloom was explosive. In October (17.10.32) he wrote to me, announcing, in effect, that he was ready for work again. The 'dictionary-slinging' mentioned in his letter involved the handling of large volumes from the *Oxford Dictionary* which he professed himself too old and infirm to wield. The wedding was of two mutual friends:

'I have a little dictionary-slinging to do in which I want help.—Could you come to luncheon Friday next—stay if you can till the later train and help me entertain some friends at tea.

'The wedding went off most successfully—I went to the reception but not the ceremony, which I hear was very pretty. But I find it too racking to go to weddings—the bride or bridegroom may not turn up, and often, according to the novels and cinemas, a female appears and flings down a baby before the bridegroom, shouting, "You are the father of my child!" and this creates an awkward situation. I didn't suppose that this was likely to happen with——, but you never know. But pure young men are very apt to shoot themselves the night before the marriage; they are not certain of their powers. This has happened twice among my relations (purity runs in the family), and a doctor once told me that no pure young man ought to be left alone for three or four days or nights before he approaches the altar. It is too dangerous. Has this marriage been consummated? Nothing else is discussed in the elegant circles in which I move.'

The prenuptial suicide of male virgins was a favourite subject of discussion with Logan. Indeed it was typical of Logan's curious attitude towards sex. 'An improper mind is a perpetual feast,' was a revealing aphorism of his; but he had neither the robust bawdiness of the public school or the public house, nor quite the unhealthily evasive dirty mind of the sex-starved. (I cannot assert with authority that Logan died a virgin—though the fact, if proved, would not surprise me. But he did not seem to me dangerously repressed—I was never afraid that he'd get himself into trouble in the park.) No—apart from the classical and familiar sort of impropriety that none but the mealy-mouthed eschew —Logan's naughty stories frequently took the form of enormous, and, I am sure, quite unreal, fantasies about the private life of actual people. He used to build up for them astonishing structures of sexual predicaments, piling difficulties, frustrations, and incompatibilities on top of each other into islands and dungeons and palaces of nightmare and Boccacian imagination. When his victims appeared—for they were often friends and acquaintances of his—walking into the house as real, ordinarily-fleshed people, the effect was to make one feel a little giddy.[1]

Coupled with this propensity, was a coy puritanical reluctance to pry into the secrets of married lives. His aphorism that I've just quoted, can be capped and contradicted with another of his. 'It's interesting to peep through most keyholes, but not into the bedrooms of married people.'

In October I sent him the typescript of a story I had written about village life.

---

[1] These odd portraits were, I think, relics of his intercourse with Henry James who, so Logan told me, pictured all his friends and acquaintances as everlastingly transfixed on enormous and inescapable predicaments; though whether Logan regaled that great man with the same fantastic improprieties, I do not know. Henry James, according to Logan, used often to say, in certain moods, 'Do so and so for me,' and Logan would oblige with a character sketch. On occasions Henry James himself would 'do' a character for Logan. 'Do Gosse,' said Logan one day; no, Henry James, for that, must be in exactly the right mood; Logan must wait; health, place, time, in fact all external circumstances must be entirely propitious. 'Never the time and the place'. 'Do Gosse', said Logan more than once again; but that unborn masterpiece of spoken prose, one to have been transmitted orally like the Icelandic sagas until it became traditional, perished, alas, in the womb.

Logan himself would not infrequently say to me 'Do so and so'; an impromptu character was then expected, as complete as the circumstances allowed. When he desired briefer information he would say, 'Give me the low-down on——', in which circumstances only salient facts were needed.

'I like your story very much,' he answered (31.10.32), 'the best thing by far that you have done in prose, though your prose might be better! But that is true of all of us. Could you come to luncheon on Friday next, and I will show you some fleas . . . .

'A postcard from Lady Hilda this morning says "No lice, but scorpions, centipedes, hornets, monster spiders and a carp that eats out of my hand." She hopes to be moved to a cave on the Arno, nearer the centre of things next week.'

I have said that in his periods of euphoria Logan used to perpetrate the most preposterous practical jokes. With the last letter but one which I've quoted, was enclosed the draft of a joke blackmailing letter; I was to copy this out, de-educating the grammar, and send it off in a dirty envelope. The victims scored off Logan in this instance by sending him a cheque made out for a huge amount above a forgery of his own signature.

An anonymous letter was his commonest joke. He once tried it on Virginia Woolf. In one of her novels she mentioned two names, male and female,—imaginary as she thought,—which happened to be noticed by owners of the names. The female name corresponded, unluckily, with that of a genuine person, not altogether unknown to the public; and, since the circumstances under which these names appeared had implications of decease, a solicitor's letter was sent to Mrs Woolf, pointing out the pain and even damage which might be caused by such a suggestion. This at least was Logan's story. It must be emphasized that the insinuation complained of (that is if any complaint—and this must remain doubtful—had actually been made) was one of mortal and not of moral frailty. Logan then wrote to Virgina Woolf in the man's name, saying that her association of him with the lady in question had got him talked about in his neighbourhood, and had so upset his nerves that he'd had to give up his job as attendant in an underground lavatory. Happening to go to tea with Mrs Woolf, Logan arranged for a friend to ring up, while he was there, and pretend to be the imaginary complainant. All went off as he planned; Virginia Woolf was called to the telephone, and told him about it.

'What did you say?' asked Logan.

'I told him to go back to his lavatory,' she answered, and then went on, fixing him, I've no doubt, with her fascinating and alarming glance. 'Now who *did* write that letter?'

'I'll make inquiries for you,' said Logan, and shortly afterwards he rang her up and said, 'I've found out now who sent you that threatening letter. Augustine Birrell.'

But the allusion to 'Lady Hilda' in that last letter brings back one of his most elaborate jokes, an increasingly complicated erection, crazy and tottering, which in more than one quarter, according to his own rather doubtful account, nearly got him into trouble.

'Lady Hilda' was Miss Hilda Trevelyan, the gifted artist. She composed in watercolour the portrait which forms the frontispiece of this book, and which, in my opinion, is the most satisfactory—if not the only satisfactory—portrait of Logan that was ever painted. She had written to Logan from Italy, where he decided to pretend that she had had been kidnapped, and was kept in a cave by bandits, who were demanding a ransom of thirty shillings. Miss Trevelyan—need I add it?—had no hand whatsoever in the preposterous joke; indeed, she only learnt about it after her return to England.

Logan kept extorting money from his friends for this charitable purpose—coppers, sixpences, or even occasionally more valuable coins. Eventually he asked me to print a balance sheet for what he called 'The Lady Hilda Trevelyan Rescue Fund'. I produced what I can still flatter myself to have been quite a pretty piece of typography, illustrated with two old cuts in the style of Bewick, one of them being printed from the original block.

Twenty-four friends were put in, with extraordinary honours, and credited with equally extraordinary subscriptions. One, Mr George Plank, described as a Senator from Utah, had given by cheque, seventy-five million pounds, and by cash, eleven American cents. A well-known hostess had the honour of RSVP. Mr Cyril Connolly, the donor of sixpence, was given the OBE; Mr Raymond Mortimer, who gave nothing, became a Methodist parson; I, a Major-General, and Privy Councillor, ending up with the Garter, the Thistle, and the DSO, was described as having taken two shillings; Sir Osbert Sitwell, who was alleged to have sent by telegram half a crown, was honoured with the Victoria Cross and the MVO; Logan himself, as Suffragan Bishop of St Leonards, had subscribed £36,969 13s. 4d; the balance in hand was ten shillings.

I am quite incapable—fortunately perhaps—of such extravagant inventions, and I was only able, at this time, to play anything like a trick on Logan by discovering in Jeremy Taylor, where he had missed it, a small jewel-tinted sentence: 'They choose venial sins, and hug the pleasures of trifles, warming themselves at fantastick fires, and dancing in the light of glow-worms.' He answered on a postcard (21.12.32): 'Thanks for the quotation. I must learn what are venial sins; I sh'd love to warm myself at fantastick fires and dance in the light of glow-worms.'

1933

I have not, so far, given any account of the way that Logan went about his work; I have merely let it be known that the first job he undertook, with me helping him, was the selection and editing of Mr Desmond MacCarthy's writings. The books that came out were excellent, and his editorial methods exciting to assist at; but what made this work so fine a part of my education was first to watch and then gradually to share in the sensibility which led him now to choose a passage and now to reject one.

But as this vicarious book-constructing came towards an end he returned to the original composition, which had never, indeed, been altogether interrupted. In 1931, soon after I started work with him, he wrote and published, as a Society for Pure English Tract, a portrait of Robert Bridges as he was connected with that Society. In 1933 he published two more substantial books, On Reading Shakespeare and All Trivia.

I think, if I live to grow old, one of the clearest pictures I retain will be of Logan, sitting in his book-lined room, and reading aloud some new work of his.

This room in Chelsea looked out on to the open space of Burton Court; across the road are plane trees through which appeared, clear in winter, fragmentary during leafy seasons, the long magnificent façade of Wren's Royal Hospital. On the few wall-spaces left were some favourite pictures—a small eighteenth-century portrait of a red-coated man, a sepia drawing by Corot, and a rather naïve painting of sailing ships at sea; there was a needlework fire-screen, embroidered by his sister, Mrs Russell, and a small hearth-rug designed by Duncan Grant; above the bookshelves were the busts of French writers which he chose when I was with him in Paris.

After his death, looking round the shelves, a friend said to me, 'What a lovely reader he was.' Indeed, I have never seen anything quite like that assembly. Popular editions of fine works neighboured rare issues of recondite compositions. Many people, however passionate as readers, are apt, like myself, too apt, to regard books as objects desirable in their material selves. Logan rather liked fine editions; yet in his room I had the feeling which I have never quite experienced anywhere else, that here on the shelves was something far more than a collection of books, namely the incarnate essence of literature itself.

A wintry sun, I think, will always be lighting this room for me, since during that time of year the outer scene was at its most beautiful—the intricately laced, half-coloured branches of the planes, drawn palely as if in watercolour across the front of the hospital—the shining misty London sunlight—and beyond all this, grey and phantasmally splendid, the great Battersea power-station, with all the huge height of its two enormous chimneys.

That room, in the light of that townscape, I shall always think of as the chief scene of my work with Logan. My position was one for which there is no regular term; I was not what could properly be called a secretary, nor, in the professional sense of the word, a companion; what I was then settling down to, seems to me, looking back, a sort of perpetual apprenticeship. Logan was just as much my instructor as my employer; I was both pupil and assistant. The money he paid me was always referred to as my allowance; its purpose was just as much to give me the requisite leisure for literary employment, as a reward for the uncovenanted help which I gave him.

He had thus contrived a situation which beautifully illustrates the particular order of his generosity. My allowance being formally unconditional, he was able to look on the assistance I gave him as nothing but a kindness on my part. Although I should have found him then the most considerate of employers, he had, by infusing such a delicacy into our relationship, made our working life together one of surpassing spiritual ease.

Even at this date (1933) he used to spend a good deal of his time in bed. He had a tray which made a sort of portable writing table. It used to get covered with letters and notes, among which he would lose his fountain pen (which seemed a lesser disaster to me than it did to him, since it appeared never to hold any ink, and had always to be dipped into the pot); at each end of the tray were two basket-work cavities, and in these he was always losing the notes and sketches which he wanted to read to me.

When he was doing regular writing I used, as a rule, to visit him

47

once a week; more often than not I would stay the night and leave the next afternoon, thus putting in two days' work. When I arrived he would sometimes be in bed writing, or else sitting close to the window, with that writing-table tray on a card table in front of him. If he was at the height of his euphoria, in later years, most of the morning would be taken up with uproarious accounts of his most recent practical joke; he would read me some extraordinary anonymous letter, or show me the all but equally extravagant responses of his friendly victims. One day, shortly before the war, he told me how he'd had a fantastic mock quarrel with a lady; as a climax, he got Hammond, the maid who by then attended on him, to buy a dead cat from the dustman and throw it into the lady's garden.

At first I would try, as tactfully as I could, to get him down to the job in hand; but I soon learnt that these vapours must be allowed to escape of their own accord. At last, however, work would be started.

He would produce a wad of writing paper, fixed together on a stick-pin, and start reading. My job was to make every criticism, however captious, which came into my head; to almost all he listened patiently, and if, for instance, I pointed out an ugly repetition of words or of sounds, he would probably say 'Of course!' and correct it. Or I might suggest cutting out some words. 'Quite right,' he would usually answer; 'look how it improves a sentence to shorten it!'

Sometimes he was held up for the right word. If I could give it him out of my head, he would often say 'That's worth a penny' (or three-pence, or sixpence; I think the most I ever got was a shilling), and hand me the sum. But if my suggestions were unacceptable, the search began; Roget's *Thesaurus* was consulted; then that golden poetic dictionary of the seventeenth century, Poole's *Parnassus*, a glittering collection of gem-like epithets arranged alphabetically under appropriate nouns. If these failed he turned to his notebooks where, carefully indexed, he had a huge collection of epithets collected during his enormous reading. 'That's it!' he would say at last, lovingly, one might almost say lasciviously, murmuring over and over again the desired and delectable adjective.

Sometimes, but rarely, he would pass over a suggestion with the faintest hint of pique, 'This is only a rough draft,' he would say, 'I shall go over it again.' But, in general—so serious and honest was his atti-tude to literature—he would consider any suggestion, as happily as a great naturalist might receive some otherwise unattainable information from an amateur.

It was a curious situation—the master seeking and receiving advice from the apprentice. I suppose he used on the whole about half, or rather more, of my suggestions; but to leave that statement unqualified would seem to be claiming impertinently and over-proudly a large credit for his finished work. In fact, I can do nothing of the kind. He worked in prose very much as Gray worked in poetry; his writings are a mosaic of other men's phrases, so sought after, so chosen, and so disposed, that the resulting arrangement became an original composition, and the voice entirely his own. That I could help him was due to a capacity, partly my own already and partly acquired from him, for noticing and retaining the sort of words and epithets which he could use; also, as I assisted at his labours, I came to know the effect he would be trying for, and thus to notice when he was falling short of it. But this is very far from claiming that I could put those words to the same use as he did, or that I could ever achieve anything like that perfection of prose which at his best he so resplendently displayed. In no way did I father any of his offspring; but I was, I maintain, quite a good midwife.

In another way, too, I can claim to have been serviceable to him. I have told how we met, coming together on the grounds of a common taste, though I was but a new adventurer and he the old scholar much travelled in the realms of gold. As I got to know him better, and my spirit approached its maturity, both through my own efforts and from his direction, it remained evident that our tastes were of the same order. With a few exceptions we loved the same writers; I had accepted, as a fulfilment of my early searchings, his attitude to the art of letters. Now every artist, I believe, has in mind, while he is at work, a possible audience, though it may consist of one man only. Art is a communication, and in an unpeopled universe an artist could do no work. In me Logan was able to embody this requisite and imagined reader. My approval wasn't necessary; my suggestions and criticisms were, at their best no more than helpful or stimulating; but I was of much service, I think, as a sea mark in his voyaging across the waters of thought and prose.[1]

[1] Most of his works, I believe, if we could only resurrect his private and uncommunicated feelings, would turn out to have been written with one particular reader in view; I can certainly vouch, however, for no more than a single case. He once told me that the first draft of his autobiography *Unforgotten Years* was written as if to please the youthful brilliance of Sir Kenneth Clark. I have had reason for suspecting that *Afterthoughts* was intended for me.

The work was by no means approaching its end when he had corrected and polished the first draft. Sentences would be removed or paragraphs added. This involved telescopic expansion or contraction of his manuscript; in fact a not inconsiderable part of his composition involved the use, literally, of scissors and paste. Two halves of a page, with an extra passage interlarded, would be fixed on to a third piece of paper; another page, with a portion dissected from the middle of it, would go through the same process. On occasion I have known a page, in its final condition, to be made up of near half a dozen pieces of paper stuck together. He was careless with the adhesive, and often enough a long passage which he wished to retain would get stuck to and obliterated by the page before it. After a number of readings, sheets would become torn away from the split pins. I have witnessed in my life a fair number of authentic marvels; not least among them is that his favourite typist was able to produce from such a chaos and patchwork of varying sized pieces of paper, written over in very bad handwriting, a perfectly coherent typescript.

As I have said, in 1933 he published, in its enlarged form *On Reading Shakespeare* (it originally appeared in *Life and Letters*, September, 1932). Even comparing the two versions, I cannot trace any suggestions of mine which he must have used; but this isn't strange, for once he had taken advantage of such hints, they became so much his own, that my part in them—accidental it seemed—was easily forgotten. When the book appeared, and I wrote him the honest praise which it deserved, he expressed his usual disillusionment, dust and ashes the work seemed, and an utter waste of time. And then the change came, and its merit became apparent once more. He sent me a postcard recording this, 'A gay butterfly has just flitted into my room, and I am taking my pen to pin it down on this card. I looked in the light of the sun and the snow at my little green book, and for an enchanted moment I saw the gleam of beauty!'

As usual, he received many letters from admiring readers; one was rather odd. Logan had hinted at some gross but recondite improprieties in Shakespeare. A clergyman wrote for more detailed information; he was an old man, he said, and such a revelation would be of great comfort to his declining years. The appeal was irresistible, and Logan gave him the requisite hints. The clergyman wrote a letter of unbounded gratitude; how the information, he said, would have pleased a certain, now defunct, bishop, who, he went on to tell, used to call out, at the time of diocesan conferences, 'Hullo, ——, and how are things at Much Piddle!'

Of the other book which he published in 1933, *All Trivia*, I can indeed, with a confident memory, claim to have noticeably influenced its form. He had decided, either on his own or at a hint from his publisher, to collect in one volume *Trivia*, *More Trivia*, and *Afterthoughts*. For this edition the text was to be revised and polished, it was hoped, to a state of more than mundane perfection; he gave me a copy of each book in which I was to mark any faulty-seeming phrase, and to make any suggestions that came into my head for their improvement.

A problem of construction remained. He was anxious that the minute essays of the two *Trivia* volumes should blend with the aphorisms from *Afterthoughts* into a homogeneous work; but this effect could never be achieved by just putting the three into a single volume. I considered the problem—for how long I don't remember. Eventually I suggested, 'Why don't you take all the pieces from all three that deal with old age, or could be considered as the opinions of old age, and put them in a fourth section at the end. As a following up of *Afterthoughts* you might call it *Last Words*. Keep the preface from *Trivia* at the beginning and use *A Greeting* from *Trivia* as an epilogue.'

That was roughly what I said, and Logan acquiesced.[1]

Other changes were made, and then there remained only the choice of a title. I suggested his keeping *Trivia*—but no, Logan felt there was a better title somewhere at the back of his mind. One morning he said as I arrived, 'I've got the title! What do you think of *All Trivia*?' I was doubtful at first about this, but soon I had to acknowledge the excellent completeness of it.

When the essay on Shakespeare had been printed a firm of publishers wrote to Logan proposing that he should make for them a Shakespeare anthology; the suggestion shocked him at first, and then took his fancy. Eventually he failed to agree on the terms offered to him (rightly in my opinion); this gave him scope to enlarge the selection, but somehow, he was never quite satisfied with it, and although it almost reached what he looked on as a final shape, the anthology was

[1] There was one curious result, which may puzzle students and bibliographers of the future. In the English edition, listing earlier issues of the book's main sections, *Last Thoughts* is put down, with *Trivia*, *More Trivia*, and *Afterthoughts* as though it were a separate work which had already been published separately. This, of course, is not the case: *Last Words* has never appeared except as a part of *All Trivia*; and, although many parts of it were revised, they had all been published before.

never published by him. Much work was done on it. I came to London every week; in the intervals we both read gradually through the works of Shakespeare, and marked the striking passages. Then we talked and quarrelled and argued over what should be included.

It was during this work that I learnt what had made Logan so superb an artist—indeed I sometimes think the only artist—in the compiling of anthologies. I once suggested a respectable passage from one of the earlier, duller plays of Shakespeare.

'No,' he said very firmly. 'It's not good enough.'

'But,' I persisted, 'it's such a characteristic example of the early plays. It would show people what Shakespeare was like then.'

'That's the mistake of all anthology makers.' he said, almost angrily; 'they put in all sorts of things for all sorts of reasons like yours, and kill the selection. The only test is the quality of the passage.'

He went through all selections from Shakespeare, beginning with Dodd, and examined every anthology that had anything of Shakespeare in it. He consulted the selection, made at the end of the last century with his sister Mrs Berenson, and her husband, and privately printed and issued in Florence as part of their periodical *The Golden Urn* (in which there also appeared his first attempt at those little essays which afterwards accumulated into *Trivia*). Various friends gave him help, in particular Sir Dennis Bray, and above all Sir Trevor Bigham.

One morning when I turned up, he said, 'Were you blind when you were reading *Titus Andronicus*? We missed two perfect lines.'

'Then you must have been blind, too,' I answered defensively.

'Oh yes, I was; absolutely blind. What can have come over us! Just listen to this:

"Oh had the monster seen those lily hands
Tremble like aspen leaves upon a lute." '

The rebuke of this exquisite discovery we owed to Sir Trevor Bigham.

At intervals during the day Logan would come back to these lines, gustating them aloud,

'Oh had the monster seen those lily hands
Tremble like aspen leaves upon a lute.'

We went all through Shakespeare and a sort of scrapbook was made of printed selections; then Logan went over the selection again, cutting and cutting. But for a long time—until near the end of his life, indeed

—I think the catch in his mind was this; he had not at first been sure how much he was selecting from Shakespeare the poet, and how much from the dramatist. Beside single lines, glittering on the page like dew, the great dramatic scenes appeared heavy, and beside those scenes, a line might seem too fragile. He named his selection *The Golden Shakespeare*, and I think this title betrays his conception—a splendour of unsurpassable poetry, but it isn't in poetry alone that Shakespeare is unsurpassed; and the portraits and drama and comedy and spiritual flashes clamoured equally for admission. Logan, while welcoming these, was altering, though not spoiling, an ideal. This I believe; but however it was, he found that catch in his mind; the collection was put away to be brooded over. From time to time, I know, he would take it out, and make improvements, and though what he left is probably the best of all Shakespeare anthologies, he never published it himself.[1]

In July of this year he wrote complaining that he had been 'rather ill with a return of his old trouble', and that he was trying a new treatment. He had found himself once again in the shadows of a cyclical depression, which persisted until December. His state of mind interrupted an innocent little joke which I participated in. Looking about among family papers he'd found, some months before, a small tract written long ago in the 1870's, by his father. It was called *As Little Children*, and described the conversion of Logan himself, at the age of 4 to a state of Justification, and at 7 years old to that of Sanctification. Logan allowed me to print a small edition of this tract, which he rechristened *How Little Logan was brought to Jesus;* he altered some disguised names in the tract back to their originals, and wrote a preface. I printed the little book in a style of large pretentiousness, as deliberate as it was essentially inappropriate; and the title-page, like the Lady Hilda balance sheet, was adorned with an original wood-cut in the style of Bewick.

His preface to *Little Logan* seemed at the time just another characteristic manifestation of playfulness—too facetious perhaps for some tastes —and quite in line with his peculiar jokes. Deeper knowledge has found deeper significance in it—how deep even now I hardly dare to speculate.

'The reading of this little tract,' he wrote, 'has revived in my mind the memory of those early experiences; my conversion in that study,

[1] The selection was eventually published in 1949 as *The Golden Shakespeare*. The material he left still needed a considerable amount of editing.

so far away in Philadelphia, and so long ago; my subsequent lapses, my dread of the great Last Judgement which I believed might arrive at any moment; and the horrible sense that just beneath everywhere I walked or sat, six inches under every floor, or pavement or plot of grass on which I played, there seethed the flames of Hell into which I might be sucked down at any moment.'

Was it an evil or a morbid sense of mine which, years later, seemed to discover—as we trace on a wall the flickering and mottling light of a fire—in Logan's own room the flickering image of flames from that so closely situated Hell?

But at this time he discussed his infantile fervours as anyone might talk over the curious fancies and fantasies of his childhood. He told me how he used to clamber on to the Philadelphia horse-trams and hand round tracts, and even ask people if they'd been saved.

'What a little prig you must have been,' I said.

'An odious little prig,' he answered. However, this sanctified primness did not, I've been told, prevent his perpetrating acts of worldly mischief, such as stretching invisibly across the road, in front of his home, a thin black cotton thread at just such a height as would knock the top-hats off the heads of passers-by.

Early in December (9th) I got a postcard from him, 'I am beginning a "happy" again, and always begin by writing letters to *The Times* (see today's issue and also a letter in today's *New Statesman*).'

1934

Sure enough, the 'happy' had arrived, to run its pleasant, accustomed and rather alarming course. Of its more comfortable aspects, I remember his discovery, which he shared with me, of Greek coins. He had been given an early Rhodian coin; but what had bewitched him was one in gold from Byzantium.

He decided to sell a book—something obscure of Bacon's I think it was—and with the proceeds, if he got enough, we were each to buy five pounds worth of ancient coins. Fourteen pounds was what he obtained, and we made our purchases. Each bought an ancient silver coin from Athens, Corinth and Tarentum; and to these we added a golden hierarchical coin from tenth-century Byzantium. On one side stands the holy Emperor, and the Virgin crowning him; on the other sits Christ on a golden throne. The glory fades a little with familiarity from all our possessions; but these shafts of light from Byzantium keep a brighter lustre than is customary. Mine has accompanied me ever since, at home and abroad, and through some rather curious circumstances in wartime England.

'I feel I want nothing else in life now,' said Logan, looking enchantedly at his. And one morning he said to me, 'I was out to lunch the other day, and I said "I've found the solution for all the woes and troubles of life", and took out my coin and showed it. They couldn't understand. They looked at me with blank eyes. They were blind and deaf. People always are.'

About this time he sent me a letter, exuberant with euphoria. Enclosed with it were three anonymous letters, which I was to copy out, and, after dirtying the envelopes, to send them off to their undeceived recipients.

One of these was to what Logan called a 'great lady' who had taken him up for a while after the publication of his essay on Shakespeare. Playing Logan's own game, I wrote an answer, and got a friend to post it in a town near to her home. Logan was intoxicated with what he took to be her response, and when, eventually, I told him that I was the writer, he didn't really like it.

'After the first stage,' he wrote, 'of my recovered madness—writing letters to *The Times*—I have reached the second stage, that of writing anonymous letters. Perhaps you can forge and forward the enclosed just as I have worded them?

'My Byzantine coin will make me I feel happy for ever—it is [a] golden key to enduring ecstasy, and nothing can trouble my everlasting bliss. I feel that I have bestowed on myself the gift the Gods gave to Orion—and you know what that was.

'I expect you Wednesday—on Thursday, as I think I told you, I am lunching in the giddy world, so you can go lady-killing and running after girls then if you like. But don't bring any petticoats into the house!'

The 'lady-killing' was an allusion to a not very funny series of jokes following on some polite remarks made about me by a friend of his; out of this he had facetiously fantasticated for me a life of huge, successful and promiscuous licentiousness. When I stayed with him he would

55

either admonish me as in the last sentence of his letter, or else say 'If you bring anyone in to sleep with you, be sure to get them out of the house before the servants are about.'

His euphoria was rather a short one, its only lasting fruit being his essay on Carlyle—already foreshadowed—and which he named, when it came out in *The Times Literary Supplement*, 'The Rembrandt of English Prose'. A true man of letters is by nature a complacent polytheist; while withholding his own incense, he respects and believes in the gods which are worshipped at alien shrines. Carlyle is a spell-binder—that I knew well enough; how, indeed, could I deny it, when Logan showed me this sentence (which he quoted in his essay)—'Again the sun blinks out, and the poor sower is casting his grain into the furrow, hopeful he that the Zodiacs and far Heavenly Horologues have not faltered; and there will be yet another summer added for us and another harvest:' or this (which he did not copy out), 'For Nature, as green as she looks, rests everywhere on dread foundations, were we further down; and Pan, to whose music the nymphs dance, has a cry in him that can drive all men distracted'?

Yes, I respected—I had to respect—Logan's enthusiasm for Carlyle, but it was a respect cold and unresponsive. Nevertheless, I think I still proved myself a serviceable audience; he was writing—and he knew it —in the face of an unfriendly fashion, and I—though I hope not a blind follower of modish crazes—I represented the sort of reader he was anxious to make a convert of. The heart might be frigid, but the mind assented; and for the library of the spirit I bought an imaginary set of Carlyle's works. The volumes rest on an upper shelf still, and the dust rests on them; but if ever I take down those books to read them, it will be because of Logan's essay.

Among his closer friends, however, there was a more notable fruit of this 'happy'. In the telling it will probably seem less entertaining than, carried off as we were in the whirlpool of his exuberance, it appeared to us at the time.

Boasting was a sport of Logan's. Sometimes, I suspect, he was blowing, however ironically, a serious trumpet; he enjoyed praise and esteem; and he appreciated, better than he liked to acknowledge, even to himself, the worldly appreciation of what he called 'the great world'. But in general his boasts were a genial mockery; and the pattern of his lighter intimate talk was often an interchange of vauntings and humiliations.

Well, one day he bought a silver cream-jug, and announced that he would hold a boasting party; and this jug was to be awarded as prize to the boast which was acclaimed the most excellent.

Logan afterwards had a record of the proceedings typewritten and sent round to the several contestants. His own boasts were that, when he was an undergraduate, Jowett had spoken of him as the best breakfast-table talker in Oxford: that the late Lady Melchett had referred to him as a man of the world: that he was the only living writer mentioned with praise in the article on diplomacy in the *Encyclopaedia Britannica*: and that, being converted as a child, his father had written a tract on that conversion which had saved the souls of innumerable Red Indians.

Save for the tract, and perhaps for Jowett's commendation, I have always felt that Logan might have done better. I had some hopes of winning myself with two boasts, first that my mother had once been adopted in the Pacific by an island queen, and second, that through an intermediary, I had, when a child, given ringworm to a high dignitary of the Church. But I confessed myself easily vanquished when a young lady announced that she had a certificate of her virginity signed by the Pope.

In June he went to France on a friend's yacht. The result wasn't quite what he expected. The hospitality was all that could he looked for; but the owner's chief passion, he told me afterwards, was painting his boat, and for this purpose they lay up in a French port, where everything about the yacht was painted, including the bath, and Logan, together with another guest, had to steal secretly off, as though for a guilty assignation, to the public baths.

He came home; the cloud appeared again; and at the beginning of July (3rd) he wrote to me:

'As you have no doubt guessed from my not writing, I have faded away into one of my intermittences and dull periods. I had a fine spring of delightful madness, and am paying for it as usual by sanity and dullness. But I don't mind paying the price, though I can only loaf and read. I can't work, but if you happen to be in town, do come in and see me. Anyhow, send me your news—have you been dried out by the drought? How is Kyrle? I hope he is all right—give him my love, and ask him to order me a copy of Carter's *Enquiry*[1]. What a sensation it is making!'

[1] *An Enquiry into the Nature of Certain Nineteenth Century Pamphlets*, by John Carter and Graham Pollard, the book which so brilliantly exposed the forgeries of T. J. Wise.

1934

We had indeed suffered from the drought; our green and silver Pang dried up, leaving an ugly wide furrow of malodorous and weedy mud Logan professed himself much afflicted. Ever after this, during hot summer weather, he used to say, from time to time, 'I worry about your river'.

His spirits gave one little, bibliographical, flicker, before he had passed altogether into his temporary cloud. I saw in a bookseller's catalogue a copy of the 1645 edition of Milton's poems—a rare and enchanting book in which some of the loveliest English poems appeared for the first time in print. *Comus* is found in it (though not for the first time), introduced by what is perhaps the most charming letter of compliment ever written, from the old Sir Henry Wotton to the beautiful and youthful Milton. This particular copy was defective, and relatively cheap because of its defects; but Logan was satisfied. 'Thanks so much,' he wrote on a postcard, 'for letting me know about the Milton. I rang up at once and bought it, and am *delighted* to have it.' For the rest of his life it stood on a little shelf in his bedroom, where he could reach for it to read it without getting up.

1935

In the spring of 1935 Logan emerged again from his gloom; as time went by these emergences became progressively more sudden startling, and dramatic. Often, as I have disclosed, they would take the form of a letter to the paper. When one of these letters appeared, if I hadn't already heard from him, I would write, asking if he needed any help, and work—or extravagant play—would start again. But in the year that I'm at present writing of, I made a not altogether happy discovery; whether from a seven years' familiarity, or from the otherwise unperceived increase of his mental affliction—and I believe now it was the latter—there supervened a period of difficulties and peevishness; it seemed as if the depression of his shadowed months was combined with the energy of approaching gaiety so as to reveal the worst aspect of both conditions. It was not a shaking of friendship, for that remained still, firm and loyal and affectionate on both sides; but it was a cloud which I came to face with certain, increasing, and, at the very end, with unendurable dread.

'What I like in a good author,' Logan wrote, 'isn't what he says, but what he whispers.' In the following letter, a nasty whisper can be faintly heard as an undertone. Does it need pointing out? In addition to the salutary lash I've alluded to before, notice the hint that my presence would not be of any help to him. If this letter were all the evidence, my interpretation would be without value and probably a sign of my own peevishness; but I learnt to recognize in such pin-pricks—which at other times were altogether playful and good-natured—an essential manifestation of his cyclical moods.

I had planned, if it didn't interfere with his work, to make a short botanical trip into the Picos de Europa, those mountains whose enormous crags arise so startlingly and with such beauty some miles inland of Santander

'By all means go to Spain——,' he answered (13.5.35), 'I shan't be able to get back to Shakespeare till the autumn. I'm getting a vol. of collected essays into shape, and no one can help me in this.

'I should be pleased if, when you didn't work for me, you would grind a bit at some work of scholarship—a life of Shaftesbury, or any subject that interests you, and get it finished. Nothing is more educating for the mind than putting through a job of this kind—whatever grip of mind I possess I acquired in my work on Wotton.

'But I don't set up to dictate—only to make suggestions.'

The Collected Essays, of course, appeared as *Reperusals and Recollections*.

A letter of happier whispers (3.6.35) was waiting for me when I got back from Spain.

'Can you remember when it was that we made our pilgrimage to Mansfield Park? Two or three years ago? I kept Chapman's letter in the *Lit. Sup.* about it, but omitted to note the date, and my neighbour Trevor Bigham wants to look it up. He is motoring me and Marjory Madan up there on Wednesday, with an order to see the house, which is to be sold by auction in a week or two.

'Marjory and I want to stop on the way to drop a tear on the tomb of Mrs Humphry Ward, but that he says he won't allow.'

Enthusiastically and happily the final work started on his collected essays; he found plenty for me to do. Sometime during the succeeding weeks, I must have asked him to alter the date of a working day; I was always, as he knew, very scrupulous about keeping to my arrangements with him, and I must have had some important reason for it.

I also, about this time, attacked, in the friendliest way, his predilection for his 'great world'.

'You wouldn't call me a snob, would you?' he asked.

'Of course I would,' I answered.

'I am expecting you to luncheon,' he wrote (21.7.35), 'on Thursday, Aug. 1st, and hope you won't chuck me again—I really have some work I must finish before I sail for Sweden on Saturday the afternoon of the 3rd, so am hoping that you will stay, as you promised, till then.

'Since I have heard (we hear everything in Chelsea) that the last time you were up you lunched with Lady Ottoline to meet the Duchess of Portland,[1] I have felt a little annoyed—not so much at being chucked, but because you seemed to think your preposterous and incredible alibi a good enough excuse to put off on me. It is polite to make one's excuses as plausible as one can; as I did when I chucked you for the funeral of my great-aunt in Kent, to which I took Lady Leslie, and where I met Lady Henry Bentinck, as I told you afterwards.

'Since you so brutally accused me of being a snob and social toady, I have scoured my mind (so for want of a better term I call it) elaborating in odd moments answers to this charge. These sophistications and rationalizations fall roughly under five heads.

'(1) I don't go snobbing often—I refuse more invitations than I accept, especially to country houses—to Mells, Taplow, Petworth, etc., which I never now accept.

'To this, however, my anti-self answers:

'(A) You don't get many invitations in London, and those you do generally accept. You aren't a real social success like Desmond, and when you are invited, it is often only at the last moment, to fill in a gap.

'(B) As to country houses, you don't go because you are afraid you will have to wear tails and a white waistcoat. Your white waistcoats are rather shabby; your tails you have outgrown; and you don't want the bother (and the humiliation) of going to a smart tailor to have a new tailed dress-coat made and fitted.

'So then I go on to my next defence.

'(2) I have never known anyone to whom this cup has been offered who has put it from his lips.

'(But, says my anti-self, Robert Bridges didn't go snobbing, and Santayana wouldn't do it—wouldn't dream of such a thing.)

'So for my next excuses, which I think are better.

'(3) It is rather fun when one is old to sip those cups of poison which

---

[1] This party—need I say it?—took place only in Logan's undeceived imagination.

would have been deadly to one in one's youth—and in age you can do this with impunity, and safe, ironic pleasure.

'(4) Why not have illusions, whether sexual or social? Is this a world in [which] romance hangs on every tree? (See *All Trivia*, p. 26, if you possess that work.)

'(5) The great world, though hollow within, presents at least the external form of a *décor* of what life might be, and ought to be—the ideal of a beautiful and happy and splendid way of living; and people of imagination ought to be able (and have generally been able) to fill out that empty form with poetry for themselves. And if there are toads to be eaten at these feasts (as there always are), there is an ironic fun in noting their odd appearances, and turning them into funny stories to tell against oneself.

'Still all this inner argument and self-defence are obvious proof of a sense of guilt, and a kind of self-contempt; and indeed I have really felt ashamed of myself this season to find that I have been treated as far inferior to André Maurois; and worse than that, to an American named Knoblock, who both are regarded everywhere as much more important than myself. When they speak, no one will listen to what I say. And yet, and yet—off I go on Thursday on one of the most snobbish expeditions I have ever made!

'So pour the contempt upon me which I deserve; and in anticipation I will now air a mild grievance which I have long nursed against you.

'I have (or at least I hope I have) always in addressing envelopes to you given you your twopenny title (upon which you set so much store); you on the other hand have never added to my name the honours which I have won in my long, varied and distinguished career. I will now tell you what they are, in the hope that you will pay more attention to this point in the future.

A.G.I. (Associate of the Institute of Certified Grocers)
R.D. (Rural Dean)
B.A.O. (Bachelor of Obstetrics)
M.O.H. (Master of Otter Hounds)
C.S.S.R. (Congregation of the Most Holy Redeemer)
L.M. (Licentiate of Midwifery)
K.H.S. (Knight of the Holy Sepulchre)

'As you know, except in the case of the K.G. (which by some oversight has never been awarded me), it is only necessary to put two titles on the address of an informal letter; the rest can be implied by a polite "etc". I am however only adding P.T.O. to the address of this epistle, as I don't know what your other honours are. If you don't know what P.T.O. stands for, I will explain it to you when we meet.'

I think it was my disputing of Logan's fifth contention when he raised it in conversation which had released these full and eloquent excuses. Was he a snob? Of course he was; but I think that this weakness was largely of transatlantic origin. I don't mean that he was the comic American snob of plays or pictures, but that he discovered in British titles a touch of alien romance, such as an Englishman could easily find in a highland chieftain or Polynesian royalty. His favourite title was a baronetcy, and it was a frequent joke of his to say that, although he didn't really aspire to intimacy with members of the peerage, most of his friends were either baronets, or closely connected with holders of that rank. It was this faintly surprised interest in English conventions which produced his ludicrous catalogue of imaginary distinctions. He used to amuse himself sometimes with questions of etiquette and precedence, and, in pursuit of such matters, he had come across these titular initials in a copy of *Whitaker's Almanack*.

While this letter was in the post I developed the symptoms of diphtheria; my attack was so absurdly mild, that I missed, in this disease, all dignity of seriousness except the name. But, as I had very lately been at one of his luncheon parties, I hastened to let him know of it over the telephone, so that he and his guests might take the necessary precautions. He wrote to me at once, enclosing with his own the noble gift of an original letter, written by Jeremy Taylor.

'I was glad to hear your voice on the telephone yesterday,' he wrote (23.7.35). 'It sounded fairly cheerful, though perhaps a little querulous, as is natural in your condition. It is good news that your attack isn't serious . . . you don't seem to have succeeded—as I did with that sonnet infection—in getting rid of your germ by giving it to anyone else. "If a mad dog bites you, bite the girl next door", is a sound principle of village medicine, but none of the people you met at luncheon here the day before your attack, are dead, or even ill yet—however, my doctor is coming this morning to give me a slight pro-phylactic injection, as I have paid for my Baltic cruise, and don't want to lose the money . . . Before visiting the land of the Bolsheviks we are going to practise blowing our noses without handkerchiefs, as that is the test whether you are a true proletarian, and I don't want to be shot as a *berjoise*.

'You will have received by now a letter full of jibes which I wrote before I knew that you were ill—my pen can't help spitting venom; but I hope that the enclosed, which you may regard as a birthday present— you are 74 I believe on the 31st—will make amends. I think you will enjoy the mingling of piety and pecuniary considerations in the letter of the Bishop of Down [Jeremy Taylor] to Archbishop Bramhall— also the mention of Lord Conway, from whose house it seems to have been written. I wish it told us how Lady Conway's headache was. How the Bishop hated the Presbyterians, and wanted to put the law on them! I don't wonder——'

This 'sonnet germ' was due to Sir Dennis Bray and his theory as to the original order of Shakespeare's *Sonnets*; the consideration of this theory Logan had successfully, in his own words, 'put on' to somebody else. I don't know if it need be added that the age I achieved on that particular birthday was not 74 but 33. A postscript followed:

'I am trying to work myself up to an heroic deed—nothing less than making a parcel of two books to send you. One is Desmond's last vol. *Experience*, so I hope your grievance about that will be dismissed from your vindictive mind.

'The other is the novel of Edith Wharton's in which she masticated and served up ——. "Churley" is the name she gives him, and you will find that I have indexed at the end the pages on which he appears. The rest of the novel isn't worth reading; indeed, just looking again at the pages distressed me sadly. She gets faintly good ideas, and treats them in a workmanlike fashion, but Good God, her style, or rather her appalling lack of that quality! After reading Henry James's prefaces (which I have enjoyed to the limit of enjoyment) poor Edith's flatness really turned my stomach—and I am fond too of the lady, and she is a generous and affectionate friend. But can one forgive such platitude of style? I can't really do it;—but still, she has a marvellous cook.

'On p. 346 of Henry James's book there is a sentence which I think must have been meant for her. "We may traverse acres of pretended exhibitory prose from which the touch that directly evokes or finely presents, the touch that operates for closeness and for charm, for conviction and illusion, for communication, in a word, is unsurpassably absent." I like the use of the word *unsurpassably*.'

My attack of diphtheria passed easily away; Logan returned from his cruise in the Baltic; after a short trip abroad I was in full health; and work began.

There wasn't any question now of saying, in the matter of his collected essays, 'no one can help me in this'. Logan, to use his genial images, cracked the whip loudly and settled down to a course of intense slave-driving. Most of the essays in *Reperusals* had been published already, and with two exceptions nothing was written specially for it. The most recent was the essay, *Fine Writing*, which was published in 1936.

The essays are all dated—the earliest 1898, and the latest 1936; but, except for the latter there is a certain falsity in these subscriptions, since everything was scrupulously corrected and re-written, and many essays were conspicuously enlarged. Attendance on this work took up most of the London days which I spent with Logan during the second half of 1935, and it lasted well into 1936. I suppose the essay which needed most work was the original introduction to his anthology of aphorisms. This essay was almost doubled in size; small selections of aphorisms were introduced into the text of it; new aphorists unrepresented in the anthology were mentioned. This work begot as tail-pieces, two separate studies, one of Dr Fuller, the eighteenth century physician and aphorist from Sevenoaks; the other, which he called *Captain Shandon*, was about Maginn, 'bright, broken Maginn', who as the Captain was introduced by Thackeray into *Pendennis*, and who had published a curious and entertaining work *The Maxims of Sir Morgan O'Doherty, Bart.*

In the pursuit of aphorisms, Logan heard of a nineteenth-century sage named Duppa. I had to look up some things for him in the reading room at the British Museum, and he asked me at the same time to get Duppa's book; if the aphorisms appeared to have any merit at all, I was to copy out a small selection of those that seemed the best to me; these, if he liked them, he would use in the essay. This plan brought about an incident which, some ten years later, was to have unpredictable and distressing consequences.

The slip for Duppa's book seemed to have been misplaced in the catalogue, and, on my first visit, I could not find it. Not long afterwards, on another visit to the British Museum, I discovered the entry, slightly out of its expected position. Logan, on the whole I think rightly, did not use the aphorisms I brought away for him. I have the little note-book now; he had kept it for many years on the shelf over his bed. The aphorisms are not altogether despicable, as these show:

> The greatest art of a quack is to time his imposture.
> When expectation is disappointed, however unreasonably, former services are forgotten.
> One who can do no harm is rarely valued for his good nature.
> He who cuts down a man's wonder creates an enemy.
> The sleep of friendship is its death.
> In language, the ignorant have prescribed laws to the learned.
> One ungrateful man does an injury to all who are wretched.

He had given me the instructions about Duppa's aphorisms in a letter (27.9.35), which concluded:

'In case a passion for work consumes you, I enclose a few notes that might be looked up in the B.M.—but about these there isn't the least hurry. I have just fetched from the London Library Wellington's *Maxims*, but as it consists of long dull extracts from his political speeches, I am afraid there is nothing in it for my purpose. Why are all anthologies and books of selections made only by the blind?'

A favourite observation of his in such matters was that most anthologies seemed to have been made because the compiler hated the authors concerned.

The work went prosperously on, and towards the end of August (31.8.35) he wrote to me:

'I am immensely relieved at the progress—thanks to you—my book is making towards the press—I did not realize how much it weighed on me, and am looking forward to further progress on Wednesday.

'Don't forget to bring up Bradley's *Maxims*—I only want to look at it—I haven't yet reached the stage of friendship which consists in taking back one's gifts. That is postponed for the present.'

There was another work, of quite a different kind, which Logan carried out during 1935. Though not a practical joke, it was much of the same order, and, like many of his jokes, got him into some trouble.

I have already mentioned that famous old lady, whose conversation was noted for its pregnant and startling irrelevancies; as Logan put it, she was a genius who had invented a new kind of wit.

A close relation of hers once explained to me—so far as such things can ever be explained—the cause of her strangeness. To her spritely intellect, I was told, the dank academic air that she lived in, was, in its essence, unbearable; accordingly, she populated it, for her mental comfort, with spirits as strangely brilliant as her own, and, for a fleshly habitation, gave to these spirits the bodies of her husband's colleagues. Stolid, serious and conscientious Mr Brown, for instance, might call on her for tea and a talk, but it was a very different character with whom she kept up a conversation. Here are three samples of the alarming methods she employed for heightening the talk:

'When someone had given a long account of successive dynasties of ancient China, she sighed and said, "How restful, how impartial!"

'Meeting in the streets one soaking day a party of half-drenched

65

people who were going sadly on a water-party, "Ah!" said she; "the river is the best place on a day like this, there are no puddles."

'Once she asked a schoolboy who had been for a walk, "Now, tell me, what did you see?" "Well," the boy answered, "I don't think I saw anything." "What!" she exclaimed in astonishment, "not even a bee?"'

Such golden fruit of almost pirandellian cross-purposes were covetously treasured, and from time to time have found their way into memoirs, or even into fiction; but many remained in oral tradition where, however, immune from moth and rust, they were still liable to other as deadly agents of destruction. Logan conceived the plan of collecting all that he could, and privately printing them in a little pamphlet. He seemed to have an inkling that he might be heading for trouble.

'What I shall say if there's any trouble,' he told me, 'is that I collected these for my private amusement, and that some unscrupulous person—that's you—stole the manuscript and had it printed. Then, I shall say, to save the collection from getting into unsuitable hands, I bought up the whole edition.'

The collection was duly made, and, so enthusiastic did Logan become, that he treated these anecdotes as a discrete art-form, and invented some of his own. I will give two of them. The first is a recension from several drafts; the second was contained in a letter to me.

'Oysters!' cried Mrs ——, 'by all means let us have oysters and the archdeacon for luncheon. I always like oysters of either sex. They change it,' she said, lowering her voice. 'So they could answer the question by which the gods of Olympus were puzzled: Which sex has most fun in the oyster-bed? All oysters know, but no oyster will tell. That's why "dumb as an oyster" is what they say, "dumb as an oyster in Essex".'

'Of course I had reasons for joining the Catholic Church,' Mrs —— said to John Bright, 'I always act on reason—like dear John Wesley. "Our Jack," said his father, "will never do anything, *nec enim crepitare*, unless he can give a good reason for it." You know what I mean,' Mrs —— said, fixing a beady inquisitorial eye on the Quaker.

The pamphlet was printed under my supervision, in Reading (for its form, I imitated the famous faked first edition of the *Sonnets from the Portuguese*); and then the more than expected little storm broke. Relations who, as it now turned out, had already shown their distaste for the plan, not altogether unnaturally protested against the little book.

'I know nothing about it,' Logan said to me. 'All I know is that I made the collection, and then some unscrupulous person stole it and got it printed; so to prevent matters getting worse I bought up the whole edition. I wonder who the scoundrel was!'

This was, of course, all part of the planned joke; but after he had repeated it several times I was astonished to realize that it wouldn't have taken much to make him actually believe his fantastic and playful alibi.

Among those who objected are people whose judgment and character I greatly respect, and for whom I have a most affectionate regard; but I must think that, on the whole, they were mistaken. It was suggested that the lady in question was made to appear unkind and illmannered, and, which is worse perhaps, that the anecdotes as edited and presented by Logan were often inaccurate.

As to the first, I can only say that it is not the impression I get from Logan's collection; and it is, I think, discounted by the fact that some of the unkindest seeming cuts were lovingly cherished and gleefully passed on by her felicitous and adoring victims.

As to the second, it must be remembered that there is an essential truth of anecdote as well as a literal. Did not Boswell tinker with Johnson's recorded talk? And were not Madame de Sévigné, Gray, and Cowper promoted immediately to their supreme epistolary thrones on the score of texts which had been stringently edited? Some of Logan's anecdotes could undoubtedly be strengthened by the correction of literal truth; some were perhaps of doubtful authenticity; but for all that Logan has deliciously embalmed a character with a high fantastic and nonsensical genius, a genius in the order of Edward Lear's or Lewis Carroll's.

But in delivering this judgment, I must also give a warning; Logan's wild enthusiasms were like charm; caught by them, one's critical faculties notably diminished; but if, as he might have said, the bug didn't bite, they were as disgusting as charm can be when it fails.

The preparation of *Reperusals* and of *Fine Writing* took up the rest of the working hours in 1935; but these hours were always preceded, and often broken, by the long discussion of jokes and playfully contrived controversies. Once he announced that, on account of his chronic bronchitis, he was going to give up smoking for a certain time; I didn't believe him, and bet half a crown that his resolution would fail.

We also had an argument about an image he had used in compiling the guilty little book I have just described. The knight in chess, he said, moved one square forward, and one to the side; I maintained that it was two forward and one to the side (or vice versa).

In the middle of November I had a postcard from him:

'I claim credit on 3 grounds.

'(1) Some proofs from the *New Statesman* arrived late here last night, and I paddled out in the rain (maids at a whist-drive) to forward them promptly to you.

'(2) I was right (I am always right) about the Knight's move—one ahead, one round the corner.

'(3) I kept my vow about smoking, so you owe me 2s. 6d. I have recovered my self-respect—a dignified but not easy-going companion.'

On December 30th I had another postcard:

'Here's a good addition to our little book, "Writing is like breathing to the Bensons. It's wonderful! but how one hates to be breathed on".'

1935, it will be seen, was a rich and notable one in Logan's life; in the history of our friendship it was notable also for a plan that he made then. He suddenly decided that he would like to visit Teneriffe, and asked me to go with him.

If he'd chosen some place that I'd no desire in the world to visit, I'd have felt in duty bound to be his companion on the journey: but to visit the Fortunate Isles, and to stay for some weeks at the foot of that great volcano, the most romantic, perhaps, in all the world! Logan suggested that since we were going to be together for something like two months, we should draw up a protocol of behaviour. Had I, he asked, any conditions I would like to insist on? The only large condition I felt inclined to make he agreed to most happily, namely that I might leave him for so long as was needed to climb the Peak. I also stipulated that I should be granted a certain amount of time on my own for exploring and botanizing.

1936

On February 3rd I got a postcard from him, saying that the *Reperusals* was practically finished.

'The P. & O.,' he went on [a curious slip, for that was not the line we were to travel by], 'won't promise to allot a cabin for Las Palmas till 10 days before sailing, but say that one will almost certainly be available. I want to get off, especially as Lady X says that I have written her a blackmailing letter, which she has put into the hands of the police.'

The joke involved was one of portentous intricacy. It started with a controversy as to what actual town Jane Austen had in mind when she created Highbury in *Emma*; of the alternatives, Leatherhead and Cobham, Logan believed in the former.

'As you will see by the enclosed letter from Lady X,' he wrote to me (8.2.36) [in which communication, for all its intrinsic innocence, I must conceal the names], 'I am getting into rather hot water, so it's as well that I am leaving these shores next week. I wrote to Lady X suggesting that she had probably written that blackmailing letter herself, or possibly the Dean of Westminster. I told her also that Lady Y Z has sent me a note saying that the scandal at Cobham was *frightful*, and that Dr A B had chosen Leatherhead for her residence on account of the purity of its atmosphere. To make my case complete I got Miss D E (whom I think you have met here), who is an accomplished forger, to forge a letter, dated 1869, from J. E. Austen Leigh, who wrote Jane Austen's memoir, in which he says that he had heard his aunt say that Highbury was meant to be Leatherhead and not Cobham. This I have sent to Lady X and have received this morning Miss E's bill for £1 12s. 7d. I think the enclosed (if you will copy it out and send it) is the answer she deserves for so extortionate a charge. While you are about it, why don't you write to F G offering to send (for a consideration) proof that Lord —— was the real father of the East End quadruplets? Blackmailers and the blackmailed must help each other, or we may all end up in Wormwood Scrubs.'

One specimen should perhaps be given of Logan's anonymous letters. This was 'the enclosed':

'Madame,

A chap as I knows has pinched from a waist paper bascot a bit wot com from your address. Hes a great pal of mine, and if you wishes to recover this compermising docerment I wil get it for you on receet of wot you charges for your forjurys (£1 12s. 7d.) wich shood be sent to me at——'

The address to be given was my own, and the letter was to be signed WELL-WISHER.

I may add that this was one of his better productions in that particular form. When I first knew him he could never, on such occasions, altogether avoid the natural elegance of his style, and I would correct his anonymous letters, by expunging the neater phrases. When I saw the specimen in question, I was able to congratulate myself that, however narrowly, I had, in one field at least, successfully influenced his art. The letter is most gratifyingly, if unconvincingly, inelegant.

The day arrived soon when, leaving behind us both blackmailers and blackmailed, we went by train to Tilbury and got on to the boat which was to carry us to Las Palmas.

I have already written and printed an account of our journey to Teneriffe; Logan I mentioned under the name of Anthony Woodhouse, a pseudonym he had given, in the privately printed *Trivia* of 1902, to its imaginary author. I did not wish—and he would very much have disliked it—to boost my own book with a familiar use of his distinguished name. So far as I am aware no one, who did not know it already, ever guessed from my published record, the actual name of my travelling companion to Teneriffe and, later, to Iceland.

But then I was writing chiefly of botanical discoveries, and description of the country as I saw it. In recording, a second time our southern journey, I seem again to be embarking on a voyage of discovery; but my quest this time is not for flowers or unfamiliar landscapes, but for the plan and secrets and motives of Logan's heart, which later on were to puzzle and trouble me so deeply.

I am perfectly aware that to many people this portrait I am drawing may appear ragged, false, and inconsistent. This I acknowledge. When the finality of death gave the occasion for judgment, ragged and inconsistent was that figure, standing so large in my memory, and which had formed so large a part of my life during eighteen years.

What, in a word or two, was he like, as I knew him in 1936 (our friendship was almost halfway through): brilliant and boring, but far more often the former: generous-hearted and generous-handed; a touch of ogre, but a kindly ogre (there was about him, right up to the fearful ending, a power, neither fascination nor charm, but with the force of both); of strong affections with something reluctant and timid in them: grateful in a most touching way of anything he looked on as a kindness; sometimes peevish and unreasonable—and what else can be looked for in man, and in a man of seventy? But above everything I recall from those sunny periods the generosity and brilliance of his spirit, the inspiration of his company, and, most of all, perhaps, the scrupulous fervency of the artist.

I, in a few months, was to be 34, and he was 71. He had taken lately to applying a particular adjective to young people (and among these, although I was approaching middle age, he classed me). The adjective which obsessed him, as words were very liable to do, was 'inconsiderate'. Other reprobatory adjectives I may—indeed I certainly did—deserve. Undiplomatic I may well have been (and what true friendship is consistent with much diplomacy?), impulsive, talkative, disrespectful, impatient, sometimes careless—all irritating qualities: to these I should not like to reason out a long defence; but, at the summing up of all things, the one reproach, so far as concerns my relationship with Logan, the one reproach that I have no fear of reading in the great book, written up against me, is 'inconsiderate'.

Among other preparations for our journey, there was a curious one I made at Logan's request. I don't usually wear a hat, and Logan once said to me, 'I don't think I like you coming to the house without a hat. It gets me talked about by the neighbours in Chelsea.' When we were discussing our voyage he said, 'If you want to come to Teneriffe with me, you must get a hat.' 'All right,' I said, 'but I think it's only fair that you should pay for it.' He agreed to this, and accordingly, as a slight practical joke, I went to an American shop, and bought a hat which could only be described by the colloquial adjective of 'flash'. Logan was a little startled, but came to admit its rather vulgar charm. I only wore it when we went on board and came finally ashore, and afterwards when I was visiting him.

We embarked at Tilbury. 'I like the idea of sailing from Tilbury,' Logan said, 'because of the wonderful speech Queen Elizabeth made there, at the time of the Armada.' And he quoted the famous phrases, 'I know I have but the body of a weak and feeble woman, but I have the heart of a King, and a King of England too.'

As soon as we got on board, Logan made up his mind that our luggage had been left behind on the quay. He fretted and fussed, and sent me many times down to our cabin to look for it, until, just when it would have been expected, I was able to reassure him that everything was safe on board.

The start of our voyage was unpropitious. On a dull February morning our liner drew out from the quay—and almost immediately dropped anchor. For two days and nights we were fog-bound in the Thames. I have confessed to some failing of tact in my relationships. I had, however, carefully made one tactful resolution. Logan, I realized, would expect a great deal of my company; I resolved, accordingly never to play bridge on the voyage, although I have always been much addicted to the game. On the first night as we lay in the obscure and silent Thames, fours of bridge began to arrange themselves in the smoking-room.

'You ought to get a game of bridge,' said Logan.

'No, I shan't play,' I said. 'Once I start playing I shall be committed to go on, and you'll feel neglected.'

'I don't always need your company,' he said. 'I can live without you part of the time.'

'No,' I said. 'If I start I shan't be able to refuse to play when some-body needs a fourth. You'll feel neglected and make a grievance of it.'

'No, no! I should like you to play. Besides, I like grievances. They make bile and help my digestion.'

I was firm. But very soon, when we were watching a game, Logan said to one of the players, 'You ought to ask him to play. He's an expert.'

This was a gross exaggeration, and in the nature of a practical joke, but since I met no one on the voyage noticeably above my standard, it didn't matter. For, of course, I was now happily committed.

Logan certainly didn't seem to worry. He used to read, or sit on deck, or sometimes in an armchair, watching the game which he once played, but had given up soon after I first got to know him. (I have a feeling that he was never a good player. All that I know about his con-duct of the game is what he told me, and it only related to his behaviour when it came to settling up. 'My friends used to say,' he told me, 'that when I lost, I took it very well, and paid out cheerfully. But if I'd won, the yellow streak appeared, and I took their money much too enthusi-astically.') Once, when I was playing for the first time with three strangers, he suddenly said, 'How do you know he isn't a card-sharper?'

An uneasy look came into their eyes. I believe they were really not quite certain that we weren't a couple of crooks working a sort of double confidence trick. It had happened once, so a friend told me, that Logan himself had been taken for a possible card-sharper. He was coming back from Italy—this was before I knew him—and, in the sleeping car he made friends with an affable stranger who shared his compartment. They were getting on famously when Logan, who at that time had a passion for piquet, said 'Do you play cards?'

'No,' said the man, and never spoke a friendly word during the rest of the journey.

72

Logan and I had to share a large cabin, with bunks at opposite ends. A slight difficulty cropped up from the start. He liked to go to sleep early and also to wake early; I like to read late in bed and to wake at the last possible moment. The dim light over my bunk did not prevent him from sleeping; but, in the morning, when he woke me with 'Are you awake?' it is not improbable that I sometimes made peevish responses. Indeed, he was in many ways an unsatisfactory room-mate. He had a habit, when half asleep, of talking to himself; sometimes he would go over large chunks of conversation from the day before. And regularly, every night, round about four o'clock, he would start up the most thunderous coughing, which usually lasted for nearly an hour. He always at this period took a sleeping tablet, and, although his coughs awoke him, this was, I think, like the first waking of an etherized patient, which afterwards is forgotten.

It was now that I first discovered how much Logan depended on little comforts—how put out he was when they were failing. He always had his breakfast in bed, and very often he would wake me by saying, out loud but apparently to himself, over and over again, 'Oh, how I want my breakfast. Oh, how I want my breakfast!'

Crossing the Bay of Biscay it was a little rough; that is, about one-third of the passengers failed to turn up at meals. Logan, who was a good sailor, as befitted an enthusiastic yachtsman, was rather anxious that his superiority in this respect should be revealed by my succumbing. But I, too, although no yachtsman, am a good sailor.

'Do you feel all right?' he shouted across the cabin one heaving night when we were in bed.

'Yes. Quite all right,' I answered.

'You don't feel at all sick?'

'Not at all.'

'You haven't even got a headache?'

'No.'

There was a pause.

'*I* call this a dead calm,' said Logan.

Our delayed start brought a little disappointment. We had been due to spend a complete day in Vigo, and another in Lisbon; we had planned to visit Santiago de Compostella at the first, and, at the second, Cintra.

A year or two before, I had come near to visiting the great cathedral at Santiago, but had failed to do so; to have seen it in the intensified air

F   73

of Logan's company and appreciation, would have more than compensated my earlier disappointment. But it wasn't to be. The day was late and rainy when we anchored at last at the end of the long bay, recalling with its atmosphere and contours the great sea lochs of the North Western Highlands. I looked rather wistfully towards the shore, but saw no purpose in taking the tender to walk, at night, for an hour or two in the rainy town.

I have a tourist's weakness for standing on deck while the shore recedes.

'I think I'll stay up until we sail,' I told Logan. He suggested that I might then be so late as seriously to disturb his night's sleep; so it was agreed that I should come down when the ship sailed, or at one o'clock, whichever was earlier. In fact, I came to bed, while we were still lying in harbour, at half-past twelve. The door was locked. I imagined that Logan, who was exceedingly absent-minded, had accidentally turned the key when he let himself in. I knocked, and he got out of bed and opened the door.

Next morning, to my surprise, he began to reproach me for not keeping our agreement. Why, he asked, hadn't I come down when the ship sailed? He'd heard the engines start up, and, after waiting and waiting, at last he became so vexed that he got up and locked me out: just to teach me a lesson.

What he had heard was the generating plant, which sounded from our cabin not unlike a ship's engines. I convinced him of this, but he was never, for the rest of his life, quite able to convince himself that I hadn't, in some way or other, wantonly aroused him from sleep in the middle of the night.

At Lisbon we made a happier call, though too late in the day for inland excursions. Lisbon: What does it mean to me? Nothing much even now: nothing more than a small vision, which, all the same, would be yet smaller had I not felt it in Logan's company. I remember a warm late afternoon, and a warm faint rain spattering the dusky Tagus: and the variously coloured cubes of houses heaped up over a hill which was rising above the shores of that fabulous river. It was dark when we went ashore; there were one or two sights which Logan, who had visited that city, was anxious to show me. I remember chiefly a wide, eighteenth-century square, built up on three sides, with the broad river black and glittering on the fourth, and in the middle, prancing and gleaming among the darkness and raindrops, a large equestrian statue. But what most of all I remember—it's hard to say why—were the earthquake-commemorating thunderbolts, cobbled in rough mosaic on the pavements, and glowing faintly under the drizzle and lamp-light.

European February was left behind us; softer airs and a harsher sun were about us; and at last, on a warm evening, just at nightfall, we disembarked at Las Palmas. A man and his wife, with their niece—a stolid little English family—teamed up with us, and we all went together to buy tickets for the small boat which was to carry us overnight to Teneriffe. I tried my newly-acquired Spanish; my questions seemed to be understood, but the answers I received were at first beyond me; however at last I made out that we had some time to wait before the ticket-office was to be opened. Our Englishman, being adventurous, good-naturedly suggested that he and I should go off for a drink. Logan had given over to me all the cash needed for our expenses; forethoughtfully, I now gave him enough of his own money to pay for our berths.

No sooner were we gone than the ticket-office opened; Logan bought our tickets and engaged our berths; but the poor lady had no money at all. Evidently foreseeing a night on deck, she looked very angrily across at Logan—so he told me afterwards—and said 'Your friend has gone off with my husband.'

'I think they've gone to get a drink,' Logan answered.

'My husband's got all the money,' she went on, still fixing on him her angry glance; 'it's very inconvenient.'

Logan looked rather crumpled when we got back; the husband seemed to put up quite cheerfully with his wife's upbraiding and further agitation and, when we were alone for a moment, he said to me, 'It's funny how worried some people get when they're travelling. They seem to think people mean them to get lost. But these people have been getting people from one boat to the other for goodness knows how many years. They *want* us to get there.'

When I told this to Logan he was charmed by such a display of simple English wisdom. But I can easily and vividly picture the scene when he was reproached by the deserted wife.

After we'd been at sea for about four days, and I had talked with many of our fellow-passengers, I said to Logan, 'I like people.'

'You'll find there are plenty of them,' he responded rather grimly. On the whole Logan didn't like people; he only really liked those who spoke his own language and acknowledged his own system of values; people among whom his wisdom was esteemed and his wit comprehended. The small-talk of good-natured philistines was something he could but seldom accomplish; his irony had no humour for them, and their usual observations no interest for him; all his accustomed openings failed. It was rather like two opponents on the same board playing, one of them chess, and the other draughts. On such occasions Logan seemed to collapse; his whole body would droop into the chair, his eyelids appeared, like Mona Lisa's, more than a little heavy, and his head sank down ponderously on to his chest.

One thing he could do, however, with people of strange interest; he would, at times, become fascinated in ways of life unfamiliar to him, and would enchantingly draw a man out as to his profession or particular interests. We fortunately had, at our table, an intelligent Irish doctor with his family, and Logan, as Boswell said of Johnson, 'had in general a peculiar pleasure in the company of physicians'.

This doctor saw through some of what can only be called Logan's little social affectations. Logan boasted to him about his depressive mania, and described his interlunaries.

'Oh, that can easily be treated,' said the doctor, bubble-pricking, 'I once had a patient like that. I used to put him right.'

'But I can't do any work for months when I'm like that,' said Logan.

'Yes, he said he felt like that.'

'But my blood-pressure drops,' pleaded Logan.

'Yes,' said the doctor. 'That used to happen to my patient. He used to say "It's quite impossible for me to go to work today; I couldn't do anything". I just gave him an injection to send his blood pressure up, and he went off to work quite cheerfully.'

In spite of this little defeat, Logan remained friendly; and it must be admitted that the doctor was in fact wrong in denying Logan's lunatic pretensions.

But at times he would come into the smoking room, and find me talking with some ordinary fellow-passengers; I used to try and bring him into the conversation, but only with rare success; Logan would shrivel into that incarnation of boredom, which, in its most wearying manifestation, must have confounded our angry fellow-countrywoman beside the newly opened ticket-office, that evening in Las Palmas.

It so happened that, for our overnight passage to Teneriffe, my drinking acquaintance shared a three-berth cabin with me and Logan.

76

Logan went straight to bed; a little later my new friend came up to me on deck. 'The other chap in our cabin,' he said to me, not having recognized my travelling companion, 'has the biggest stern you ever saw in your life.' This remark of his, unlike the other, I thought it wiser to keep to myself.

In the morning I looked out of our cabin window, and saw through warm February air the black and intricate volcanic cliffs of Teneriffe; and during that inevitable and boring wait on foreign arrival—a wait for luggage to be got ashore, and for some kind of transport—I saw, hovering over the roof tops a grey cone which I knew must be the warm summit of El Teide, the storied and enormous peak.

It was during this little period of boredom—a boredom extinguished for me by my excited perception of a new climate—that I understood one base little ingredient in Logan's finer motive for so generously bringing a companion with him. He seemed quite incapable of managing the practical affairs of travel; things were altogether different from the time, six or seven years before, when he had met me like an intellectual guide, in Paris.

He deflated on to a bench, and vented complaints of trivial misery. I thought it best to ignore these, and, in no very great time, we were in a car, with all our luggage, and driving uphill, on our way across the island to Orotava. On either side of the road was a country of stones and declivities, bearing a vegetation altogether unfamiliar to me. Among the strange shrubs I looked for the only Canary plants I knew about, the giant echiums; and my eagerness inspired Logan's always sympathetic interest. And then we reached the crest of the hill.

Sudden and huge and unlooked for as a vision of Paradise, an immense dome of light silvered incredibly over the sky ahead of us. Chatterers both, we had nothing to say for a moment. The ecstasy of sharing an ecstasy needed now no utterance of agreement to confirm it. The genial and pure and tremendous beauty of the ice-burnished peak, stealing equally into both our spirits, induced in us, travelling together towards it, a mystical union of joy. Then, as though a gay Olympian, disclosing for a moment, with no sinaitical terrors, his large beauty, should veil himself again with 'That's enough for the moment', the Peak, at a turn in the road, hid itself behind some inconsiderable elevation.

In travelling, the spirit seems at times to lag behind the body; mine, primed with volcanic anticipations, had outstripped Logan's for a little;

but now he was well up with me. We noticed with equal delight the exquisite pink stars beside the road, of wild cinerarias; and we delighted together when, perched green among the green leaves of the trees, wild canaries sang their native song for us.

The cinerarias Logan usually referred to as freesias; if I quietly corrected him, he would remark, 'When I say "freesias", I mean "cinerarias".' Such errors of nomenclature were common with him. He claimed to have been at one time an indefatigable gardener. His enthusiasm I should not attempt to question, but I cannot think that he was ever such an expert as he often wished to imply. Nevertheless he was the most rewarding spectator in horticultural affairs. I often used to bring him up particularly exquisite flowers from my garden: gentians, hardy cyclamen, narcissus species collected abroad, or beautiful cultivated daffodils, in particular what I sometimes think the loveliest of all cultivated flowers, that great white daffodil called Beersheba. He would have these flowers in a vase close beside him, and would keep looking at them with an expression which hardly fell short of ecstasy. I remember his excitement when he told me how a friend had shown him that strange, lovely American alpine, the Lewisia. But one flower he professed to value above all others. 'If I had nothing else to do,' he would often say, 'I think I should spend the rest of my life growing hepaticas.' Had this ambition been realized, he could certainly have lavished a fine display during the early spring; but for all the rest of the year his garden would have been a dull one. There was, I suspect, a certain artificiality about his cult for these exquisite flowers; perhaps it was the name which really charmed him. I once showed him in our garden where, at the roots of a copper beech I had prosperously naturalized hepaticas of varying shades from the Cantabrian Mountains, the Pyrenees, and the French Riviera. He was breathless with an altogether proper appreciation; nevertheless, he frequently asked me afterwards, 'Do you grow hepaticas?'

We spent about three or four weeks in Orotava. It was the first time I had been so long and alone together with Logan. How did we get through with it? Pretty well. But I found the germ of small difficulties that later on were, I think, to darken and enlarge. Although his wisdom never turned into pedantry, Logan's wit might lapse at times into facetiousness, and his narrative gift into insupportable anecdotage; in fact to keep always in his company was not reconcilable with lightness of heart and pleasantness of manner. It was necessary, during so intimate and familiar an association, to preserve a slight but rigid independence. This Logan occasionally resented.

Perhaps this last paragraph redounds to the credit of neither, and I must point out emphatically an aspect of the case where Logan shines in spirit, almost saint-like. I have said that on our travels he intended to pay all expenses. He did more. He had said to me, 'I once travelled with a rich cousin of mine. She paid all our fares and hotel bills; but the little expenses, when you travel with rich people, the tips and so on, come to so much, that it was really more than I could afford.' Accordingly he used to give me pocket-money to cover the lesser costs of our travelling. Had I not, for my own satisfaction, spent on the sly a little of my private money, I could, with no disquiet have set out and returned without sixpence of my own in my pocket. But Logan carried out this arrangement with so graceful a generosity that the receiver was almost made to feel more magnanimous than the giver. Others who travelled with Logan under the same circumstances had, so they have told me, experienced the same delight, and, I think I may add, the same surprise; though generosity is happily no infrequent virtue, generosity of so fine a quality is rarer than that precious jewel, virginity, that rare jewel, as Logan wrote of it, so prized in Heaven, but so rare, they say, on earth.

Logan, in *Trivia*, painted a remarkably true picture of himself; but in this, as in some other accomplishments of his, he showed himself up for a magazine of problems. How is this self-portrait—so acute, so bravely remorseless, so accurate—how is it to be reconciled with an almost unsurpassed self-blindness? To many, and indeed to most of the problems in Logan's character I have discovered at least provisional answers; but this contradiction—this dichotomy, as I have called it—is a problem to me insuperable. Would an expert diagnose schizophrenia? I can't say. All I know is that in Logan these contradictions most decidedly existed, and that his reactions at different times to the same situation could be disconcertingly and sometimes exasperatingly unpredictable. (I do not mean according to the state of his cyclical depression or elevation; to one very familiar with him these differing states could be foreseen and usually dealt with.)

In Teneriffe, I wasn't aware of these problems; only in the light of later troubles, and backward searching of time, do I see how, on this occasion they first began, although unrecognized then, to reveal themselves. But for the most part of our sojourn in the Fortunate Isles, the halcyon built, and the lotus was in blossom. There was one small ruffle, indeed, which I took for no more than a cat's-paw. To explain the cause of this, I must go back a little into my own past.

I had, at this period of my life, made several trips into Spain—without knowing the language. This disability was often exasperating, not on account of the practical difficulties it gave rise to, but for the solitude it imposed upon me. Friendly faces would appear betokening affable spirits, an old woman with her cows on high pasture, a young horseman in a field of strange daffodils, a goat-herd among crags, a potter in a woody recess of the peaks—and always the barrier of incomprehensibility was there, making deathly solitude out of a peopled nook. I learnt something of the language; when we went to Teneriffe, I could read without much difficulty, speak a little, and understand the answers if they were spoken slowly enough. (Logan's habitual observation was, 'I'm like Edward Lear, "he reads, but he cannot speak Spanish".')

Steeped in and possessed by the air and beauty of the place, I resolved it should not be for me such a needless solitude as were the Asturian mountains. I made friends with a native of the island; my choice was accidentally more appropriate than at first I realized; for he had the pale skin and hair, so noticeable in the Canaries, and which almost certainly denotes the aboriginal blood of the Guanches; he, like his home, was at once Spanish and African. Sometimes I would see him in the evening—we might go down to the shore, where there was a small bar; the air would be soft and the stars blazing; the lanterns of fishing boats, like moving stars, flickered more palely out at sea; near at hand the rollers of the Atlantic thundered and hissed into a glimmer of faint light over the blackness of the volcanic sands.

Logan seemed rather pleased than otherwise by my small personal excursions into this strange new world we had found ourselves in. But one night, perhaps because he had been bored at the hotel, or, more likely, through some unaccountable stirring of the spirit, he seemed faintly vexed. He didn't say anything at the time, but next morning he said:

'Do you think it wise to go off and neglect me, as you did last night?'

'Wise?' I responded.

'Well, when you have a friend who might leave you a lot of money, do you think it's wise to neglect him?'

This was the first time that Logan truly shocked me.

'But do you really want me,' I asked him, 'to behave differently to you so as to get money out of you when you're dead? If I thought of things like that, it would make a friendship impossible. It would be ghoulish. At any rate what you let me have now and you've promised me for life may not be an enormous income, but it's enough for me.'

'I just put it to you like that,' said Logan evasively.

Nothing else during our whole stay was said in the same temper or in the same vein. I took it, as I have said, for a cat's-paw. But that small flurry on the waters was not, as I thought then, the imprint of Zephyr; it was the barely perceptible sign of an otherwise imperceptible earth tremor, the presage, though long to be unfulfilled, of a huge moral cataclysm. Better forgotten, I resolved, and put it, so far as I could, out of my thoughts. I wonder now if, had I reflected more deeply, I should have seen how irreconcilable was this little stain with the generous and enchanting character of my companion. For I think that, on the whole, our abode in Teneriffe was the happiest period I ever passed in Logan's company.

The spell came upon us when we first saw the Teide. The afternoon that we arrived we walked down to the beach; on our way to the shore we passed a romantic grove of palm trees, ranged, in two double columns, like the pillars of a temple, with a shadowy and gleaming fountain at one end for the altar.

The rollers flashed like glass, and glittered with the whiteness of snow, in sudden drifts of foam, up on to the black sands. Black cliffs rose of ash and lava, plumed with curious plants among which, fat and spined and leafless, grew up in angular beauty, that strange spurge, *Euphorbia canariensis*, for all the world like a giant cactus.

Chronology, which can shape the most shapeless narrative, plays little part in my memories of Teneriffe. One day was very like another, and necessity fixed no date for any particular excursion. In the morning we usually went down to the sea past the pillars and shadowed leafy vaults of the palm-tree temple; on sunny days I would bathe, and then sit on the black sand with Logan, and gossip. I taught him to drink at the little shore-side café, where we used often to meet fellow-guests from the hotel. Logan, being at his best, worked up human interest in these; in particular he was fascinated by a quavering-voiced woman who used to tell of very odd adventures. In one—whose thread was rather tangled—she told us how, on a sea-cliff in the West Indies, she had come on a naked young man; since there was no hint on her part, nor suspicion on ours, that her relations with this apparition were improper, the significance of his condition always escaped us. On another occasion, she told how, travelling by steam-boat up the Irrawaddy, she had gone ashore for a brief walk; returning, she found the jungle path completely blocked by an enormous buffalo with a crane standing on its head; at that moment the steamer's whistle blew; so, pulling her skirt up over her head she plunged into the jungle to evade the curiously bonneted monster; in consequence she was stung on the behind by a hornet. To such adventures we listened entrancedly.

One day, somebody mentioned Budleigh Salterton. 'The last time I was in Budleigh Salterton,' she quavered out, 'I was nearly hit by a thunderbolt.'

Then it was, as a dream fades at the opening day, that faded away as truth, for us at least, the whole fantastic life she'd been beguiling us with. Logan tried to make out—but I never believed him—that he'd had earlier suspicions.

'That crane on the buffalo's head,' he would affirm, 'always seemed a little too much for me.'

On ordinary afternoons Logan would have the nap that was his invariable habit during most of the years I knew him. I would then go for a walk, sometimes with my local friend, but more often alone, botanizing. Logan, queer though it seemed to the friends of his latest years, had once been energetic in outdoor pursuits. He had gone after bears, and fished in the Rocky Mountains (I remember his almost startled response to the rippling rings in our river of rising trout); he was interested in birds. Botany had never taken hold of him until sympathetically he came to share in my excitements. When I returned with curious plants he would ask me about them, relishing their strange forms and various shades of emerald. Not only did he sympathize with my hobby—he seemed to look on it as a sort of distinction, boasting of it to our fellow-guests, and adding sometimes—which wasn't altogether untrue—'he writes about it'.

In the evenings, after nightfall, we would usually stroll off into the town. The air, comforting with soft influences of the Crab, was warm in the darkness. Stone benches and trees surrounded the main square of the town; low against lamplit branches the sky seemed to rest like a dark ceiling. It was carnival time, defiantly in Lent, to celebrate and emphasize, as we supposed, the success of the anticlerical popular front. Young people walked round and round in groups—the girls in one direction, boys in the other—strumming on guitars, dancing to their music or singing their native songs, easily and thoughtlessly as birds.

I at the time, like many of my generation, was freshly intoxicated by the poems of Lorca. It was likely that I would be ravished more than Logan by that Iberian music; but he, sharing through my eyes and ears what his own may have missed, succumbed as completely as I did.

As we returned we would see, in the darkness and tarnished gold of lamplight, young men 'plucking the turkey', as the saying goes, leaning against the sill and talking to a sweetheart who sat smiling and gracious in the window.

And books? Literature was not the prime object of our journey, but it was natural for us that we should often talk about books. Logan carried out his usual odd practice when travelling rather farther and for a longer time than usual. For many weeks before setting out he accumulated, unopened, copies of *The Times Literary Supplement*; these, on the ship and in the hotel he opened and thoroughly read.

I had brought, among other books, a Keats, and, in bed at night, with as careful an eye as when I botanized on the cliffs and slopes of Teneriffe, I searched for rare treasures among the earlier and less familiar poems. I showed my discoveries to Logan, and with one he was particularly pleased. It is from the early poem *Sleep and Poetry*,

> The glorious features of the bards who sung
> In other ages—*cold and sacred busts*
> Smiled at each other.

The words I had underlined enchanted him. 'Cold and sacred busts', he intoned, and, as always when a phrase had bewitched him, 'Cold and sacred busts', he kept on repeating, 'Cold and sacred busts'.

I discovered for myself, too, and recalled to him, a poem which he had known and half-forgotten, the posthumous, unrhymed sonnet *What the thrush said*.

> 'O fret not after knowledge—I have none,
> And yet my song comes native with the warmth.
> O fret not after knowledge—I have none,
> And yet the Evening listens.'

These lines brought into his eyes quite unmetaphorical tears. A long time after this he played a practical joke with them. He read them aloud to an intelligent literary editor who, so Logan affirmed, used to declare at one time that Keats turned his stomach.

'Of course,' said Logan, 'he thought I was trying to put on him something that had been written by myself, or by some friend of mine. They wouldn't do at all he said——'

Unwisely forgetting our little discovery in Teneriffe, he tried, at the same time, the same trick on me, sending them on a postcard with that editor's opinion on them, and asking for mine. I answered on a postcard, 'I quite agree with ——. These lines turn my stomach as much as the worst excesses of that intolerably over-valued poet Keats.'

Strange vegetation, waves whitening along black sands, wild canaries, the natural beauties of dance and song—these were the background of our days; but beyond them all and above them all brooded, often invisible, serene in its far-off and tremendous beauty, the warm-hearted, glassy peak. Sacred it seemed, and as if possessed with some more than mortal spirit, and altogether fittingly chosen by the pale-faced aborigines for the seat of their god Achaman.

The shining peak was not often to be seen from Orotava; frequently a ledge of cloud lying against the mountain slopes extended almost to the edge of the land, so that, at times, only the beaches and cliffs were in sunlight; and even on clear days, lower elevations, or little dead volcanoes, and the embanked slopes of long-cold lava flows concealed the greater elevations of the island. But every now and again we saw that icy glitter, high in the clouds like another world, all mysteriousness and unsurpassable beauty.

West of Orotava lies the small harbour town of Garachico. Thither we motored one day. The place is visited for the sake of an old Spanish fort on the quay, a pleasant little building, emblazoned with decayed heraldic sculptures, such as may often be seen, remote and romantic, in little, obscure, Spanish towns. Peaked and puckered waves stretched out from the quay, but of a strangeness, for those billows were black and cold and silent and motionless; the quay might have been Charon's whence only for hell did passengers embark; none but infernal boats could ever drop anchor in the roads of that little port, for it was filled up with lava. When we turned back from that extraordinary spectacle, clouds, which had been covering the heights, blew apart, and there, swaying with that delusive movement which the passage of clouds can give, there, in the light of silver and crystal, hovered the warm and icy cone.

Before this little trip, I had already explored beyond the great valley of Orotava (the vestige, it is believed, of a vast ancient explosion), on

botanical excursions in the company of Don Juan Bolinaga, custodian
of the botanical gardens. More usually I went alone with him; but
sometimes Logan came too, and on one of these expeditions—in search
of a very rare narcissus—I sat in the back of the car, squeezed between
those two large, corpulent, elderly men, Don Juan and Logan.

My Spanish wasn't good enough for regular talk, and we conversed
in French. This led me to a curious discovery. Remembering with what
authority Logan, some years before, had displayed Paris to me, and
knowing how expert he was in French literature, I was surprised now
to find out how little habitude he revealed in speaking the language. I
had to interpret for my two companions.

'What are those trees?' Logan asked once, as we passed a distant
cloud of pink on the hill-side. Don Juan declared them to be peaches;
when he heard me repeating this in English to Logan, he shook a
roguish finger at me and said, 'That's a word you must never use in
Spanish.' I was able to please Logan with the explanation, which it
would not be decorous to set down in print; the uncomprehending
reader, who desires an elucidation, must look for it among Spanish-
speaking friends.

We picnicked that day on the edge of a little village, among flowery
slopes, far above the coast road, and well away from the tourist-
frequented parts of the island. We had a longish walk from here to my
narcissus, and Logan was to drive round and meet us at the foot of a
deep ravine. When tired, but with some precious bulbs, and wet from
newly falling rain, we approached the car, I was worried lest Logan
should be in a state of not unjustified impatience; we were nearly an
hour late; the ponderous but amiable Don Juan was very weary by
then, and making slow progress; with less than southern courtesy I felt
bound to hurry ahead to appease as best I could my disappointed companion. But I found Logan in a mode of the most sweet and charitable
patience.

To indulge a little Elizabethan whim, we stopped at a small bar and
drank some Canary wine, in homage to the memory of Ben Jonson;
we found it disappointing, and were disillusioned as to the more
material delights of the Mermaid.

And then the day came for my ascent of the Peak. A car was hired,
and Logan, who intended to come with me as far as it was possible to
drive, had invited Laurence Binyon and his wife to come with us.
That Binyon, one of the saints of literature, with his exquisite taste and

exquisite talent, should have been in Teneriffe then, was, for such a journey as this, an inestimable benefit. Another guest had somehow got into the party—we didn't quite know how; this was a talkative and good-natured and boring Swede; he was continuously joking, and though his jokes were nothing to laugh at, he himself was very laughable, and, since he took our laughter for testimony of his wit, courtesy was undisturbed by our involuntary rudeness. The last passenger was my guide.

The road climbs for six or seven thousand feet through fertile country, and then breaks suddenly, at a point named Portillo, into a very strange landscape. Just above the regular level of the more persistent clouds is a desolate plain, known as the Cañadas. Rather to one side of it rises the final substance of the Peak, the last five thousand feet or so; bounding the rest of the Cañadas, and proving this place to be in fact the relics of an enormous crater, is an arc of high cliffs. The plain itself is a wilderness of ash drifts and lava flows in various states of disintegration; dotted about are countless little cold volcanoes of white and yellow and black. The vegetation is inconspicuous, for it consists principally of a leafless broom, the retama; but in spring, I have been told, these dead-looking bushes burst out into fragrant drifts of white and pink, interspersed with the golden yellow of a different broom.

I had made this trip once already with Don Juan, who had shown me rare plants and various botanical curiosities; most particularly we had searched for and found in the Cañadas, in the valley formed between them by a black and a white volcano, the first shoots of a very rare echium.

Logan, while not troubling himself much with the intricacies of botanical nomenclature and classification, had, as I have said, eagerly concerned himself with my private interests. 'Tell us about any interesting flowers we pass, Bob,' he said, as we approached the wilder regions. 'But don't tell us too much.'

I probably did tell them too much. I called attention to the groves of Canary pines, great evergreens that wither at the slightest frost; I pointed out the woodlands of giant brooms, thick-boled, and with silvery leaves, and bright with tassels of large white flowers; I talked a lot about the giant heaths, just coming into flower and which, as forty-foot trees, darkened the hill-side about us. But most of all, as we passed the black cliffs of a little valley, I discoursed about the greenovias, curious house-leeks which grew there, like roses of cloudy green jade mounted upon black porphyry.

We were in that bank of clouds which rests so long and so frequently, at about 6,000 feet, against the flanks of Teneriffe; thinning out, and luminous with sunlight was this cloud when we drew up on the edge of the Cañadas at Portillo. Frost had sheathed with glassy ice the retama twigs, and, as the cloud continued to disperse, these shrubs glittered strangely conspicuous in the gradually pervading sunshine; and, while the rays loosened them, falling splinters of ice tinkled on to ash and lava. Suddenly the cloud-fringe parted and the Teide in all its wonder and symmetry blazed out against the sky. Binyon clutched Logan by the arm. 'Look at that!' he gasped, and then, after a pause added, 'Did Dante know about this?'

Soon the whole region was clear save for occasional tatters of cloud; the peak was all ice, it seemed, and streaked here and there with lava flows; only the highest little cone of ash, called the Piton, was free, because of its inward warmth, from ice or snow; and over it fluttered up now and then translucent puffs of steam.

Such beauty and grandeur gave an air almost of sanctity and we were none of us inclined for much talk as, in full view of the mountain, we sat down to a picnic meal—none of us, that is, but the Swede, who chattered incessantly and imperturbably.

Soon, as the guide told me, it was time to be off; we had some way to walk and climb before nightfall.

While we were getting ready Logan said, 'There's a very large blue chaffinch which lives up here. Ask the guide if he knows anything about it.'

'Yes,' answered the guide in his slow easy Spanish. 'But it's early in the year for them. They should be nesting now, on the other side of those cliffs in the forests of Vilaflor.'

Well, I probably shouldn't see this bird; but if I did here would be a pleasant memory for Logan to share vicariously with me. I resolved to be on the watch for it.

We drove to the end of the road, thus saving about two miles' walk, and, leaving the party, I set off with the guide on my mountaineering adventure.

Logan arranged to meet me, the next day, and at much the same time. That I was deserting him for 24 hours needed no apology. He was charitably pleased with my pleasure, and, I think, he enjoyed—as in the case of my botany—the mild distinction he made of it in the hotel. And it was fully according to his plan that the Peak should become a large and dazzling element in our memories.

'It was quite exciting,' he said afterwards, perhaps with a little irony, 'seeing you disappear off into the desert like that.'

When I had first said to him that I wanted to make the climb, he had been all enthusiasm and complacency. 'Of course you may,' he said. 'I think it's to see the Peak that I want to go. I've wanted to see it ever since I first read those lines of Donne:

> "Doth not a Tenarif or higher Hill
> Rise so high like a Rocke, that one might thinke
> The floating Moone would shipwracke there and sinke?"'

Other Canary literature we had studied; I had dug up Burton's phrases, from the *Anatomy of Melancholy*, 'The Pike of Teneriffe, how high is it? Seventy miles, or fifty as Patricius holds, or nine, as Snellius demonstrates in his *Eratosthenes*?'

Logan had unearthed a curious and rather ineffective allegory by Dr Johnson, entitled *The Vision of Theodore, the Hermit of Teneriffe*. I was able to show a finer, old discovery of mine, of which, I think, he had known nothing at all. This was *The Man in the Moone* written by Bishop Godwin at the end of Elizabeth's reign—the first and one of the best of scientific novels; it describes the adventures of Domingo Gonsales, a proud Spanish dwarf, who, marooned on St Helena, trained and harnessed a flock of birds which are called ganzas; these carried him on short excursions through the air: on his voyage home, being shipwrecked off the Canary coasts, he escaped by means of his ganzas, which carried him to the summit of the Peak, and thence, starting their migration, to the moon, where he had some curious adventures.

Cyrano de Bergerac, following the hint of Godwin, wrote another lunar romance. His hero met the dwarfish Gonsales and the inhabitants, taking disparity of size as evidence for difference of gender, shut them up in a cage together to breed.

I had an early eighteenth-century collection of authentic travels among which Godwin's novel was curiously reprinted. At Logan's request I took this volume with me, and on the ship he read the story. He was enchanted with it, and I remember his being particularly taken by the phrase 'my fortunate misfortunes'. On the way home he left the book behind in our cabin (he had had it in his luggage) and it was lost;

he never showed quite the vexation over this that I'd like to have seen.

I will not tell here what I have already told, my private experiences on the Peak; let it suffice that next day, tired and scorched and very thirsty, and with one finger frost-bitten, I emerged from the desolation of ash and lava, and found Logan waiting for me in a car. I had one particular satisfaction in that, a very little time before, the guide had said suddenly, 'Look! The blue bird! The bird of the Peak!' and there I had seen, balancing on a retama twig, bright and beautiful amid the deathly landscape, a big blue bird, as big, I seem to remember, as a thrush.

We ate some sandwiches at the little café. It is an unavoidable rule of Spanish courtesy, when eating before strangers, to invite them to share your food; the offer is good-manneredly declined. There were some workmen in the café. I had the greatest difficulty—I don't know why—in quietly persuading Logan to make the proper gesture. He was, for the moment, in one of his social collapses, such as he displayed when he was bored or embarrassed by the company. He seemed not to hear me at first, so I said, louder, 'It's bad manners not to offer some food. They won't take it.' With an expression half blank and half afraid he jerked a bitten sandwich at the workmen, who politely murmured a refusal, and convention was formally satisfied.

Clouds were ahead as we drove away, and on their tattered fringe a rainbow brightened and arched itself triumphantly above the road; it seemed to me at the time a fitting gateway from a region which had so lately enriched my mind with mystical riches of such incalculable worth.

'When I've had an experience like this,' said Logan, 'I like to sort out my memories; it helps to preserve them.' And so we talked over, and defined, and embalmed all that seemed richest and loveliest in the visions we had partaken of: and I told as best I could what wonders I had seen and felt; of how the shadow of the peak at evening had risen tremendously until it encompassed the whole night; and I told how, just before dawn I had seen, on opposite horizons the Plough and the Cross, with four planets between them; I told of the crater, scorched and sulphurous with steam, or jewelled with icicles: I told him about the blue bird of the Peak: what did I not tell him? The Peak of Teneriffe surpasses in beauty all mountains that I have ever seen; some years later Binyon, when I talked it over with him, could hardly maintain that Fujiyama itself was more beautiful.

G   89

But the time came at last when we had to set off northwards for the bleaker airs of England in March. One day had to be spent on Grand Canary and, with a car, we explored what we could of that less beautiful but nevertheless lovely island. Three particular memories we brought away: a camel ploughing, to remind us that, although in a province of Spain, this was also Africa: a hoopoe, Logan's first sight of one—a surprising fact to me, for Logan had travelled much in the Mediterranean, and I was familiar with this bird as a denizen of hills and woods on the French Riviera: and lastly and most impressive, a huge crater, with a whole farm and its fields and pastures in the bottom of it. After the Peak, the memories which Logan came back to most often were the palm-tree temple of Orotava, and this enormous and spectacular crater. (I still have live specimens of a plant which I collected on its lip.)

After this glimpse of a strange island, we went with our luggage and memories on board the homeward-bound liner.

One thing, however, less desirable than luggage and gleaming memories, Logan had taken with him. We had not sailed far from the Fortunate Isles when an infection appeared on the heel of one foot, confining him to his cabin. To lay up in bed was never a hardship for Logan; I fetched him old-fashioned forgotten novels from the library, and carefully ordered his meals, and used to sit and chatter to him, but——

This 'but' introduces the danger I had foreseen but could not now escape. Many of our outward-going friends returned on the same ship with us, and among them were my particular bridge partners. Since Logan's affliction was, according to the doctor, more inconvenient than serious, it was impossible to avoid playing. Logan decided to feel neglected. One afternoon I went to see how he was and found him still asleep, although the time when he usually ended his nap was over.

When at last I found him awake, he said, 'You've not been to see me since just after lunch.' And when I told him the truth, that I had twice found him asleep, he said, angrily, 'I was *not*. I've not been asleep the whole afternoon.' (He said to me, another time, 'It always upsets me if people tell me they've seen me asleep,' a feeling that is not unusual.)

An angel, I suppose, and I am not one, might have sat with him all the time; but he wouldn't have liked it. He enjoyed a good chatter, but couldn't do without several hours' reading every day. Nevertheless he conceived a mild obsession about the wickedness of my bridge-playing.

As we drew near England, he began to dread the journey by train from Tilbury; accordingly I ordered a car by wireless, to take him in comfort to his home. On the last morning of the voyage, just before he was quite awake, I heard him, as often before, muttering to himself. Suddenly some distincter words came up; '*You'd* better go in the train; you might get a game of *bridge.*'

This was my first experience of what I called Logan's 'traps'. They were not, of course, actually traps; it was one half of his disynchronous character resenting what the other half had approved. He was never aware of these inconsistencies in his spirit. They were disconcerting, for it was never possible to be sure that some quite accepted way of behaviour might not suddenly arouse his indignation.

However, wakefulness restored his good temper, and we got comfortably and happily away with only one mishap; my collection of plants got left on board. I thought they were lost for ever, and lamented particularly my narcissus bulbs, the first, in all probability, that were ever brought to England alive; they turned up of course quite safely in about a week's time.

Before I left him, I told Logan that I knew of no words or phrases which could begin to express my gratitude for the delight our journey had given me.

'Don't try,' he said in an amicable tone of voice, 'I don't like gratitude.'

Nevertheless, as soon as I got home, I tried to put something of my feelings down in a letter; during my night in the hut on the Peak, I had improvised a short poem which I wrote in the visitors' book there; these lines I worked over and enlarged, and I sent a more finished version to Logan with my letter; he answered (16.3.36):

'Certainly I have said that I don't like gratitude, but how little one knows oneself! Nothing literally could have given me greater pleasure than the letter which came from you this morning—my irrational self had taken on the boat the notion that I had been tiresome and had got rather on your nerves and I had made a real sorrow out of it. But your letter has blown away the clouds and the peak of our friendship is as bright as ever—a great wonder and delight to me. Incredible, yet there it is! I really must believe in its existence.

'I am so glad that your plants arrived—I have been worrying about them. My doctor keeps me in bed . . . I don't at all mind a bed-ridden existence, and in bed you will find me when you come to London. I shall love to see you, but won't be able to do any slave-driving for some little time I imagine.

'I think your poem one of the best things you have done—you have actually caught in words the strange, unbelievable Dantesque beauty of that incredible mountain, which, as you say, it seems to need a special sensibility to appreciate. Binyon, I believe, felt it too.

'With very best love and gratitude—equal to anything you can feel —for your kindest of letters.

'(I am sending you a copy of *Fine Writing*—Rose Macaulay is amusing about it in the current *New Statesman*.)'

The joys and excitements of Teneriffe—and perhaps the poisoned foot—hastened the state—whose advent in any case was inevitable— of an interlunary and under these depressing circumstances, the proofs of *Reperusals* began to turn up. Only on these occasions did Logan send for me. With his approval I had two short botanical holidays—one to the Lakes in spring, and another, in July, to Scotland. Each time I arranged to come back at once if proofs arrived. I was duly summoned by a telegram from the Lake District.

When I went to Scotland, sheets were being corrected at intervals for an American edition. In July Logan seemed to be under the impression that an autumn edition might still be published in the United States. However, it was amicably arranged that I should go to Scotland, and, after a week, if I found that sheets had arrived, I was to come back at once.

Accordingly, I rang up, from Perthshire, without saying where I was. Some sheets had turned up.

'I'll be up tomorrow,' I said, still without telling where I was; the journey was quite possible. But when he found that I was still in Scotland, he told me, happily as I thought, that three days hence would do just as well. I was caravanning with friends, and there was no need, he told me, to leave them so suddenly. But when I visited him I found that he had scrambled through this particular batch and had sent it off. He was evidently determined on a grievance.

In September *Reperusals and Re-collections* appeared, and I was, as usual, presented with a copy—he gave it me on the 9th; I wrote my appreciation in a letter and on the 25th his acknowledgment of it arrived:

'I too rather like the book, now that [the] nightmare of proof-reading is over. I'm glad you like it, and the reviews and letters I get are most flattering. But there are toads in every dish—Sisam writes from the Oxford Press that I have misspelt *meconopsis* on p. 64. Fortunately this I can correct, as the book is being reprinted. But why didn't you notice this? Also I suspect a little scorn and mockery in your attribution of "penetration" to me, which I think unkind. We all have our failings. I have some other grievances against you, which I will tell you—if I remember them—when we meet . . .

'I have emerged from my interlunar cave, and am deliciously crazy again. I put it down to the Great Pyramid, which, according to the British Israelites, foretells the future, and indicates that on Sept. 16th a new period of happiness and prosperity would descend on England. On the day following, the 17th, I woke up another person, so am inclined to believe in the Pyramid. One must believe in something, and this pyramidal prophecy is the only prospect that gives a gleam of hope in this universal scene of woe.'

These misprints—and they were, I think, no more than every author finds inescapable—became a recurring and unextinguished grievance. A few days later he wrote to me (2.10.36):

'A sudden longing to go to Chartres has come upon me—the result, I suppose, of the thirteenth century history I have been reading. I shall only want to go for five or six days, and wonder whether you would care to come with me as a travelling guest. You would have to arrange about tickets, hotels, etc., and behave yourself, or try to behave yourself or at least successfully deceive me. This ought to be not impossible for so brief a period. I think I can afford to pay for us both before I retire into the poor-house. I should like to go [the] week after next, before the cold sets in or France collapses. But if you have another holiday, or a series of important bridge-parties, no doubt I can find another companion, though I should greatly prefer to take you, doubtful though you may be on longer expeditions . . .

'I had a visit from a devil yesterday who came to point out a number of other misprints in my book. These are like boils on my behind, which is now liberally spotted with them.'

He was out of his cave, but cheerfulness hadn't yet come fully upon him; this was the kind of letter and the kind of temper I expected at such a period; better times, I knew, were on the way. I agreed, of course, to visit Chartres with him, that building as transcendent among cathedrals as the Teide among mountains.

Mrs Russell, Logan's sister, had lately become dangerously ill; about the same time his other sister, Mrs Berenson, had come to London with her husband, and taken a house. Logan removed there from his afflicted home. I went one day to see him and stayed to lunch. The house belonged to Lady Horner, and was full of pictures and drawings by Burne-Jones.

Logan was in bed when I arrived. He discussed our trip to Normandy. He was not in a good mood; this was much as I had expected, for I knew he would still be shadowed a little by the penumbra of his periodic eclipse. But he was rather worse than usual, and for the first time I experienced a portion of real venom in his attacks.

'I thought at first of not asking you to come with me,' he said.

'Why not?' I rather unwisely asked.

A long attack followed about my bridge-playing in the liner; 'I don't blame you, of course,' he ended. 'Like all young people of your generation, you're inconsiderate.'

As I have already granted there were various reprobatory adjectives which I probably deserved of Logan (this was not a boast masquerading as confession); but, as I also said, the one I will claim never to have earned is 'inconsiderate'. However, at last the undeserved adjective had been uttered, and it was never hereafter to be altogether laid aside. Once a word had possessed Logan nothing—no logic, no evidence, no feeling—could ever again free him from its influence. He was largely slave to a sort of moral etymology.

As the day wore on his temper improved—I knew from experience that I could count on this. When we went downstairs, and I was introduced to Mrs Berenson, he asked her if she admired Burne-Jones.

'Often,' she answered. 'You can't help admiring him.' There was a painting in the house so beautiful, that her husband and she, with all their proud collection of Italian pictures, would very much like to possess it. We decided to have a look at it, and another guest, a man, came with us. We found upstairs a large cartoon in charcoal—pleasant enough, but it left me, rather ashamedly, cold. Could this be, I asked myself, the sort of thing to convert the unconverted?

'Does that strike you as an exquisite masterpiece?' inquired Logan, in a tone which betrayed to me the same doubts as my own.

'Yes, it does appear to me strikingly beautiful,' said our fellow guest.

'What do you think, Bob?' asked Logan then, looking at me.

'I'm afraid it doesn't move me as it ought to,' I answered.

'No,' he responded. 'I don't feel it either.'

'We must be wrong,' I said, and he agreed.

I didn't like to admit my failure to Mrs Berenson, but Logan was less bashful. 'We didn't,' he said, 'like your Burne-Jones as much as we ought.' And then we found that we'd made a mistake, but not one of appreciation. We'd been looking at the wrong picture. To the right one we responded just as we should; it was a lovely, romantic and jewel-like panel of Hero, bent over golden flames of the fire she was lighting as a guide to Leander; Burne-Jones had painted it as a screen to put in front of a hearth in the summer.

In the afternoon I went with Logan to his room—for work, as he said, but in fact mainly to chatter and to discuss again our trip to Normandy. We arranged that he should first stay with me for a few days. He brought up the same grievances, but by now he was in full cheerfulness, and reproaches of the morning became the afternoon's jokes. I was able to defend myself.

'In fact,' said Logan, when I'd finished, 'you're perfect.'

'Of course,' I said.

'Then how do you account for giving me these grievances?'

'But you need them to make your bile work; you've often told me so. I only do it for the sake of your health; some one less perfect than me wouldn't think of it.'

'Then I suppose I ought to be grateful,' said Logan.

And then we did a little work. He began reading aloud to me some autobiographical sketches; he planned to make a book out of these, the book which afterwards appeared as *Unforgotten Years*.

'Look out,' he said, when he started off, 'for passages where I get too playful or arch. I've been reading these aloud here, and Berenson says that my chief fault—every writer has a special fault which he tends to fall into—well mine, Berenson tells me, is a tendency to become too facetious. I think he's right.'

When I left him to catch the train, he gave me three letters for the post; by some unhappy accident I left two of them behind, and was forced to write him a letter of apology and explanation; he had left London.

'I am delighted,' he answered from the country (13.10.36), 'to have been able to make you eat some mud and give you some dim sense that your character and conduct are not always, in every respect, absolutely perfect . . .

'I am quite happy to stay here till Saturday, though the corridors are cold and the bath-room untidy beyond imagination. If you will make out a railway itinerary for me . . . I will conscientiously follow your instructions, and try to be a well (or ill) behaved guest for a few days before we go, as I hope we shall be able to go, to France.'

He was writing from the house of his niece Ray Strachey. She made a hobby of building, and had invented a method of constructing the walls of a house out of compressed mud. To demonstrate her invention she had built by this process part of her own home, and had therefore named it The Mud House.

We had been planning to travel about Normandy by train, and, where it was necessary, to hire cars. It occurred to me now that it might be pleasanter and more convenient to take my own car; but this car of mine was a small one and it might not, I was afraid, be comfortable enough for Logan. So I wrote to him now, making my suggestion; I would, I said, come over and fetch him, and as it would be a fairly long journey, he could then decide if he would be happy to tour Normandy in it. I also, in this letter, defended myself over the matter of the letters, developing facetiously the theme of my perfection.

'It will be angelic of you,' he answered (15.10.36), 'to come for me on Saturday—I hate railway trains and stations; and to buy a ticket I always feel to be an act beneath my dignity. I enclose instructions how to find this habitation of mud—if you can read instructions, which I never can, as my thoughts always wander. But being the Perfect Being which you so modestly boast yourself, I dare say you can accomplish this. I would be quite willing to accept your theory of yourself, did not my imagination, that boundless faculty, suggest less annoying ways of giving me grievances I require than mislaying letters for the post, or keeping me from sleep on steamers. But perhaps the acute annoyance is needed to give poignancy to the grievance . . .'

Mrs Berenson was also staying at the Mud House. At lunch Logan demonstrated a very curious peevishness. He and his sister got on to reminiscences of their remote childhood.

'Can't you tell us some story against Logan?' I asked. Logan, I should add, almost invariably liked having his leg pulled—so often, in fact, that I can only recall two or three occasions when such behaviour annoyed him. This was one of those occasions, though I was not the offender.

'Oh yes, I know one,' said Mrs Berenson. 'It was when he was about five years old. A friend of mine and I had just got bicycles—velocipedes we called them in those days——'

'I don't like this story,' interrupted Logan, and deflated with vexation.

Mrs Berenson took no notice of him. 'Logan wanted to play with us, and *we* wanted to ride our bicycles, so we said to him, "If you want to play with us, we'll tell you what to do; lie down there and pretend you're a worm." So we bicycled round and round the yard, and whenever we passed Logan, who was rolling about on the ground, we said, "Look at that nice worm." He was quite happy.'

'I don't like that story,' Logan repeated, seriously and sulkily. This little trickery must have been contrived about 1870, more than sixty years before.

In the afternoon I drove him to my home. He professed himself quite satisfied with such comfort as he found in my car; later, however, he made quite a little story out of it.

'Bob said we could use his car,' he told people, 'and I pictured to myself a nice comfortable little saloon; but when he turned up, what do you think I saw? A *racing-car*, which went everywhere at seventy miles an hour.'

This description, considered either as praise or reproof, was unmerited. All the same, I was surprised that he so cheerfully and so enterprisingly fell in with the plan. My car was a small sports model, and whenever I got Logan into it, I felt as though I were squeezing a foot into a shoe too narrow for it, or putting a very large egg into a very small egg-cup. I did once or twice, on the long straight roads of Normandy, touch seventy; but if we went 'everywhere' at any particular speed, it was more like thirty-five to forty miles an hour.

'I'm a car-snob, you know,' Logan said when I first got him into it; 'is this a smart car?'

'It's not exactly smart,' I said, 'but it's what's called racy.'

'That'll suit me,' he said, 'so long as people look at us.'

During the few days that he stayed with us, the season of difficulties, I noticed, was not quite over. He tried perhaps, as he promised in his letter, to be a well-behaved guest. But on one occasion at least he wasn't so well behaved.

'You know that trip you took to Scotland this summer?' he said. 'Well, it cost you two thousand pounds.'

I can't quite remember what my response was to this astonishing observation; he explained it.

'I was making my will about that time: I was going to leave you those houses of mine in Chelsea and then I thought, "No, he doesn't deserve it," so I changed my mind.'

Threats are dangerous to friendship, and such particular threats intolerable, for a money value is attributed to what cannot be valued in terms of money. I think it was after this that I tended sometimes to become off-hand with Logan on inappropriate occasions—for fear of setting a material goal to disinterested behaviour. I answered with what dignity I could muster, that Logan was only pledged to leave me the allowance he was now giving me, together with his copyrights and his books which had been finally included in the agreement; as to anything else he was free to do as he liked; but I added that such things should never, never be spoken about, and that, in any case, the penalty seemed rather large for a short delay which he himself, all unasked, had sanctioned. Kyrle took a severer line, and gave him a harsh lecture on manners—and one, I think, that was not undeserved.

For almost the only time in the course of our friendship, I saw that Logan was ashamed. He made a remark to me later that was half-apology and half-explanation.

'I've got no grievance about that,' I said. 'You're perfectly entitled to do whatever you like with those houses. But you oughtn't to have told me about it.'

'No,' he agreed. 'I shouldn't have told you.'

This outburst had, later on, some curious elucidation.

At lunch one day he told us about his prostate operation. He had been advised that the world-expert on this ignominious gland was an American surgeon, and accordingly for the first time in many years he revisited his native country in order to undergo the operation. It was not a success and, when he was home again, he had to go for treatment to a London doctor.

'I said to him,' Logan told us, '"I suppose you're very pleased to find a failure of ——'s"', and he said he was delighted.' Or rather that was how he had meant to tell the story: but in the meantime an odd thing had happened. His head sank to one side; he found great difficulty in speaking, and kept saying, over and over again, 'He said, "Oh, I'm de-*lighted*." Oh, he was de-*lighted*. He said "I'm de-*lighted*".' For a moment I became alarmed, thinking he must have had a stroke, of which he seemed to be manifesting all the symptoms. Then I saw what the trouble was. I had poured him out a little whisky, leaving him to fill up with plain or soda-water, as he pleased. Intent upon talking, he had absent-mindedly and without looking taken the whisky bottle, not the water jug, and filled his tumbler right up; so eager was he to talk, that he had not even felt the strength of the spirits as he gulped them down. Being a most moderate drinker the consequence was sudden and extreme. He had become very drunk. It didn't, as I hoped, have any interesting effect upon him. All he did was to keep on repeating incoherently, ' "Oh," he said, "I'm de-*lighted*".'

His usual afternoon sleep put him right, and when he found out what had happened, he seemed to think it as much a joke as we did. Once or twice after this, when he had made a joke attack upon me, I retaliated with this story. Then one day he said, as he had to his sister's tale of the worm, 'I don't like that story.' Afterwards, he remonstrated with me. I pointed out that the story was in no way to his discredit, upon which he said that because of it people might be inclined to impute to him graver vices—a turn of thought which has always remained quite inexplicable to me. After that I denied myself the pleasure of exposing his inebriate past.

On the whole it must be granted that, during this visit, he was an ill- rather than a well-behaved guest.

We crossed by night from Southampton to Havre, and, after pleasantly breakfasting in that port, where people kept on telling us how unlucky we were not to have seen the *Normandie,* we set off in the delicate autumn sunshine, between white cliffs and the wide luminous river, up the Seine valley; crossing by ferry, we turned back to Honfleur. Our tour in Normandy had begun.

Honfleur was a charming little port, across the estuary from Havre, like an old village beside the park walls of a mansion. The shadow of his depression had cleared, and Logan was in the highest of spirits— sometimes embarrassingly so. We each had our hair cut in Honfleur. Logan tried to chatter in his abominable French; he brought up domestic politics—a rather unsafe and not always courteous subject for foreigners to discuss—and gave the barber to understand that a bloody revolution was expected to break out at any time, in Paris.

When he was tidied up—so far as he could be tidied up—Logan went off and left me.

'Why does he talk like that?' asked the puzzled but luckily unoffended barber.

I managed to laugh it off, and satisfied him with, 'Il aime les histoires qui font peur.' Which was true; though sometimes the discomfort he attempted was less benevolently intended.

From Honfleur we drove to Caen where our first night was spent. Some letters which I wrote to Kyrle at this time happen to have been kept; I was amused at some of the things and events they recalled.

'All today,' I wrote from Caen, 'Logan has been all right, talking about subjects and discussing things, when he is very pleasant and good company.' (This was praise too tepidly given; on such occasions Logan could be the best company in the world.) 'But after supper tonight,' I went on, 'there was a very bad outburst. One story, which I thought very good when I first heard it, four years ago, went on steadily from 8.45 to 9.45. I bore up, but it was rather like a dog barking at night—dying down, and just when it seems to be stopping, off it goes again. It was also rather like several copies of the same newspaper, torn up and scattered higgledy-piggledy. First the story went through, and then different parts were repeated over and over again, in quite a chaotic order. I thought when he was tired it wouldn't happen, but it did!

'Logan's French is quite unbelievably bad. The French can't understand it, and I have to interpret.'

The next morning, we went to look at the two matchless Norman churches, the Abbaye-aux-Hommes, and the Abbaye-aux-Dames, built respectively by William the Conqueror and his wife Matilda; in these the purity and austerity of Norman architecture more beautifully reveals itself than in any other buildings known to me. The huge splendour of Durham is lacking, it is true; but in these two early churches the classical spirit, which blossomed so strangely in the North, shines with a mysterious and inescapable light amid their faultless proportions.

The perpetual taking of sleeping-drugs had begun to affect Logan; this principally showed in a weakness of the ankles, which made walking difficult. He often needed support as he shuffled about and, on this tour, I saved him by taking the car wherever it was possible, driving even the shortest of distances. But we couldn't drive inside churches and he soon became tired; while we were in Matilda's church, he sat down on the base of a column near to her grave, and went irreverently off to sleep. Nevertheless, coming away in the best of moods, he clearly showed how much he had felt the stern beauty of the two churches.

Our next stop was at Bayeux. We arrived in the evening; after supper, I explored the town; a fresh and pleasant obligation had fallen upon me, one that, henceforward, I was always to feel when I was going about with Logan; I wandered around the town and into the Cathedral, looking for sights which I thought likely to please him; I knew, by now, what would probably take his fancy, and was thus able to save him some laborious and unrewarded sight-seeing.

I saw by street-lights some ancient houses, well worth a look in the morning; and then I found the Cathedral, open still, and darkly lighted. Some festival was in preparation, and all shops and businesses in the town seemed to have prepared shields for a procession. These shields were appropriately adorned in a style that seemed at once contemporary and timeless; their appearance at first sight was antique and heraldic, and then it could be seen that armorial decorations had been made with goods which would now be on sale; on one were collars, together with a cap such as would be labelled in the window 'très sport'; on another were electric light bulbs and patterns of flex; and every one of them purged by a sacred intention from all vulgarity or semblance of advertising. I stood near the bright altar and watched the devout pray and bow, and then drop into a little basket their written and material petitions to an immaterial being. Then, warm with that strange and holy light, I went back to Logan with my discoveries and the promise of delight for the morning.

The famous tapestry has overshadowed in most minds the other beauties of Bayeux. The small town is of great charm, and the small cathedral, as I discovered in the morning, quite fulfilled the presages I had drawn the night before from its candle-lit interior. Just to the south of it is the beautiful, classically designed old palace of the Bishop. Here the tapestry is kept, stretching its fabulous length up and down and around a large room. Need I add that this work is not in fact tapestry with woven designs, but a very long piece of embroidered stuff?

Logan looked at bits of it, and then sat down while I examined it, every now and again calling his attention to details of special charm or beauty. Meantime he was contriving a sort of conversation with the curator who, being used probably to foreigners, understood more of that strange talk than most of his compatriots.

Logan had made up his mind, and not without reason, that Blum was a great man; but when he said it he usually hoped, I think, that he was going to shock one of Blum's opponents. The curator, however, listened most complacently to the praise of his Prime Minister; he even volunteered, by way of contrast, some fun at the expense of President Lebrun whose chief asset, he gave us to understand, was a delightful grandfatherly manner when he had to kiss children.

Logan then got on to food; he said we were going to Mont St Michel next, and what should we ask for there? 'Lamb of the salt marshes,' answered the curator. 'Agneau de pré-salé,' and he kissed his hand in an ecstasy of platonic greed.

The weather darkened after we left Bayeaux, and when at last we saw, towards evening, that miraculous rock, it rose black against the silvery water of a stormy sunset. On the way we had passed in sight of Avranches, and Logan reminded me of the Bishop he had written about so briefly in *Afterthoughts*, '. . . Huet, that gay old Bishop of Avranches ("*flos Episcoporum*", a German scholar called him), who lived to be ninety-one, and read Theocritus every year in his favourite month of May.'

My night's exploration was less happy than at Bayeux; Mont St Michel, it seems, for all its great beauty, is dead; the great buildings can only be visited with a guide; there was nothing for me to find out, after dark and alone. Logan appeared tired; the food, we had already decided, was not what we expected; the lamb was just lamb, and the famous omelettes more than half a fraud. In a rather disgruntled mood he went to bed.

I was sleeping in the next room, and, as in foreign hotels, there was a door between. In the middle of the night, half-aroused by Logan's titanic coughing, I was suddenly startled by a loud crash. He had coughed himself out of bed. I was getting up to help him when he called out to me, feebly. I found him lying on his back, like a sheep in a hollow, and quite unable to get up. I performed the not inconsiderable task of raising his enormous bulk, and left him.

The next morning he declared himself too weak for any excursion; indeed, the one thing I had made sure of the night before was that Logan would be quite unable to climb the many steps of the rock. However, after inquiries at the hotel, I managed to engage two men and a carrying chair for him, and the party of tourists went round with this unusual addition.

When he was set down in the great hall of the Mount, Logan said, 'Yes, this does strike me as very great architecture. What do you think?'

I wasn't sure yet—hadn't altogether surrendered; but as I looked now the huge beauty seemed to beacon out, like sunlight, over the stern gothic arches and austere massive pillars of the nobly proportioned place, the 'Merveille', the Wonder; and once the idiom of that strange pile of buildings had become plain, I could see, and could share with Logan that Miltonic beauty which stirred, not so much ecstasy, as a solemn and all but mystical response.

The guide seemed fascinated by the sight of Logan in his carrying chair, and addressed all his information to him. Logan, it appeared, felt bound to respond, and kept repeating, with his head sunk down from encroaching fatigue, 'Oui, oui, vraiment.'

We reached the highest platform. The ancient gothic church has been curiously embellished with a not unlovely, Italianate, eighteenth-century façade, the slight antiquity of which compelled the guide to belittle it. Logan seemed to be getting sleepy now, and, under the fixed eye of the expatiating guide, his responses became odder. 'Oui,' he said, 'Oui, yes, vraiment,' (slowly nodding his head), 'oui, yes, really, oui, yes.'

We had now seen all the considerable buildings of the mount. On the way down, beside one of the lesser lights, Logan suddenly said, 'Bob, I'm getting bored; I must go back to the hotel.'

Everything stopped while I explained this to the guide. Keys had to be fetched and the whole party delayed and inconvenienced. This, while much embarrassing me, left Logan altogether unperturbed.

I was worried a little about his health. But he assured me that I needn't concern myself, and that his falling out of bed was nothing to trouble over. I was not convinced, and suggested that we shouldn't leave till the next day; but he didn't like the hotel, and determined on our going. We set off on a rainy afternoon; Logan was anxious to get on to Chartres, but I insisted on stopping early at Domfront. This was the town where Cotman once painted some of his loveliest water-colours; but the weather didn't encourage sight-seeing.

Logan appeared unwell in the evening, so I borrowed a thermometer from a friendly old woman who seemed to be running the hotel. It was marked in Réaumur degrees; after a long calculation, I made out that his temperature was just above normal. Again I pressed him to stay on; but he was firm, and since, next morning, his temperature was normal, we decided, after he'd had a good rest, to set off in the after-noon for Chartres.

There is, I truly believe, no other building in the world where so complete and so limpid a delight is to be felt as in and about the cathedral of Chartres; the Sistine Chapel, perhaps, and the Parthenon in its prime—these alone could be reckoned as its peers. The exterior design of this cathedral is outstripped in perfection by others, by Salisbury in our own land, for instance, or by Durham; the ancient removal of the ancient western front has robbed the great church of utter perfection. But at the southern corner of that front rises still the impeccable and antique spire; on its porch smile as though from beyond all scenes of the world, and with joy that was never of the flesh, those quiet figures of stone. And within! Varying with the varying gleams of day, glitter resplendent all the jewels of the Revelation, fiercely in many of the lights, more delicately in the triple West window, the loveliest object, surely, ever accomplished by the hands of men. Nor is there any terror here or sternness as in other churches, no hell-dooming Jehovah, no menaces of terrible judgment; there broods here only in sweetness and serenity and all loving kindness, peacefully, the Mother of God.

The Trinity makes only the most perfunctory and formal appearance. For Mary the fane was built, who, so it was believed, could turn to mercy all the dreadful sentences of her Son. And still, with her infinite complacence, she shelters in her temple the shrine of a coarser and more ancient immortal.

On the dark evening of our arrival I went round to the Cathedral, mysterious in the obscurity of lamplight; the interior symmetry of the building melted into the chaos of a night which had blinded all the brightness of the windows. But in one nook of the shadowy Cathedral there was brightness still; round and about the pillar shrine flickered and flared innumerable tapers; and every now and again one of the devout would add a star to that waxen galaxy, and having kissed the black pillar, would silently withdraw—that pillar, sacred relic from what incalculable antiquity, when aurochs roamed in the forests of Gaul, and the legions were less than dreams in the savage hearts of their forefathers.

Next day, before Logan was up, I was back in the Cathedral, and later in the morning we went round there together; I pointed out my particular choice among windows and statues; I showed him the pillar-shrine, bright still with candles and attended by worshippers; we sat down and looked about us in a mood that was almost one of wordless worship.

Logan had been during our journeyings—he admitted it—rather querulous, but not, he was good enough to add, with me. The beauty of Chartres seared and soothed all these troubles away. We visited the Cathedral again during the afternoon, to observe the windows under a differently hanging sun, when the most ancient and most beautiful patterns, those of the Western lights, blazed out with a more emphatic splendour.

We went out and sat in a café.

'If we could find a bookshop,' said Logan, 'there's one particular book I should like to buy you. There was a nineteenth-century poet whose name I can't remember now, though I know it perfectly well— damn it! what was his name? He wrote one book of sonnets, just one book which he polished for years, until he'd made it quite perfect. If I could choose what book in literature I might have written, I'd choose that. I'd rather have written it than any other book in the world.'

Being profoundly ignorant then in French literature, I didn't realize, as now I should, that he was referring to *Les Trophées* of Heredia. Logan's copy is now in my possession; on the flyleaf he has written, 'The book, of all the books in the world, that I should have wished to have written.' This choice, I think, illustrates most admirably both the defects and the merits in Logan's heart: his boundless worship of beauty and perfection—and that curious decrepitudenizing fear of the heart's depths. In nineteenth-century France alone, *Les Fleurs du Mal*, surely, or some book of Verlaine's ought to be a preferable choice; but those revealed chasms, which Logan could never bring himself to explore; and then, how much pleasanter to have been Heredia than Verlaine, or Baudelaire!

Logan's angelic voice was upon him; his little peevishnesses, his impatience at petty discomfort and small inconvenience had somewhat exasperated me, and made a barrier against respect; but now I could easily understand again the pride and pleasure which I felt in his company and in his friendship.

And indeed, warmed by the fires of art, not only his intellect became undulled, but his heart too. It was now that he acknowledged, apologetically, his querulousness; and that evening, in the hotel, he went farther, attempting to expunge an earlier offence. 'Logan,' I wrote to Kyrle a little later the same night, 'has just confessed to me that *before* we went to Scotland it was already too late for the American edition to be published in autumn! What do you think of that? I must say, he looks ashamed. He calls it an imaginary grievance; but if he was telling the truth, it had rather violent material consequences.'

The most curious feature of the whole affair is that he was not, as it turned out, telling the truth; he admitted eventually that when he made his outburst, he had already sold, or was preparing to sell, the houses in question. Self-deception is a common vice, but with Logan, at this stage of his life, it was turning into self-hallucination. There is one thing I am sure of in this respect, namely, that when Logan declared how disproportionately he was punishing me, he really believed, first, that I had wantonly held up the American publication of his book, and, second, that in doing so I had deservedly forfeited property to the value of two thousand pounds. And neither of these propositions was true.

The impulse of his attack had been, I believe, very little to do with my behaviour, but was rather some inward discomfort of his own. A tendency was growing in Logan, and one which in the end was to become overmastering, to make of his friends scapegoats for his private troubles; and the closer the friend, the heavier was the load imposed upon him.

Chartres, dazzling the memory, outshone and blurred the images of other marvels, much as light, accidentally let in, can blur a photographic plate; but we had transcendent memories enough to justify our little tour when we set off, happily in sunlight for Rouen and Havre.

On our way I discovered a fresh angelic nook in Logan's character. Years ago when his father died, his mother would, according to the will, have lost a large part of her income, which was to pass on to her children. Logan and his sisters told her that everything but what they had at the time was hers for life, and they paid the surplus regularly into her bank.

'And how she enjoyed herself with it!' he added with delighted relish.

Soon after he had told me about this, and when his demeanour had become all sweetness, we approached that great castle, so superbly placed and constructed by Richard Coeur de Lion, Château Gaillard, the Gay Redoubt, looking gaily down from its cliffs on to the Seine and Les Andelys. We stopped to marvel, its beauty appearing to the full in the light of this golden autumn day. Through bright green precipitous turf, rounded bluffs of the whitest chalk were echoed by the preciser curves of the fortress towers; and above, in a pale blue sky, these were echoed in their turn more faintly by the swelling luminousness of occasional small clouds.

I have said that we had gathered memories enough, but there is one ungathered memory which I shall always regret. Logan had realized at one moment that we were not a huge distance from Vétheuil, by Giverny, where he had often stayed during the 'nineties; the lovely Miss Kinsellas had been there, and Conder, and Roger Fry and Lowes Dickinson; and how much of his heart had Logan left there for ever? These were the days when he was first setting out to learn what he so often called 'the lovely art of writing'; then it was that, in Paris, he had sometimes posed for Whistler, burdened with a monstrous fur coat, 'standing in', to use a modern phrase, for a nobleman, perversely celebrated under the name, which will be remembered long after his own has been forgotten, the name of M. de Charlus.

It couldn't be done; Logan seemed cheerful enough, but, for all that, I couldn't be altogether satisfied about his health and I contrived it so that he should only have fairly short drives to put up with; a visit to his old haunts would most probably have altogether exhausted him.

For he had indeed deceived not only me but himself as well; soon after he got home an attack of bronchitis developed which was more than a little serious. Whether two or three days' rest at Domfront would have prevented this, I cannot say; it is not unlikely that he would in that case have fretted himself into the illness, that must, in any case, have already been germinating in him.

He had to spend about a month in bed in the charge of a gay and efficient Irish nurse. He seemed perfectly happy whenever I saw him, cracking jokes as gross as he dared with the nurse, and grosser still with me. As soon as he approached convalescence, his practical jokes started up again. The principal one this time involved a lady whom Logan professed to suspect of a guilty and unbridled passion for Mr Berenson. Eventually, of course, I, as usual got dragged in. Early in December he wrote to me (6.12.36), enclosing a long and elaborate threatening letter:

'—— was in here yesterday and threatens me with a libel action. I think it wise in these matters to take the first step oneself, so I should be obliged if you would copy out and send her the enclosed. I don't think it will let you in for any danger. What line are you taking about Mrs ——? I think the British Public will swallow it—it can swallow anything, and come to take beautiful views about it. Anyhow the whole affair bears the mark of the cinema world—a world in which I think we are coming to live more and more.'

We were now in the climax of the abdication. After the Prime Minister's broadcast he sent me a postcard (11.12.36):

'Will you inquire for me sometimes about lodgings in Iceland? Mr Baldwin's broadcast last night turned my stomach, and I feel inclined to leave this land of unfathomable hypocrisy.'

To amuse him, I sent, just before Christmas, a slightly improper French novel. I had printed at home as a Christmas card my poem on Teneriffe; I had worked over this, and added to it, so that it now comprised other aspects of life as well as my vision of the highest peak. I sent this poem with the book. He answered on Christmas Eve:

'What a delightful book you have lent me! a little too much patriotism and *ma mère* for my taste, but that seems a necessary ingredient in French novels. But the rest of the book is fascinating, and gives me quite a taste for *la crapule*. Alas, I am too old for that sort of thing, and must finish my existence on the high plane on which I have lived it. I dare say that on the whole it is a preferable one and certainly my declining days are extremely pleasant. Such days are after all a part of life, and it is well to prepare for them.

'I have read several times the verses on Teneriffe you sent with the book, and have liked them better each time I have read them. You are undoubtedly a poet, and have turned this bit of experience into literature—a rare and indeed unique phenomenon in these days. As I have a taste for that sort of thing I am compelled to take from my store of grievances or reserve this special one, so here is my formal withdrawal, signed and in my own writing. You had better keep [it] for reference, if the subject comes up again—as it may!

'Of course I should love to see you next week, but don't feel under any obligation to come to see me. You need your holidays, and I should hate to have you break down! . . .

'With the most dismal greetings of this dismal season.'

In reference to the last paragraph, I should perhaps explain that, owing to his illness, I had not done much work with him since our return from Normandy.

But there was no vice in these insinuations. He was in the best and kindest of spirits. Once after I had made some mock attack on him, which I cannot recall, and which would almost certainly not be worth recording if I could, he said, 'How you torment me! How can you bring yourself to make all his last years miserable, as you do, for a poor, invalidish unhappy old man?'

'How miserable have I made you?' I asked him.

He paused, and then said, 'The last few years have been the happiest years of my life!'

1937

After this illness it became obvious that Logan had reached an age when he needed properly looking after. Accordingly, when the nurse left, a special servant was engaged, half-nurse and half-lady's maid. Everyone who knew Logan during the last years of his life knew Hammond. A friend of his old age once described her in my hearing as a sort of female Sancho Panza; this was more than a passable witticism; it exactly described their relationship. She took a large part in his jokes—it was she who bought a dead cat from the dustman and threw it into a neighbour's garden—she adored him with an unexcellable devotion, which was for all that superficially critical; she would expostulate, answer back, and scold; night and day she gave up to him, running errands and always, at all hours, ready for the summons of his importunate bell: and in every way looking after all his enormous corpulent body as though it were a baby's.

About this time the Society for Pure English, mainly, I believe, on Logan's prompting, had offered a prize for an essay on a set subject. Three or four of the best essays were sent to Logan for his opinion as to the prize-winner. He got me to read these, and asked which my choice was. There wasn't much difficulty; one seemed to me of a different order of scholarship to the rest. My opinion, I found, coincided with Logan's.

When we went to France, we had visited, on leaving and on returning, some friends of Logan's who lived not far from Southampton. (Logan was afterwards to declare that they had said, when we first left them in my car, 'There's the last of poor Logan!') One son, Michael, an invalid, with tuberculosis and an enlarged heart, showed great literary promise, and indeed, more than promise; his unhappy death, during the war, following a chill, bereaved England of a writer, unrecognized, but of very great individual talent and integrity. I had been lucky enough, since my introduction by Logan, to make friends with the family; Michael had been advised, for his health, to spend the winter in the south of France, and his parents had asked me to go with him on the journey, a suggestion which, of course, I proudly and happily fell in with. I told Logan about this, saying that it would necessitate my coming up to him one day earlier than we had arranged. My journey with Michael would mean my being away for just under a week.

About the same time I had sent him some faintly improper postcards —not Paris pornography, but the sort of comic vulgarity which can be bought sometimes in seaside tobacconists. I don't remember what my 'claims' were, but can only be sure that they were humorously founded. *Marjory Kempe* was a remarkable fifteenth-century autobiography lately discovered and printed. 'Ronald' was my cousin, Sir Ronald Graham, formerly ambassador in Rome.

'Wednesday,' he wrote (6.2.37), 'will suit me just as well as Thursday, but if it is terribly inconvenient, don't hesitate postponing and visit [me] next week, though I shall miss seeing you awfully. But I am so glad that you are looking after poor Michael, that I shall hate to interfere with this . . .

'In the meantime I shall make a careful calculation, to set against your claims, of the damage you do to my moral character by sending me obscene postcards—the sum keeps mounting up . . .

'I have had a letter from Lascelles Abercrombie who is as enthusiastic about that essay on compound adjectives as we were. So the prize is to be allotted to him and his essay to be printed as a S.P.E. tract. I have written to the author . . . to find out about him.'

He goes on to lugubriously prognosticate that the author will probably turn out to be stodgy, old, married and father of a large family, and a bore.

' "It is like that in the life", as a foreigner of my acquaintance always used to say.

'Will you ask Kyrle to send a copy of *Marjory Kempe* to Lady Hamilton. . . . She writes in a note received this morning that she is ill in bed, but has an immense party this afternoon which she hopes to get through by means of dope and rouge. I feel I owe her a debt for bringing me and Ronald in connection. He has just been here, and was as delightful as ever. But I wish he didn't think Aldous Huxley the finest living writer. However, as I have said already, "It is like that in the life".?

Logan had composed an epigram for *Afterthoughts*, and cut it out before printing, 'I don't like diplomats'. I am glad that this elimination was practically justified by a relation of mine. As for his opinion of Mr Aldous Huxley's work, the reader must settle for himself whether that was the fruit of reflection or of prejudice.

In the early part of the year he relapsed into his gloom. He had lately, with very great kindness, tried, but unsuccessfully, to persuade a publisher to issue my poems. In reporting his failure he wrote (18.3.37), by way of comfort, 'nothing really good is ever accepted by the first publisher to whom it is sent, as I know by the fate of my *Trivia*, which met with several refusals.

'I am still a ghost and a very dull one. But if you are in London do look in.'

After he emerged, the rest of the year was taken up with the putting together of *Unforgotten Years*, and I visited him regularly.

To assign an ultimate standing to our contemporaries is a dangerous, chancy undertaking. Who is the Rogers of our day, and who the Keats? But Logan, I certainly believe, had the sort of intellect and talents which earn an everlasting niche; if those talents were satisfactorily employed, as I believe they were, he will be remembered, undoubtedly, as the author of *All Trivia*, which, if it keeps any place at all, is likely to be esteemed in English literature a little lower than the aphorisms of La Rochefoucauld, or the *Charactères* of La Bruyère in France. His other works will be carried along with *Trivia*, but one, in my opinion, more conspicuously than the rest, his partial autobiography *Unforgotten Years*.

Wise men had seen the obvious cones and craters and lava-flows of Auvergne for very many years before an inspired observer deduced their volcanic origin. When Darwin first propounded his theory, Huxley said something like 'Why did I never think this out for myself'; he'd had all the facts before him. For almost a year I lived in the childhood and youth of Logan; and yet when, a year later, the catastrophe came, I with many of the clues in my hand, was taken utterly by surprise.

How much of the truth was there in these reminiscences of Logan's? A truth, I think, more complete than is usual in such composition; at

III

any rate, there were no falsehoods. He wasn't writing up his character. But there is a large reservation.

Numberless are the similes of Man's life. May I liken it now to a raft, floating upon unplumbed, yet transpicuous deeps? Some men spend their lives on the edge of the raft, gazing down into those infinite waters. Logan sat plumb in the middle, intent on his letter game, and facing no more of that unfathomable ocean than the occasional flurries of surf that sometimes flashed inevitably across his vision, and these he didn't like. To gaze out upon the breadth, or to search probingly into the profundities of that ocean, was to him an unspeakable horror.

When one of his books was published—I forget which it was: probably *Afterthoughts* or *All Trivia*—a reviewer compared Logan to a French abbé of the eighteenth century. From the quality of his work, and of the mind he revealed in it, this was a natural comparison; nevertheless, I believe it to be utterly false. If there is a case in literature parallel to Logan's, the only one that I could name would be Cowper's. Logan, of course, was never afflicted with any dreadful or terrifying illusion; but having, by the fineness of his discriminating instinct, perceived that deep and alarming feelings were not a matter for his pen, he turned with a consequently greater intensity upon the lighter themes which he worked so consummately with. The limitation, it must be realized, was not essentially a matter of art; it was not a case like Jane Austen's two inches of ivory. It wasn't that he could not deal with deeper themes, but, in effect, that he dared not. This I believe to be the clue to his artistic nature. The unspoken fear was an incentive which heightened immeasurably the apparently trivial matters which he wrote about most often. Without this emotional limitation, he might never have perfected his prose to the same degree; on the other hand, I think it not impossible, that, with a spirit less crippled, he might have proved himself the peer of Donne, Sir Thomas Browne, and Jeremy Taylor.

I have found it strange to reflect that in all our years of deep intimacy —an intimacy in which no subject on its own was unmentionable—I never made Logan a full confidant in any private trouble of the spirit. And yet, as I can see now, it was not so very strange. Sorrows and perplexities of the heart were matters not allowable in his life; instinctively I had avoided them.

As I shall record later on, Logan found it intolerable to witness activities which he couldn't account for. I share—though to a less passionate extent—that weakness of his. To me, some explanation, although not altogether certain, is better than no explanation at all. I find a slight consolation in being able to accept for the truth, at least provisionally, some cause of Logan's subsequent aberration. In offering a solution to the problem, I may add that in this particular case, I am not alone in reckoning them as at least approaching the plausible.

It is requisite for all animals, when they achieve maturity, to leave the fold or the nest; the bird becomes fledged; the fawn forgets and forsakes its mother. In the more conscious and artificial society of humans, parental ties are usually not altogether broken; yet it is well, even in the happiest of families, for the children, as their childhood recedes, to break, however delicately, with their mothers, and to escape, as adults, into a mainly unguided freedom. Among normal people, a new relationship, as happy and as strong in affection, frequently and fortunately takes the place of the old.

Unforgotten Years is a history of escapes, from religion, from business, from America, from sordid ambition. But there is no record of escape from the silken cord of maternal chains; nor, in fact, did Logan ever make such an escape. After living alone for some years, he returned to the nest, and shared a house with his mother. Indeed, when he first lived alone, it had been as a neighbour to his parents, whom he was continuously visiting.

His old mother, for all her passionate religion, had brought her children up with tact and forbearance, training them chiefly to be happy; and when, as young man, Logan went back to live with her, this tact became more delicate than ever, so that she neither questioned, nor interfered with his ways of living. But it is evident, I think, that the thread between them—the biological thread—had never been severed; Logan was never at heart free from her; and when, as an aged woman, she died, his Oxford friends were astounded by the intensity of his recoil, and his dazed manifestation of a deep affliction startled them.

Psychologists tell us that in such circumstances the impulse for an escape stays on, unsatisfied; by the process known as transference this impulse may be assuaged from time to time by quarrels and breaches with people who are, as it were, proxies for the now unattainable mother. And I, as I am firmly convinced, was picked on a number of times for this unhappy function. His sister too, after devoting a large part of thirty-five years to looking after him suffered the same; and indeed towards the end of his life more than one old friend became a character to be escaped from.

About the fiery religion of his parents, which was inculcated into the children, Logan writes with irony; and his eventual loss of faith he narrates gaily, telling how 'One Sunday afternoon in June, when I was up in a cherry-tree picking cherries, the whole supernatural scheme of things seemed to fade away into the blue sky, never to return.'

That is the surface truth, no doubt; but there's far more to it than that. Let us see what he lost with his faith. In his own words 'a sense of Salvation, Sanctification, and exemption from the fears of Hell and the fate of others [which] filled my little heart with a felicity more exquisite than any, I think, that I have ever felt since then'.

These words must be accepted literally; the intensity and power of that holy and delirious conviction cannot be underesteemed. But one fruit of salvation was carried curiously into that new universe, which he liked, so he said 'as immense, grim, icy and pitiless as possible'; this spoil of salvation was an almost complete freedom from the sense of guilt. 'I may do,' he has written, 'I have undoubtedly done, things that were foolish, tactless and dishonest, and what the world would consider wrong, but since I attained the state of Sanctification at the age of seven I have never felt the slightest twinge of conscience, never experienced for one second the sense of sin.'

This, strange as it may seem, was very near to the actual truth. Logan might admit to errors in matters of ascertainable fact—or even of aesthetic opinion; but I cannot recall three times in the course of nearly eighteen years' friendship when he behaved as if he knew he was morally in the wrong. I once had occasion to remonstrate with him over a not inconsiderable perfidy. At first he denied the grounds of my complaint; but when material evidence proved him to be wrong, his reponse was to say, blandly and quite cheerfully, as though he were solving a moral problem, 'I haven't the slightest feeling of guilt'. (The occasion was a broken promise; perhaps he had already recognized the weakness revealed in him then, for one of his unpublished aphorisms reads "When I've promised a thing, I feel as if I'd done it'.)

Now, what did he gain by his loss of faith? A free intellect, and freedom for that irony of spirit which made possible the writing of *Trivia*. But one thing he did not gain. Logan had, I believe, both in feeling and in the flesh, like his father, a passionate temperament; but he never lost, until too late, the puritan ethics sucked in with his religion, and which had prevented the free indulgence and satisfaction of that temperament; and much of his life, in consequence, was taken up with a timid, uninspiring and unremunerative austerity of the flesh. In fact, for comfort and ease of the self-indulgent mind, his loss was greater than his gain.

All of this I believe, and much of it I know to be fact. What I am now adding is conjecture, for it involves a part of Logan's mind which was never directly revealed to me, and whose state I can only indirectly deduce. But I believe there was always lurking within him a dread that, in this enormous change of outlook, he might just conceivably have been wrong, that he had as it were imprisoned his immortal spirit, while giving no freedom to his mortal flesh. 'Never grant that you were mistaken', a terrible inward voice was always ready to whisper. And so it came about that no malease of the spirit, no unhappiness, however slight, no vexation, must be attributed to any fault of his own.

The sanctified boy was liberated from all sense of guilt; what if the faith-abandoning man should feel it? The hidden line of thought can be easily fancied. Follow it up: Could this little distress or that be the consequence of rejected faith, and the harbinger of guilt? And what if it were? We are back to the same dread doubts. 'Never,' the heart would whisper, 'never allow that you were wrong.' A different decision would involve something very like damnation.

It was from such a reason, I believe, that he was more than ordinarily inclined to temper his affection with dislike. Where we love, however slightly, we can suffer. To Logan as to anyone else a friend, though an occasion of pleasure, was also a risk and sometimes a cause of pain; the balance is usually to our advantage, but Logan was too often aware of possible distress, and he resented the occasion of it. The moments of pain, however mild, were danger marks. There was hatred in his affection, and in his heart always a fear of deep feelings.

It would be altogether out of character if such thoughts took their way in his conscious mind. But, as uninterpreted feelings, some such wordless reflections, I verily believe, were working in that half translucent zone of the mind between acknowledgeable thought and the dark regions where deeper passions lurk and incomprehensible images.

To scatter the blame thoughtlessly on to blameless people is an easy instinct of men; just so a dog bites the lifeless trap that its foot has been caught in. To Logan it was more than easy to obey this impulse that only too frequently we all of us obey; to resist it, to admit, in some instance of sorrow or discontent, his own culpability, was to admit as I have said, if the thought were too thoroughly pursued, something no far from actual damnation.

But, it may be argued, there are people bound by a mother-fixation or who have lost their faith, and no very distressing consequences follow. So I must reiterate that Logan was already possessed, mildly, by a known type of madness: that the continuing sanity of his father had not always been a matter of certainty: and I think it not improbable that the long poisoning of his bladder, and the long continued reliance on sleeping drugs, may have deleteriously affected his brain.

I have told how Mr Berenson pointed out to Logan his besetting danger of over-playfulness; this playfulness, not always happy, was, I believe, an evasion of dangerous deep feelings. Perhaps the best chapter in *Unforgotten Years* is the chapter about Walt Whitman. Logan explained to me that he intended this for a serious interlude, contrasting with the gaiety and irony of other chapters. It is interesting to follow this attempt at high seriousness; at every touch of solemnity the writer seems to shy back again into his more comfortable irony; only in the concluding paragraphs, where he describes the effect on him of *Leaves of Grass*, is the purpose completely realized. But then, aesthetic feelings were the only feelings which he could, with comfort, deeply and solemnly experience.

The habit of scholarship still persisted which Logan had perfected many years before, when he was writing his life of Sir Henry Wotton. In looking for sources of fact for his autobiography, he read through old letters of his mother's, and re-discovered, in the process, that she had been a remarkable letter-writer. He told me a great many anecdotes about that formidable, wise, affectionate and saintly old woman.

Anyone who has written about his past can tell how the very act of such writing is a powerful aid in itself to the re-discovering of time that has long gone by. The manner of his telling these maternal anecdotes seemed undoubtedly to imply that he was speaking on the sole authority of long persisting memories lately returned. In one or two cases, this was the truth; but I have lately discovered that most things which he told me about his mother were also contained in her letters. Did he, I often wonder, really remember these incidents or had he only just learnt about them? And if that were the case, did he come to believe, as I was certainly led to understand, that they were now a part of his

emembered life? I don't think that he was trying to deceive, but I
hink it very possible that he may have deceived himself.

Another, and odder form of research was involved in the preparation
of this book. Logan's parents—need I say?—had been famous and successful evangelical preachers; but his father, serene on the crest of the
wave, had been suddenly overwhelmed by a scandal involving female
disciples. When he arrived at this part of the story, Logan became irre-
evantly fascinated by the subject of religious eroticism. He told me
one odd and unprintable story about the circumstances under which a
famous nineteenth century sage had composed a very spiritual book.
He sent me to the British Museum to transcribe the accounts of curious
antique relationships between priests and virgins, and other similar less
virginal associations. Such affairs, it seems, were sometimes to be discovered within the bounds of Victorian piety. Of the information I
collected for him he used just enough to make a witty paragraph or
wo about his father's misfortune; perhaps the happiest result of my
little research was the choice of a word to describe these sanctified
goings on, the word 'loving-kindness'.

1938

1938 was an to be an eventful and calamitous year. It
saw the publication of *Unforgotten Years*, and the
conception of his last book, *Milton and his Modern
Critics*; it also saw for a short time, after serious illness, the complete
overturning of his sanity, a hurt from which his spirit never properly
recovered.

At the end of 1937 I sent him my fifth book of fiction. Except for the
first, in which he discovered promise, he had not, on the whole, been
pleased with the novels I had written. Frankly and inoffensively, but
sometimes severely, he had criticized them. This past disparagement
brought a zest and a relish to the approval which he now gave to my
latest venture. With the generosity which he always displayed when
he liked a work, he bought copies of my novel, and distributed them
among his friends.

'I thought you were on the wrong tack,' he said, 'when I read your
other novels. But I see now that I was mistaken. You are a novelist.'

1938

(It is not proper for me to discuss my own work. But I have to say that I think Logan's original judgment was probably correct. And indeed, if he rightly imputed merit to my last novel, that merit lay in those very qualities whereby it departed most from the qualities requisite to proper fiction. My novels were, I hope, at least respectable things; but they were, at most, the careful work of a man working out of his proper medium.)

'But now,' he went on, 'I want to give you some advice. You don't go about enough. If you want to be a good novelist you must get to know more people. You stay at home too much. Why don't you come to London more often, and stay there and go about seeing people.'

The perversity of this speech was far greater than might appear. In the first place I was living more completely than ever Logan did the sort of life which in principle he most preached up and praised—a life, however far short in accomplishment, at least, in attempt the life of Fitz Gerald or Flaubert—I lived quietly, as I still do, with one friend in the country, studying and reading, and learning as best I could 'the lovely art of writing'. Was it some lust of power or possession which made him resent the ivory tower he had so firmly and decidedly planted me in—made him resent it so much that against all his principles he tried to put me fair and square back into a world, which in any case had never at any time become my natural home.[1]

The second inconsistency is more obscure. I had had for many years a very dear friend, who had lately died, leaving a gap which still, even now, gives me a feeling of bereavement. Logan for various reasons greatly disliked her, and one trouble I often had was to make him see that she ought to be generally a forbidden subject of conversation between us. One great sin he accused her of was a capacity for interfering with the lives of her friends, 'eating them up', as he put it; this took the form, he asserted, of breaking up friendships and wrecking marriages. (This was not, I may add, after years of close and affectionate friendship, the impression she left with me.) At his not very wise bit of advice, I couldn't resist sticking a pin into him.

'What would you have said,' I asked him, 'if —— had said that?' The thrust went home.

[1] However strongly he approved of the ivory tower, he was often ready to find fault with its occupant. Some years later Logan and I happened to be lunching with another friend of his, whom he suspected of looking too much after the main chance. In unimaginable counterpoint Logan attempted throughout most of the meal to be at once talking me out of an ivory tower and our host into one.

'That's not fair,' he cried out, and went on to justify himself, insisting that he had nothing to say against my way of life, and indeed that he thoroughly approved of it. I didn't follow up my little attack.

Few people can have understood their own motives less than Logan did. Whatever his impulse, he certainly believed that he was giving wise advice. And it must be remembered that the one thing which he valued far above all others was art. If I had the talent, or the promise of talent, which he believed in, he would, if he was able, persuade me to give up all private happiness and obligations, if by doing so that talent could be improved in quality; and there he could believe, would lie the only motive of his advice.

'The trouble with you,' he once said to me, 'is that you'll get mossy with happiness.' (This, in spite of his aphorism, 'Happiness is a wine of the rarest vintage, and seems insipid to a vulgar taste'.)

But he was able, with a good heart, to take the other point of view. During the war when both the comforts of my life and the size of my income began, as with most other people, to diminish, he asked me how I was putting up with it. I told him that, in myself, and when not considering the state of the world, I was perfectly happy.

'Yes,' he said with a tone of affectionate approval, 'you've got happiness inside you.'

At the beginning of the year, having given me some references on 'loving-kindness' to look up in the British Museum, he followed it up with a postcard (3.1.38): 'When you are at the B.M. will you look up in the Peerage to see whether the Duchess of Sutherland, whom my grandfather saw purchasing a rug in about 1850, was the same who rescued me at Broadlands in about 1872. I am afraid chronology will not allow it.'

'Is it you or your sister,' he added to another postcard at this time, just before my sister's wedding. 'who is getting married on Wednesday? My memory isn't what it was.'

It will be deduced from these sentences that Logan was coming to the height of his euphoria, and life was to be gay once more.

This gaiety was quite untarnished by an attack of bronchitis, which mildly beset him. When he was recovering, he decided that he would like to visit Holland in March; as usual, I was asked to go with him. He became obsessed, however, by the fear, that during the night's crossing, I might leave him to get a game of bridge. Luxury steamers, he had decided, were not the ships for us to travel on together—even for a night.

The result of this obsession, however, was a happy one. We found ou
a line of small cargo ships which sailed from Ratcliff to Rotterdam
and which could take a few passengers.

Shortly before we sailed he wrote to me (4.3.38):

'. . . Will you come up Wednesday morning, and we can have ar
early luncheon here and take a taxi together to the steamer? To mee
you at the steamer would be too great a strain on my nerves—I nevei
believe that people will turn up on such occasions, owing to some
dreadful experiences with —— . . .

'I don't think that the below is a nice way of talking, but Hammonc
tells me that it is habitual in your class.'

'The below' was a newspaper cutting about a law case between twc
women, in which one of them was alleged to have said 'You are a
filthy, dirty adventuress . . . I know you, you are a street woman and I
am a peer's daughter.'

When I saw the boat, it looked to me like one of those which, on a
Channel passage, one sees all but disappearing into not very large
waves. But since we were both good sailors, this didn't matter;
and, as it happened, no storm arose, either going or returning, to
test us.

I was a little worried when we set forth on this trip, for Logan was
barely out of convalescence. He had brought back a poisoned heel from
Teneriffe, and from Normandy an attack of bronchitis. Holland in
March seemed to me a little unpropitious, and I resolved to take as few
risks as possible. I perfected my system of scouting around picture galleries, and of searching for lovely aspects of a town; then I would show
Logan the pictures I was confident he would like, and no more; and
hiring cars I took him to see carefully-chosen buildings.

He was very weak at this time, and had to lean on my arm when we
visited churches or picture galleries; I was careful to make him rest
every afternoon, and lie down in the evenings. During his afternoon
sleep, and sometimes in the evening, I took the private recreation
which, as I have already told, was necessary—and particularly so when,
as now, his physical state demanded so continual and close an attention.
I was determined that no grievances, even so frail as those which were
born on our southern trip, should have any chance of coming to birth.
I looked after him—I can truthfully boast—like a mother.

On visiting a small gallery in The Hague, I made the acquaintance of
an Anglophil Dutchman. We knew practically nothing of each other's

language; but, with the aid of a dictionary which I had with me, we managed to exchange a number of ideas. Following my usual custom of trying to see more than the material shell of a country, I met him from time to time. I told Logan about it, and he, being in high spirits, began fantasticating an imaginary background for my friend; I played up, and we carried on the sort of conversations which friends entertain themselves with, but which are not in the least funny when repeated. One day when I came in from exploration he said, 'I've just heard from ——. You know he has a Dutch wife, and he knows all about your friend. He tells me that he comes from the lowest criminal classes of The Hague.' I made an appropriate and equally fantastic retort.

We visited The Hague, Amsterdam, and Delft. At The Hague we went to a restaurant which had been recommended both to Logan and to me, by different people, as the best in Europe. The food was stodgy and expensive; and we maliciously consoled ourselves with the thought of our misguidedly aspiring friends, eating poor food in a snobbish and bogus rapture. (The best food in Holland, we decided, was to be found in unpretentious fish restaurants.)

The famous paintings and artists of Holland are a substantial part of the world's intellectual spirit; but to see in quantities and for the first time the vast and amazing fruit of that culture, the fruit, at its best, of so short a flowering season, is an experience that startles and enlightens, like the discovery of a new world, or the inception of a passion that will never die. Logan's company made of these experiences an ecstasy. Over one picture only did we disagree.

I couldn't respond as I should to Paul Potter's *Bull*. Had it been the work of an obscure painter, I might have rejoiced in it as a discovery; Logan, however, clearly saw in it the accepted greatness that I was blind to. But to write of what we saw in Holland requires a pen skilled in the criticism that I am not master of; I can but record our private adventures of the spirit, the tremendous and rugged creations of the old Rembrandt, above all in the *Bridal Couple* at Amsterdam; the pleasant surrender to the too popular yet perfect loveliness of Vermeer, Terborch and de Hooch; the crocuses in fields and parks: and, more privately, our surprise at the solemn, melancholy, and splendid beauties of old Amsterdam, which came upon us so unexpectedly.

When we arrived there, I had left Logan to rest, and gone exploring. A friend had told me that I shouldn't like Amsterdam, and to my amazement I found a beauty unlike anything I'd ever seen before.

I

'This is one of the most beautiful towns in the world,' I said excitedly to Logan when I got back.

'Nonsense,' he said, 'it can't be. We should have heard about it.'

But he agreed with me, as I knew he would, when I had taken him round.

In this last city, having both of us fallen in love with the country, we decided to experience the intimacies of a smaller town, and engaged rooms in a hotel at Delft, there to pay our homage to William the Silent, to the old potters, and to Vermeer, although none of his work is to be found in his native abode. In the meantime, a shadow from the outside world fell terribly across us. Hitler marched into Austria.

We were still in Amsterdam. I heard the bare news, and wondered if we were going to war. All English and French papers were sold. How could I find out? I hit on what I still think was an ingenious device. I took a pound note to a bank. If we were on the point of war, English money would be hard or impossible to exchange. Without hesitation I was handed over Dutch currency, and I knew that still we were at peace. But our first afternoon at Delft was polluted by Hitler's voice, howling out, loud as damnation, from loud-speakers.

In Delft, I bought myself, as a memento, a pretty eighteenth-century tile (the finer work of the seventeenth century seemed unprocurable). When I showed it to Logan, 'You must let me pay for that,' he said; 'I'd like to give it you in memory of our visit. It's been a perfect trip.'

It had, indeed, been a perfect trip; Logan had been gay, friendly and good-tempered (only for a moment, when we first got to the quay at Ratcliff, had he betrayed a sign of vexed agitation; and that was not altogether unjustified, for the tide was inconvenient, and it looked for a moment as if he would have to be hoisted on board by a crane); when, coming home, after a calm night at sea, we steamed up the sunny Thames, he was in better health than when we set out a week before. I had enjoyed myself equally with him, and this time, I thought, there would be no reproaches, no regrets, and no grievances.

I am suspicious of easy explanations given by psychology, and I have no more than everyman's knowledge of the science; but I am driven again to seek clues from that science. Were Logan's bodily afflictions of our other trips due to some uneasy stirring of the spirit? Did he resile from care and attention, as he never properly did from his mother?

While we were coming up the Thames he said, 'Were you telling me the truth when you said that you'd made friends with a Dutchman?'

'I wasn't altogether telling the truth,' I said, 'because I invented a lot that I told you. But it is true that I made friends with a Dutchman, and managed to carry on some sort of conversation with him.'

'I don't believe a word of it,' he said.

He was convinced in a curious way. The Dutchman got the idea that he would like to get some sort of a job in England, and he wrote to ask for my help, help that it was quite impossible for me to give. To find my address he went, evidently, to our hotel at The Hague, where we had both registered under Logan's address. My letter, accordingly, came to Logan's house. He was convinced.

Logan as I have said came back from Holland improved in health. The escape whose need I have surmised was not possible through sickness; therefore some occasion for reproach was necessary. Accordingly I underwent the most extraordinary attack for the 'lies I had told him in Holland'. If an acknowledged fabrication be a lie, then I was guilty; and some such principle may have lurked still in Logan from his early Quaker upbringing; though my offence was fanciful, there probably was something in Logan which would once have reckoned as sinful my facetious inventions. However, he tried to rationalize his attack. 'How can I ever believe you when you tell me such lies?'

At this very moment the contradiction in his character appeared.

I had just finished a book on British wild flowers, and he read through the typescript, 'picking out fleas'. He approved of the work, and praised it generously. After I had attempted a rational expostulation with him, he ended this scene. 'I must finish this. I find it's very interesting. I think it's one of the best things you've ever written.'

The grievance subsided, although it did not perish at once and altogether. Work on *Unforgotten Years* approached happily to its end. Logan was in high spirits.

'Desmond,' he wrote to me in one letter (2.5.38) 'is in great trouble as his favourite tom-cat gave birth to a litter of seven kittens on his armchair on Saturday. He feels that the cat has deceived him grossly as to its sex, but he is fond of the animal, and doesn't want to hurt its feelings. He believes however that cats can only count up to five, so he is going to have two of the kittens removed, letting the other five live in his armchair. It doesn't seem to me a wise arrangement, but wisdom in the practical affairs of life isn't exactly Desmond's gift.'

Although my 'terrible lies in Holland' produced that extraordinary outburst, they evidently had not engendered in Logan any great reluctance towards me as a travelling companion. Just at this time he conceived a plan, as strange in its monstrous bravery, as ever, in their time, were Samuel Johnson's Hebridean projects.

I came up one day to find him examining advertisements for cruises. 'I've got a feeling,' he said, 'that I should like to visit Iceland. Would you like to come with me? You'll have to behave yourself, of course.'

I have a sort of belief, founded on little more than a half-intuitive feeling, that he picked on this unlikely expedition in order to please me, and to make up for an unduly prolonged succession of peevish moods. There seemed to be in his voice, when he made the proposal, a tone which I had heard before when he was suggesting some plan which, he already knew, would be to my liking. For he was aware, I am sure, that Iceland was a country with a romantic appeal for me; so strong a passion, however unlikely of satisfaction, cannot have gone unmentioned between us; for ever since as a small child I had seen in a book called *The World at Home*, a misleading, stylized woodcut of the Great Geysir, Iceland had been to me a land of dreams and day-dreams.

'There's a cruise,' Logan went on, 'which goes to Iceland and Jan Meyen, and the ice-barrier and Spitzbergen. But I don't think it would be safe to take you on a cruising liner. I'm terrified of these bridge-playing friends. I know they'd get hold of you, and I'd see nothing of you for the whole of the trip. What do you think?'

He looked at me with an expression not unlike anger. I thought before I answered him.

'No,' I said, 'it probably would be dangerous to go on a cruising liner. But it might be all right if we went on something rather like the boat we went to Holland on. I don't mean a small boat like that. But if there were a large cargo-boat, with comfortable cabins, and very few other passengers, it would probably be all right.'

Logan took this idea enthusiastically, and wrote to the firm which had engaged our passage to Holland. When he got the results, he wrote to me, evidently rather doubtful about the trip. On the back of this letter were stuck three newspaper cuttings, supposedly applying to me; the first was the report of a trial for theft, in which the prisoner pleaded 'Something must have snapped in my brain': against this, Logan had written, 'Beware of these brain-snaps'; the next was without comment: 'Inordinate vanity and love of dress have been your downfall. You have started on a very dangerous road which, if still followed, will wreck your life and lead you, as it has thousands of others, to ruin and disaster'; the last was an ironically chosen passage in praise of darts, a game to which, as Logan half-disapprovingly knew, I had become addicted. Newspaper cuttings, it will be seen, had become for this year a sort of seasonable obsession.

When I next saw him, he was evidently very much set on his Icelandic plan. Perhaps, after all, he thought, the difficulties he was imagining were no more than imaginary. Almost without volition we ordered a taxi, and found ourselves at the travel agents, ordering on the 2,000-ton *Gothafoss*, what looked like a two-berth cabin. The journey was decided on.

My book on wild flowers was published now; it was beautifully illustrated with photographs, and with drawings and lithographs by Mr John Nash. A friend of mine, given to flowery ways of life and expression, had telegraphed his approval, 'Your flower book is a heavenly, blissful thing'; the comic thing about this, as I told Logan, was that the gratifying message was stolidly read out over the telephone by the local post-mistress. I sent a copy of the book to Logan.

'Thanks for your beautiful book,' he wrote to me, enclosing an irrelevant cutting (29.5.38), 'which has this moment arrived. I expect to find it a "blissful, heavenly" book, like ——. Thanks also for the poems of —— —— [a gifted contemporary poetess], which I must now read, though I should much rather read Agatha Christie's *Appointment with Death*.

'I am reading *Letters from High Latitudes* and getting excited about Iceland. But Binyon, with whom I spent most of Thursday, is against Iceland. He says that May Morris was once put up in a cottage there for a night and was given nothing for supper but rotten last year's blubber. Also he says that now you can go everywhere in motor buses which are always crowded with people who vomit all the time. I don't think that sounds at all pleasant.'

We prepared ourselves more carefully for this journey than for any other that we'd made. I got all the travel books on Iceland that I could find, and Logan read some of them. I even made faint preliminary attempts at learning the difficult language.

'I like putting new places on the map,' he said to me one day. 'When we come back, no one will listen to anything we say about it, unless we cram it down their throats. But we shall know what "Iceland" means.'

Another time he said to me, 'Will you take to reading the Sagas?'

When I answered that I probably wouldn't, 'I think,' he said, 'you'd better read *one*; then you can tell me about it, and save me the trouble of reading it for myself. I'm told that *The Story of Burnt Njál* is the best.'

'All right, then,' I said, 'I'll read it. It'll probably be frightfully boring.'

'Frightfully boring, I should think,' he replied. 'And you'd better take care it doesn't get hold of you too much. I believe there are no bores in the world like Icelandic bores.'

I read Njál's saga—and was caught up in the strange, slow, violent airs of that remote and magnificent literature—a literature which, although he excitedly accepted my judgment of it, I could never persuade Logan to read for himself. And whether I have become an Icelandic bore is perhaps, as Logan might have quoted from Sir Thomas Browne, 'a question too sad to insist on.'

Eventually, in the middle of July, we set off. The voyage started un-propitiously. We arrived in the darkness of late evening at Hull, and drove down to the quay, to the little *Gothafoss* which was due to sail late on the next morning. We went on board, and asked for our cabin, the two-berth cabin we thought we had engaged. We were shown to a very small cabin—one with four berths in it. I expostulated, but two of the bunks were undoubtedly numbered according to our tickets. Logan sat heavily, despairingly, down on a suitcase. 'We've been swindled!' he said.

I thought the journey was off. I suggested our spending the night comfortably at an hotel; we could then go first thing in the morning to the office of the shipping company and try to have things put right. I hadn't in fact much hope of any alteration being made; but this seemed the best way at the moment of dealing with Logan. He fell in with my plan.

I didn't think so close and uncomfortable a confinement at all suitable for Logan—he was nearly 73—and I said everything I could to prevent him setting forth out of consideration for me alone.

'Well,' he said, 'we'll see what happens in the morning.'

In the morning, driving in a taxi to the office, he said with an air of great wisdom and experience, 'The thing to do on these occasions is to threaten and bully. I shall tell them that we've been swindled, and that I'm going to write to *The Times* about it.'

At that, a prospect of great embarrassment beset me. I didn't think Logan's plan at all a good one. Nor was it.

To the independent northern spirit of a Hull shipping clerk, a letter to the London *Times* was a menace to be easily faced; at Logan's allegations of a swindle, he pointed out firmly but reasonably that the company could not be blamed for the mistake of a travel agency. And then, with the plan in front of him, he asked, 'Which cabin did you engage?'

'That one!' said Logan, plumping his finger down, recklessly and at random, on to the plan.

'That's a four-berth cabin,' said the clerk, upon which Logan deflated.

With diplomacy of which I shall always be proud, I managed to soothe the clerk without offending Logan. Then I asked if there were any possibility at all of our engaging a two-berth cabin; to my friend, I said, money was no object. There were, of course, no vacant berths at all on the ship.

Logan rallied suddenly; I realized that he was as eagerly set on Iceland as I was. We would go, whatever the circumstances. This triumph of the spirit over discomfort, in an old man, feeble and invalidish, showed something like courage, and a courage to be seriously commended. Very few elderly people, fond of their comfort as Logan was, would have set so adventurously forth as he did now. 'We'd better go,' he repeated, and back we went to the *Gothafoss*.

I arranged our luggage, and Logan sat down on his berth which was underneath mine. 'It's worse for the Jews in Vienna,' he said.

The discomfort, of course, was only relative; we were warm, and pleasantly fed; our quarters were dry and clean. But it must be remembered that Logan was accustomed to spending long hours on his bed, asleep or reading: that the weakness of his ankles made it difficult for him to get about: that he had become used to and dependent on Hammond's devoted attention: and that he was always uncomfortable in the presence of strangers.

One morning, indeed, I heard him murmuring to himself below me, slowly and deliberately, in his half-sleep, 'I'm——not——*perfectly*—— comfortable.' But his conscious outcries—there were two of them— had no direct connection with the luxury of his physical circumstances.

After our first luncheon at sea, Logan went below for his usual nap. In an hour or so when I thought he would be ready, I went down to see how he was getting on. He was sitting up at the head of the berth, in the space beyond the end of the protecting rail, his behind spreading out at the back of this rail, and his feet on the floor; a look of preposterous anguish was on his face.

'Bob!' he said, 'I can't get up, and I must go to the water-closet!'

I pulled him up, and when he had eased himself, he came back and sat down again.

'There's an Icelander in with us,' he told me, 'he saw me struggling, and he did *nothing*. And I was *bursting*.'

Imagining that he couldn't raise his weight forward, I devised, and showed him a method whereby, after putting one leg over the rail, he could heave himself up. But next morning, when I went down to see if he was dressed, he said, 'Look; I can get out of the bunk quite easily.'

My theory as to the mechanical difficulties was unfounded. All he did was to stand up, and his behind rose easily over the rail.

'You see,' he said unrebukefully, 'your elaborate scheme yesterday was quite unnecessary.'

The other occasion of his crying out was yet odder. After my breakfast one morning I went down to the cabin (Logan breakfasted in bed).

He groaned and quivered and said, 'Oh Bob, I've had the most awful morning.' He looked quite ill. Was there, I wondered, a doctor on the boat? I was a little frightened, and asked him what was the matter. 'It's that Icelander,' he answered; 'he's just unpacked all his things, and rearranged them, and put them back again. He didn't want *anything* out of his case. I've been watching him. I couldn't see *any* reason at *all* for what he was doing. It was awful. I can't *bear* watching behaviour without *any* explanation to it.'

Unfortunately our Icelandic companion rearranged the contents of his luggage more than once; and each time was as dreadful to Logan as the first. However, apart from this, he adapted himself magnificently to our circumstances. He loved the sea, and would sit, watching the waves, or delightfully talking. One day he handed me a periodical—*English*—and said 'Read that, and tell me what you think of it.'

There was an air about him as though he had shuddered; the subject, I somehow felt, was one that might have entertained him had it not been so shocking. To my melicious and more frivolous spirit, the article was not enjoyable. It was an exhilarating detection of sham scholarship, and disclosed the biggest howler ever perpetrated by any man with a claim to a knowledge of Latin. This was the rendering from Propertius of *Cimbrorumque minas et benefacta Mari* (The threats of the

Cimbri and the meritorious services of Marius), which had been Englished as 'Welsh mines and the profits Marius had out of them'. The nearest approach to this I heard many years ago at my prep. school, when a boy translated 'nisi' (unless), assonantically as 'nicer'.) The victim—I had almost said 'little victim'—of this intellectual birching was that learned, and not altogether untalented poet, Ezra Pound.

'Do you want to keep it?' I said when I had finished the article.

'No,' he answered, 'it's too painful. Throw it into the sea.'

We could almost have expected to see the cold Northern Atlantic bubble and hiss, as this burning exposure floated away on the surface of its billows.

Pound was one of the more asinine of Milton's detractors, and I suspect that from this article Logan received the first impulse towards his last book, *Milton and his Modern Critics*.

And so we fared northward, happily, save for occasional groans from Logan at the spectacle of the baggage-deranging Icelander, and spending much of our time on deck where, on the third day out, strange birds welcomed us to the outworks of the frozen north, as arctic skuas floated about the ship, spying out for scraps of rejected food.

The skies and the winds, whether in calm or storm, were all pleasant; there was, however, as I found, less comfort in the dining saloon. There were here two long tables down each side of it; at one of these sat the English-speakers; at the other, the rest of the world. We were therefore obliged into an intimacy with our fellow travellers. At first I could get Logan to talk to no one but myself; and speaking to me, in his faint discomfort, he almost wantonly displayed his worst aspect.

'When people tinkle coronets in the conversation,' he had written, 'I am inordinately solaced.' But 'solaced' is very far from the qualification I should give to my feelings when, talking most distinctly to me alone, he banged and waved coronets at that long dining-table. There was no doctor with professional charms to distract him. Fortunately, however, I discovered and made friends with a man sitting opposite to us; he was not only intelligent and enlightened, but he knew Logan's books and had read them.

With this opening, when I revealed it to him, Logan managed to enter into more general conversation. Most of the time, after this, I was at my ease, but every now and then he made unfortunate sallies. My new friend met them as cleverly as that Irish doctor on our journey to Teneriffe.

'Can you explain this to me?' said Logan at one meal. 'My grand
father started a bottle-factory in America. It's still in existence. I hav
nothing to do with it, and yet they keep on sending me cheques. Nov
how do you account for that? It's a mystery to me.'

'There's a clause,' my friend answered, putting on a very stolid look
'in the American Constitution, by which private property is protected
and may be passed on to heirs. It's under that clause that you ca
receive the dividends from property which you've inherited.'

Some remarks, stupid in form, can be as witty as the neatliest turne
epigram.

Usually, however, Logan talked seriously, and, more, he listene
with careful attention; for our companion had already visited Iceland
and had much to tell us which we wanted to know about the country
and the ways of its people.

Before setting out, I had got into communication with an Icelande
named Stefán Stefánsson. He was partner in a travel agency, and I ha
made inquiries about trips ashore. At Reykjavík he came on board th
ship to meet us.

Logan began to display his usual impatience on arrival. After a tal
with Stefán—with whom I eventually struck up a close friendship—
we planned to hire a car for the three days that the ship was in Reyk
javík. We were to spend one night at Thingvalla,[1] site of the earlies
European parliament; on the following day, I was to leave Logan a
Thingvalla, and, spending one night by the Great Geysir, to visit after
wards some wonders of the interior; then I was to join Logan agai
for the third night at Thingvalla. The next evening we should go o
board again, and, on the following day, travel to the north, and
eventually, return in the same ship to England.

Stefán took us to a hotel, and, having ordered a car, returned t
have lunch with us. He gave me advice about the trip, but I notice
that Logan was not happy. After lunch, we waited in the dining roon
for the car—waited longer than was pleasant to him. He began to ge
very peevish.

'There must be a better hotel than this!' he said, to which I was abl
to make no comment. Then he asked, 'Where's your friend gone?'

[1] This is the curious anglicized form, being the genitive of the correct nominativ
Thingvellir. Having learnt a little Icelandic, I shrink pedantically from this word; but, as
disciple of Logan, I must follow his golden rule, that wherever a foreign name has a wel
used English form, that is the form to use.

having taken a mistrusting dislike to Stefán, and transferred his
indignation to me.

'He's gone to fetch the car,' I said, 'and give instructions to the
chauffeur, I suppose.'

'I don't trust that old man,' said Logan. (Never was a more inappropriate judgment. Stefán did me much professional service, and then
refused to take a penny for it; 'When a man takes an intelligent
interest in the country, I don't want to be paid,' he said. All I could
get him to accept in the end was an old silver snuff-box, which he
couldn't refuse, as I sent it to him from England.)

Stefán soon appeared. 'How soon do you want to be going?' he
asked.

'At once,' Logan shouted, with an explosion of fury. I was very
much embarrassed, and said nervously, 'We'd like to go as soon as it
can be managed.'

Stefán went away, and not long after returned, and Logan, at last,
groaned into the car.

At lunch, Logan had asked Stefán about birds. 'There are arctic
terns,' he had answered, 'nesting on an island in the lake here in
Reykjavík; if you like, I will make them go round that way, and then
you can drop me. They are sometimes called sea-swallows.'

We stopped by the lake, and there they were, flocks of those lovely
birds, swallow-like gulls, hovering fearlessly and chattering with their
beaks over our heads, or swooping, with the infinite grace of swallows,
over the waters of the lake.

Their flight and beauty charmed in an instant all vexation out of
Logan's heart. After watching for a time entranced, we set off for
Thingvalla. Scarcely had we left the town when I saw to the south, in
pyramidal perfection, black against that pale blue sky, an undisfigured
cone.

'Look at that volcano!' I said.

Logan looked. 'Never judge anything by the first few hours,' he said,
a piece of advice he was more in need of than I. But now he was in a
state of beatitude it was beautiful to behold.

We drove across a desolate upland; curiously shaped mountains
were on each side of us, streaked in many places with snow. After we
had traversed about five and twenty miles, the chauffeur stopped, and,
looking over his shoulder, said, 'Thingvallavatn'.

We got out. We were standing, I discovered, on an ancient lava

131

flow, black, and hard, and ropy-surfaced. Through a dip in the plain
we could see a broad lake, with mountains beyond, and two small
cratered islands rising out of it. The dark landscape was strangely and
dimly coloured in red and blue and green, like the reflections of a sunset. We were on the edge of a valley, carved by no river, but brough
about by the fall into hollow caves of a lava field; the broken edges o
the plain were torn into wide gorges. Down one of these gorges we
were soon driving; the road then wound across the lava to the small
hotel. This fallen plain is shattered into deep clefts, in each of which
slept in its silence and chill, serenely, the clearest water.

We engaged rooms, and had tea, and I took Logan upstairs to rest
while I wandered out, exploring and botanizing. When I came back
he was sitting out of doors; I sat down beside him, and expounded my
discoveries. Then, hardly speaking, we looked about at the amazing
spectacle. To our left were the romantic gorges, and the crystalline
water of the broken lava—scenes where wild chieftains once bound
themselves into a law-pursuing community. Far away to the right, lazy
small clouds whitened sunnily over steam-jets. In front of us, among
inlets of the lake, paddled happily two kinds of phalarope, the grey and
the red-necked; and everywhere about us, arctic terns soared and
swept and hovered.

After a long silence, 'I hope,' said Logan, 'this won't make you un-
faithful to Teneriffe.'

In the morning, I went to his room.

'I'll be back tomorrow evening,' I said. 'Don't worry if I'm late. And
if you get bored here, or feel uncomfortable, just go back to Reykjavík, and leave a message here for me.'

'So you're going to desert me?' he said with facetious pathos. 'Well
don't worry. I shall be quite happy without you. When you get back
you'll probably find that I've settled down here. I think I shall spend
the rest of my life watching the terns.'

Logan had almost eight years to live still; but that was the last time
ever saw him invested in all the strength and truth and security of ou
friendship; for when next we saw each other the germ was already in
him which was to make so fearful an alteration in things. I have de
scribed—perhaps with undue emphasis—the difficulties which often
cropped up in our relationship; I may have treated with too much
irony—but that would have been Logan's way—the comical aspects o
our mutual life. It is natural perhaps, in such a retrospective inquiry, to

ollow the tastes and principles which I imbibed from Logan. I told
im, and more than once, that I respected him; 'For heaven's sake don't
o that,' he would answer, 'I don't want to be respected.'

'How do you want to be treated, then?' I asked him on one such
ccasion.

'I like to be made fun of: but not cruelly. Treat me with affectionate
erision.'

Often, when he was in a mood of overflowing friendship, he has said
o me, 'I like your mockery.'

Nevertheless, he himself, surprising as it may seem, was given to
dealism. Not a few times, when I had pleased or helped him in some
nanner, he would say, 'You're perfect to me.' As my narrative will
ave betrayed I, with all other humans, fall far short of perfection;
ut for him there was a particular danger in making such assertions. By
ver-estimating my character, however absurdly, he was laying himself
pen to inevitable disappointment, and a disappointment in that way
vas bound to react unhappily upon me. This I often explained to him,
ut with a uselessness that was equal whether he was in a good mood
vith me, or a bad. Coming north on the *Gothafoss* I pleased him in some
natter—I forget the actual circumstances—and he said, 'With all your
aults, I couldn't do without you.'

'That's the way you ought to think about me,' I said. 'It's perfectly
atisfactory, and there are no risks.'

When I think of that evening at Thingvalla, and that morning when
left him, it seems to me that, in our friendship, we should have been
lestined to accomplish in Iceland something higher and more complete,
ven than what so happily befell us in the Canary Islands. But our des-
iny was broken by a most horrible and unpredictable catastrophe. An
dventure that should have heightened and perfected our friendship
urned to something abominable that was the shaking and eventually
he destruction of it.

Late on the next evening, after visiting places of beauty and marvel
uch as I had never before seen, I came back to Thingvalla. I remember
hinking to myself, 'If I were a perfect character, I'd say nothing to
ogan about the wonders I've been seeing without him. I might even
ry to pretend that it was all a bore, and hadn't been worth doing. I can't
lo it. I can't hold my tongue. But I really must apologize as fulsomely
s I can, for having had such a time out of his company.'

An English-speaking man met me at the hotel door.

'Your friend is gone,' he said. I hardly had time to think: 'Logan must have got bored here, and gone back to Reykjavík. I've time to join him tonight,' when he went on, 'He is sick. They have taken him to the hospital.'

I drove back full of the most unpleasant forebodings. But at the hospital, late though it was, I managed to get some information from an English-speaking nurse. 'He is not very bad,' she said; 'he has an attack of bronchitis.' I might, I was told, come and see him on the following afternoon.

I went to the hotel, where we had lunched so unforebodingly two days before. Everything gets known in Reykjavík. Stefán had heard about Logan's illness, and, shouldering the burden imposed by three hours' acquaintance, he had taken the trouble, in his kindness, to order a room for me.

The next morning I went to the *Gothafoss* to cancel our berths and remove what was left of our baggage. In the afternoon, I went up to the hospital and visited Logan. He was cheerful, and didn't appear gravely ill. He told me that he had been watching the terns when he felt what he described as being like an attack of lumbago. His memory of the attack was to become more and more confused, and even now, it was evident that his recollections were incoherent. He had somehow got up to his room, and undressed and gone to bed. The night must have been delirious, and he now accepted the memories of that delirium.

'I had an awful night,' he said; 'I kept ringing for the steward, but he never came.'

Next morning the hotel people became alarmed. With an access of meanness which was more than a rarity in Iceland, they didn't send for a doctor, in case there should be no one to pay his bill; instead they rang up the British Consulate. Mr G. Turville-Petre, the Icelandic scholar who was then attached to the Consulate, came out, and discovering Logan's condition, telephoned for an ambulance. Logan always spoke with appreciation of the 'scholarly young Englishman' who rescued him.

When I first came in, he said that he had been expecting to see me in the morning; 'I thought you must have gone off on the *Gothafoss*.'

I was startled by such a fantastic, though passing, misjudgment of my character; and it still appears very strange to me that after ten years of close friendship, Logan should, even for a moment, have supposed

ne capable of so callous and inconsiderate a desertion. But the
:hought seemed to have stirred no malice, and he received complacently my explanation that I had been informed he couldn't be
visited until the afternoon.

When he had told me what he could of his adventures, he said, 'Now
I want you to promise me one thing; I want you to go on in the
Gothafoss to Akureyri. I'll be quite all right, and when you get back,
you can pick me up here.'

This, of course, as I told him, was out of the question, and in any
:ase, even had I felt inclined to do so, it was impossible now, as I had
:ancelled our berths, and removed the rest of our luggage from the
:hip.

'But you'll be awfully bored here,' he said.

'Not a bit,' I answered; 'I'm never bored in a strange country. And
it any rate, when you're better and out of hospital, I can desert you.
There are some lovely trips to be done from here. I might even get to
:he edge of Vatnajökull.' (The great ice cap which spreads itself over
:housands of square miles along the south coast.)

'Yes,' he said, 'I'd like you to see that. But I wish you wouldn't stay
here now.'

I saw the doctor, who advised me not to cancel our berths home; he
:old me that they had diagnosed Logan's cystitis of the bladder, and his
:hronic bronchitis; I was thus assured of the care and reliability of the
hospital authorities. Then, having got permission to visit him whenever I liked, I went back to the hotel.

The next day, a Saturday, Logan was improving; there didn't seem
:o be anything to worry about. The Sunday was my birthday, and,
after carefully sounding him, I decided to go off for the day with
Stefán to visit his old home at a place called Krísuvík, on the south
:oast. (This wasn't just a sentimental journey; there was then at
Krísuvík a very spectacular mud cauldron which I wanted to visit.)
Dn the way out, in the morning, I called in on Logan; he was rather
quiet, but there was nothing to cause me anxiety. I saw with great
pleasure new aspects of Iceland, and the spouting, bubbling mud
:auldron, with a titanic steam jet at one edge of it, was all that I could
have looked for. We got safely back in the evening. But at the hotel
a man came up to me with an anxious expression. The hospital had
been sending for me. I drove straight up there. Logan's illness had
:urned to double pneumonia, and he was desperately ill.

He was very weak when I saw him, and delirious; his temperature was 103; suddenly one of his old stories started up; in the middle of it a young assistant said, 'He should not talk too much; it would be better if you were to leave him.'

I knew that he would talk until the story was finished; I explained this and waited only till the end of it. I find it difficult to describe the ghastly effect of this recital; the story went through with all the accustomed chuckles, pauses and asides, exactly as he might have told it at a luncheon-party; and yet he was so ill, and so delirious, that I was not sure at first whether he knew me or not.

The illness ran its expected course; each day he was a little weaker each day the periods of delirium became longer; there was no reason to suppose that he wasn't dying.

Logan made a worthy scene of it. He seemed quite unafraid.

'I've been trying to think out some appropriate last words,' he said one morning. 'And this is what I say—"I've done with life, and it really was worth living".'

Another time he said, 'I suppose I ought to be thinking of my golden throne.' And then he added, 'Eternal Bliss—what an awful idea.'

He had resolved at one time to leave his body for dissection; and now he told me to find out if he could do the same in Iceland. I felt bound to perform this grisly task, and I hoped he would forget to ask me about it. He didn't forget, and I was able to assure him that his wishes could be carried out. (In his last will, stirred by I know not what reluctance, he undid this resolution, and arranged that he should be cremated.

He was hopeless at making the nurses understand what he wanted when he tried to ask for things.

'She's learning,' he said about one, 'she knows now, when I ask for things, that "a glass of water" means the *Saturday Evening Post*.' (He had brought a copy of that periodical with him for light reading.)

At last one evening, three or four days after the danger had begun I left him so weak that it didn't seem possible I should find him alive next morning.

Madame du Deffand wrote on her death-bed to Horace Walpole 'Vous me regretterez, parce qu'on est bien aise de se savoir aimé.' On that score alone there was occasion now for a night-time of weeping But I thought of far more than the friendship of ten years that Logan had so prodigally given me; I thought of all his kindness and generosity of his jokes, of the excellence of his company, of all that had gained him so many friends, and had kept them so long; the very faults that had vexed me at times seemed only pathetic now—something to pity in him—and curiously endearing; I knew what I had never doubted, how easily and deeply I had returned his friendship. I am not ashamed to record that I wept on my bed that night, as I said to myself, 'Logan is dying.' It is a tragic irony to reflect that in little more than a week, his death would have come like a blessing to me.

For Logan had not done with life. A curious change began to come over him. He was so weak that he could not move; but vigour returned to his speech, and with that vigour there was an increase and spread of what I took for delirium, until not for one moment was he rational. Some days went by before I learned the true nature of this change; the pneumonia was over, his temperature was down, but he had gone mad. The doctor was overworked, and I didn't often see him. One day, however, he waited especially for me.

'I am worried about his reason,' he said to me. 'The pneumonia is over, and his temperature has been normal for some time; but I am afraid that permanent damage has been done to the brain.'

Logan, though in no pain, was in a condition of great physical discomfort; his weakness and his weight made it quite impossible for him to move; he lay as if paralysed. His earliest complaint was against the roughness of the nurses. I knew little of Iceland and, although I had good reason to be confident of the doctor's skill, I didn't know anything about the standard of nursing, and I was worried. One morning a nurse came in with a bowl of liquid food for him, a pleasant-looking, pretty girl. She could speak a little English. Logan refused to eat. Gently and tenderly as a mother, she held a spoon to his mouth, and he swallowed the contents; then another spoonful: he shook his head —and swallowed. She kept on. Once he interrupted by shouting an obscenity at me. 'What does he say?' she asked, proving, fortunately, that she hadn't understood. And she kept unwearyingly on, until the bowl was empty. When she went out he said to me, 'That's the roughest of them all.' I was reassured.

Owing to his weight it was impossible for him to be moved smoothly when they washed him or the bed was being made. Their work in shifting him he reported as violence. 'The nurses,' he said one day, 'have been rolling me about, and pummelling me and almost kicking me'; and a short time after he said, 'Did I tell you the nurses have been kicking me? That can't be good for a patient!'

Very soon his dissatisfaction extended to me, deepening, as reason progressively failed, into a terrifying and abominable hatred. He began with complaints which might have been due to no more than a venomous peevishness; I wasn't troubling about him, I was neglecting him; if I really cared for him, I should get him moved to another hospital, where he would be comfortable. And then the attacks became altogether crazy.

'There's one comfort in all this,' he said slowly one day, 'that the whole thing is your fault.'

'How could it be my fault?' I asked.

'You know those lies you told me in Holland? Well, these things leave a germ in one, and in me they've come out as this illness.——knew all about your friend; he was one of the lowest criminals in The Hague.'

A lady, who had suffered some months of insanity, once told me that the most dreadful thing she could remember of her experience was the seemingly infinite extension of time. Twenty years, she said, appeared to go by during the course of a single day.

Logan used to be washed in the afternoon, and during the process—which took about twenty minutes to half an hour—I would go out for a short walk.

These strolls were soothing and refreshing to me as the air which a diver ascends to breathe. I used to wander on to the fringe of the open country at the edge of the town. Westward, I would search for the great ice peak which sometimes glimmers upward above the bay like the huge pale ghost of a pyramid; inland was the black heath-land leading to Thingvalla, edged by hills on which the snow still lay in streaks, and beyond the black and rising level could sometimes be discovered the gleam of an ice-cap. Southwards lay the strangely profiled Reykjanes peninsula; over a gap, where I knew lay the cauldron of Krísuvík, I would attempt, but always in vain, to descry the shimmer of steam. The ground was of ancient lava, smooth and scarred by long decayed glaciers; and the dark stone was patterned by small plants such as one finds on the heights of a Scottish mountain: in cushions of yellow-green, with its rosy pin-head flowers, the moss campion, and small pallid annual gentians, and a bright chickweed, and, filling clefts with black wiry stems, the least of all willows jewelled the stone with emerald-coloured sequins of its glittering small leaves.

Once after I had just been out like this, Logan said, 'How long is it since you've been to see me?'

'Not an hour,' I answered.

'Many, many days, you mean. Here have I been lying all this time alone, and you never came to see me. I sent the nurse to ask you to come, and she tells me you said (and, nodding his head, he shouted my imagined answer) "No, I won't." So I asked her to see Kenneth Clark, and he said that of course he'd come.'

Sir Kenneth Clark ran curiously in his mind. In an early stage of his madness he said to me, 'How did you come to visit this very interesting country?'

I thought at the time that this was a piece of playfulness which he might easily have uttered in his sanity. I responded by describing our journey.

'But aren't you,' he said, 'confusing yourself with Bob Gathorne-Hardy?'

On my astonished 'I *am* Bob Gathorne-Hardy,' he looked at me with great surprise, and said, 'Why so you are. What a very funny thing. I thought you were Kenneth Clark.'

It must be over thirty years since I first met Sir Kenneth Clark; but it has so fallen out that we have never known each other well, and I doubt if I have met him more than three times in Logan's company.

I had tried to persuade myself that this was all the result of delirium —the doctor had not yet told me of his fears—and it seemed almost incredible to me that so old a man of Logan's invalidish disposition should still be alive after so long and so violent a fever. And then I learnt that the fever had subsided. I have known few occasions of greater horror.

I used to spend a large part of each day with Logan, visiting him in the morning, in the afternoon, and, for the first week or so, in the evening. He rested early after his lunch, so that I was free for about an hour in the afternoon; as his craziness became worse, I discovered that he always got more violent towards the evening, and eventually it became insupportable to visit him then. He didn't notice any difference. A number of times his night nurse rang me up in the morning to say that he was insistently asking for me. At first, when this happened, I hurried straight up to the hospital. Each time I found that he had alto-gether forgotten his summons. After that, I used to tell the nurse that I would come at the usual time; he never noticed.

It was evident that he badly wanted my company, though he took strange advantage of it, pouring out a spate of abuse and accusations. The half-hour's walk to the hospital became for me like the scaling of an all but unscaleable mountain. I used to find myself walking very slowly, as though up steep slopes, and loaded with an enormous burden.

It became a physical labour to pass through the doors of the hospital; and when I got to his room, unable to watch the dreadful expression of his face, I used to put my chair behind the end of his bed.

His delusions began to be centred around outside forces, and imprisonment. Sir Kenneth Clark, Logan told me, was at the head of a fascist plot by which the constitution of Iceland was to be shortly overturned; if anything were more improbable than Sir Kenneth Clark being me, it would be his appearance as a fascist leader.

Then, one morning, as I came in, Logan said: 'Look here, I want you to get on to the police at once; there's a rogue in the town, called Bob Gathorne-Hardy; he's got me kidnapped and shut up here, and now he's trying to get ransom out of my relations.'

I had once been professionally advised that it was a mistake to contradict mad people; they should, I was told, be humoured.

'You know him,' I said to Logan, 'he's like you; he's always playing practical jokes. I'm sure that's all he's doing now.'

'No, no, he's not; he's perfectly serious. What I'm afraid of is that my relations will pay. I don't want that to happen. You must go to the police at once.'

'Well,' I said, 'I'll make inquiries when I get back this evening, and let you know the result.' I knew that all this would be forgotten the next time I saw him.

'You won't have any difficulty in finding him, will you?' said Logan with a curious change of tone; 'he's got the same name as you.'

About this time, he frightened me by declaring that he was suffering from a retention of his water. I asked for the doctor to be sent for. He came at once, and, after a careful examination, told me that everything was functioning perfectly well. I tell this trivial incident only because I believe that it may illustrate to the expert some part of his troubled spirit inexplicable to me, for during his last illness, he made the same imaginary complaint.

After a period of this horrible and stormy gloom, I came up one morning to find him in a state of elation that was, I felt, even more dreadful.

He started, as usual, with a reproach.

'You've done nothing about those steamer tickets I told you to get!' he said. 'There's no time to be lost in ordering them. And find out what port we're sailing from, because it's *very* smart and we must have our evening clothes sent. One must follow the world. And there's something in being received as a great man. People get to know one's on board, and ask for one's autograph. I *hate all that*, autographs and photographs. But one must follow the world.'

This exaltation and megalomania persisted for some time, and he used to punctuate his remarks with dreadful, cackling chuckles that to me were unbearably horrible. And then he passed to a stage, wilder yet and still more irrational, speaking in the language of 'mad scenes' from Elizabethan plays or Italian opera.

'How is it,' he said slowly one day, 'that I find I've been legally bound——' here followed a long pause, during which I expected some delusionary complaint of legal trickery, but which he ended, loudly and suddenly, with 'to a bootmaker!' 'I find,' he went on, 'that I've been apprenticed to a cobbler, which gives them a legal hold over me, so that they can keep me here. Now who can have done that? It wouldn't be my sister, Mrs Russell. Such a thing would never enter her mind!'

In a mood of a gayer delusion which, however, started with indignation, he said, 'Do you realize that all I've seen of Iceland is that door.' Then he went on, 'Do you know what's on the other side of it? The mortuary! Just the other side of that door, there are rows and rows of dead bodies. They don't want me to find out, and they think I don't know anything about it.' Then he began chuckling, and said, '*You* look. They'll be very angry, but they can't do anything to *you*. Go on! Go on! have a look.'

There are people who find intolerable the sound of a high wind at night; its unceasing raving stirs melancholy feelings and harsh dreams, making their sleep restless and uneasy. There was no release, in Logan's company then, from the daylong utterance of his delusions; on and on went that dreadful voice, weak in the early days, and strengthening as the bodily illness began to diminish.

At first, as I have told, there was a period of unbroken melancholy; then there followed a time, unbroken too, of hideous gaiety. But as physical strength increased, there seemed to be a further disintegration of intellect. The miserable and the gay moods succeeded one another with unpredictable frequence—'happys' and 'interlunaries' coming out in fragments. Other particles of his mind would also appear. In any of his moods, grim or uproarious, anything might start off one of his 'set pieces', his particular stories that I knew so well, too well indeed. When he told them now—interludes amid ravings—they came out, as on that first night, exactly—but exactly—as he would have told them in his sanest mood, with every little pause and aside and premeditated hesitation. The mock-sanity of these occasions was more ghastly to me, I think, than anything else of horrible or ghastly that I experienced during this period.

Looking back it seems to me that I was perpetually struggling to catch hold of the true Logan, the old friend whose company I had so much loved and delighted in. In vain. I was having lessons in Icelandic, a language in which there are curious changes of vowel-sounds. Could I use this to rouse Logan? One day I tried. I asked him about Grimm's law under which these changes are beautifully systematized. At any other time, however difficult or embarrassing his mood, a question like this would have started Logan into an exposition which displayed his intellect at its finest. There was just a stirring, a faint shadowy semblance of his real self. He tried to answer my question, became confused, and slid back into the delusive world of his madness.

Charlotte Brontë once told how she had laid a sprig of heather on the pillow of the dying Emily. 'I remember,' wrote Mrs Gaskell, 'her shiver at recalling the pang she felt when, after having searched in the little hollows and sheltered crevices of the moors for a lingering spray of heather—just one spray, however withered—to take in to Emily, she saw that the flower was not recognized by the dim and indifferent eyes.' It was a pang of that kind that I myself felt when Logan's true intellect gave, as it were, a slight trembling movement, and then sank down again and vanished.

The consequence of my watching and the troubles of my mind, ought, I suppose, to have been expected; but it came unexpectedly to me. I began to notice a strange increasing weakness in myself; I slept badly; and then, at last, a night came when I didn't sleep at all, not for one single moment of that night which never through all its length darkened out of twilight. I walked up next morning to the hospital, very slowly; happening to touch my face, I found that it was wet with tears. I'd had more than my body would allow me to put up with.

When the doctor had visited Logan, I followed him out. He looked at me, and took me into his room, and I told him about my state. I remember that I had to hold my chin with my hand to keep myself from weeping. Logan, for all his abuse of me, needed my company. Would the hope of his eventual sanity, I asked, depend on my still visiting him? If that was so, I would still come, but I should require, for the first time in my life, something to make me sleep. The doctor reassured me, saying that the only danger was that material damage might have already been done to the brain (a possibility which it seemed had all too probably been realized).

'You cannot go on like this,' he said. 'Go away into the country for several days. Do not come back this afternoon; it is a beautiful day; take the bus to Thingvellir. And tomorrow you can go away into the country somewhere.'

'He'll be very angry with me,' I said.

'No,' said the doctor, 'I will see that he is angry with me,' and taking me back to Logan's room he displayed the most inspired example of tact I have ever witnessed. This is how I described it the same day, in a letter to Kyrle:

'He said to Logan, "Do you trust me?"

'Luckily Logan is pleased with the doctor, so he said "Yes."

' "Mr Hardy is ill," said the doctor, and when Logan asked what was the matter with me, he said, "Something in the chest" (which is all Logan can understand), "and I have to be very careful. Mr Hardy wants to stay up, and I tell him he must go to bed. Who is he to obey?"

' "*You*," said Logan, very loudly, with a spiteful look at me. So that should clear me.'

The doctor then said, 'Then Mr Hardy is to go to bed until I say he may get up?'

'Certainly,' said Logan, and, for a while I was free. The doctor wrote a prescription which, I found out, had a large proportion of bromide in it; he evidently wanted to be sure of not having *two* mad Englishmen on his hands. Another complaint, though it may well have come from the same cause, unfortunately took away some of the dignity from my affliction; for I had to consult the doctor, at the same time, about a painful attack of what Logan once described, in a letter which I have quoted, as 'emerods'. For this, as well as for my sleeplessness, he amiably prescribed.

I found Stefán, and he undertook to get me a car, and generally advise me about a recuperative trip. I decided to go as far as I could along the south coast. There was one most interesting saxifrage which I might find there; and I should have visions of a small geysir, of huge waterfalls, and mountain-ranges of ice.

The next morning, Stefán came to see me off, and to give last instructions to the chauffeur, the same I had driven with when Logan first became ill; he had also taken me to Krísuvík. Suddenly the beat of Stefán's voice told me that he was quoting poetry. He turned to me, and spoke in English. 'Bjarni here has been asking what you have been doing; he had been away in the north. I have told him, that like Illugi on Drangey, with his brother Grettir, you have been sitting by the sickbed of your friend. There is a poem about it. It says "Dapur situr daga langa"; that means "Sadly he sits day-long". I will show it to you.'[1]

My escape into the country undoubtedly saved me; each night I slept better, and, on the last, for nine hours on end. That journey and its discoveries I have already described; I will only record one incident here, as showing the nearly unbalanced condition of my own mind.

It had so happened, when I saw the Great Geysir fling up in thunder and splendour its two hundred foot column of water, that just about the same moment Logan was first taken ill at Thingvalla; and just when I was watching, at Krísuvík, the mud-cauldron bubble and spout, with the steam-jet screeching deafeningly in my ears, Logan's temperature was rising to a degree that was nearly the death of him.

[1] He was alluding to the death of Grettir the outlaw who, according to his saga, while lying sick on Drangey, a small island in the north, was surprised and killed by his enemies; his brother Illugi, refusing quarter, was killed with him. The poem is by the nineteenth-century romantic poet Jónas Hallgrímsson; Stefán afterwards sent me a selection from his works, with this particular poem marked. Since he always gave so romantic a comparison to my watchings beside Logan, I may be pardoned, perhaps, for giving a free paraphrase of this poem.

> Trembles a phantom peak
> On a threefold race of the tides;
> Blue and broad above the middle firth
> A crag-toothed mountain rides.
>
> Drangey looms on the deep
> Where rocks din with the sound
> Of sea birds, and the spouting whales
> Press and plunge around:
>
> Where long and lorn on Drangey—
> How long since!—night and day,
> Watching in grief his death-drawn brother
> An outlaw's brother lay.

On this trip I saw the little geysir Grýta sparklingly display, in a thirty-foot plume, white steam and silver lances of water-drops, and I suddenly found myself thinking 'What has this done to Logan?' If my strangely conceived superstition was true—namely that the revelation in my presence of violent subterranean heat would have an effect on the health of my friend—there were now only two things left to hope for, either the death of his body or the recovery of his mind; the first, as I found when I got back after five days, Grýta had not contrived, but towards the second it might be held to have made a considerable contribution. I discovered an almost miraculous change in Logan.

The doctor had told him he could go home; at the prospect of escape, delusions and brutality began to fade. It seems probable that, at the time I left him, the uncontrollable effects of his madness were becoming capable of control. I asked the doctor what had happened.

'I decided to treat him rough,' he said. 'He was being difficult, when I told him that if he did not behave himself, I would move him into a ward. I know these selfish old men. He has been spoiled, and thinks the whole world has been arranged for him. It is best not to give way to him,' which, of course, was what I had been doing all along.

The doctor, with kindness that seemed characteristic of his race, had, as he told me, already arranged passages for us, on a boat leaving shortly for Copenhagen.

I went to Logan's room. He was not in proper control of his right mind (nor, for many weeks, did he achieve that control); but he was in quite a different condition to what I had left him in. Clouds of delusion appeared from time to time, but the dark unbroken fog was largely scattered.

He attempted a spit of the old venom.

'I've learnt from this illness,' he said, 'that nobody really cares for me, and I don't care for anybody.'

I couldn't cite my own case from which, in the recent state of my health, I had good evidence to contradict him; it wasn't the time yet to tell him of the small and necessary deception we had practised. I reminded him of an occasion when he and his sister were seriously ill at the same time; the unwary announcement to her that Logan was in danger, caused a shock which imperilled her own life, and noticeably lengthened her illness.

'I've always had my doubts about that,' he said.

'You've no justification for any doubts at all.'

'Then why hasn't she been in to see me?'

I thought it was now time to try the doctor's tactics. I told him that I had been in continuous communication with Mrs Russell, and that, at her request, I had sent her a cable every day. Then I said, 'I'm not going to allow you to talk like that; if you keep on, I shall go away now and leave you.'

The effect was like magic. Logan was quiet for a little, and when he started speaking once more, it was on a different subject, and in a sweeter vein.

Another time when I was with him during this early convalescence, he recurred to one of his delusions—I forget now which it was. Rather fearfully, I thought I would try to control him.

'That never happened,' I said. 'It was just part of your delirium.'

To my relief and satisfaction he took this quite calmly.

'What you've got to learn,' I went on, 'is to be sure of distinguishing what is from what isn't.'

He seemed to accept this happily, as, in fact, I believe he did; there were just beginning to work and stir in him the feelings of an enormous penitence. But these were not outwardly perceptible yet. All I perceived was a rather curious and pathetic humbleness. How did I take it?

A doctor once told me that the occasional deformity of bodily organs is of great value to anatomists, for by the strange view thus granted to them they can the better understand the structure of the organ in question. Such a deformity of the spirit I had lately seen in Logan, all his evil points revealing themselves in huge and hideous caricature. I had beheld a monster. Was it possible, I began to ask myself, to keep on the old affectionate familiar terms with Logan? This question didn't trouble me for long. As I regained my spirits, and Logan returned towards sanity, this particular problem vanished into thin air. For all that, I was like a man who has been through an earthquake; never afterwards could I be sure that the solid ground might not tremble terribly again. And indeed, never again could I feel with Logan, as in the past, that old and absolute security.

In trying to account for some of Logan's vagaries, I have called on—so far as I could—the resources of a very modern science. To explain my feelings towards him after this catastrophe, and the great change which took place in him, I can only use, I find, the symbols of long-discarded superstitions.

Logan, it might be said, was always attended by an evil genius. He had the common faults that we all of us share; but added to these, and different in kind from them, were his unpredictable enormities, some of which I have recounted. These, it seems to me as I look back, might easily have been reckoned as due to the promptings of a devil. But hitherto they had only been promptings from the outside. In his madness this devil entered right into him, through a breach which the sickness had made, and which, it seemed, was never to be repaired. At any time during the rest of his life the devil might take charge of him; it was to be no longer a question of obedience to exterior and malignant whispers; he would always be liable to various degrees of a very dreadful possession.

Death brings a completeness as well as a finality to the life of a man; and only in the face of that completeness was I able to deduce what I have just been telling. At this time I believed in the possibility of Logan's entire moral recovery; and never, during his life, was I able to correlate the various deformities of his character. Then, if an awkwardness arose beyond what normal friends might look for, I was apt to resent and be hurt by it. Now, in the rediscovery of his past I can take a more affectionate and charitable view of him. Those words and that occasional behaviour of his which, in another man, would have been difficult to forgive, these I can now properly estimate. I can see now that all which was exceptionally unpleasant in Logan was indeed a part of his madness. The germs and little foreshadowings which I have told of were—I can see it now—beyond his control, and not to be judged morally. We are apt to look on the best side of a friend as the true side; in Logan this was actually the case. A man's character is, I suppose, a summing up of all his behaviour; but in human intercourse we do not reckon with what a man acts or talks of in his sleep. And the actions which strains of madness prompt, are, morally speaking, no more than somnambulistic. But such conclusions were beyond me while Logan was alive, and particularly so in my shattered state when at last, after so much tribulation, we embarked and set forth to voyage southwards from Iceland.

I have painful incidents to record still, and what, from anyone else, would have been the sharpest of cruelties; and—for the heart cannot reason—I was to be hurt by them as though they were torment carefully devised. But I can see at last, and take comfort in the thought, that what my friend acted in the possession of his demon was not the action of my friend.

147

1938

We had a stormy time of it, when we left Iceland, voyaging through outrageous gales. Logan was in the care of two nurses. I found that I had a scunner of him, and only when he sent for me did I pay him a visit. We were, indeed, a sorry couple. My devotion was exhausted for the time being; but Logan, it appeared, had nothing to blame me for; when, at his summons I went to see him, his mood was always one of pathetic and almost obsequious humility. This, I must confess, re-assured rather than melted me. The strength of a man, lost and be-nighted, may endure through wanderings and trials and vicissitudes, until at last he discovers the way again, and reaches home; but then, for hours, or for days even, he may find himself unable to move. My case was very much the same. Day after day I had forced myself up to the hospital at Reykjavík, had done so until my health was almost broken; and now all that I could claim of self-sacrifice in me was exhausted. The time had arrived, I felt, to be wisely and thoroughly selfish. Logan never on any occasion betrayed any resentment at this, but he was very soon finding fault with other people.

Our friends in England supposed, I believe, that I was in almost as bad a state as Logan, and they had arranged for his niece, Dr Karin Stephen, to meet us in Copenhagen. The party ended more elaborately than I expected, for when the boat drew in, I saw on the quay, as well as Dr Stephen, Hammond and Kyrle.

Dr Stephen had ordered a room in a nursing home for Logan. This institution took up only one floor of a large building. The occupants of the flat overhead, by a most unfortunate mischance, celebrated that night, loud and late, their return from a holiday. Logan, I think, never forgave his niece for this unforeseeable accident.

Voyaging between Reykjavík and Copenhagen he had been all sweetness and quiet; crossing from Esbjerg to Harwich, he began to get excited.

He was on deck, and I was sitting beside him, when Dr Stephen came up.

'Karin!' he shouted, and kept on in the same loud, crazy, carrying tone, 'I want you to tell me if I'm a dope fiend. For years I've been taking sleeping draughts. And now I can't sleep without them. Am I a dope fiend? *I can't sleep without them.*'

I have always hoped that of the passengers within hearing, everyone was a Dane and ignorant of English.

Kyrle and I had already arranged to visit some relations of mine in

148

the Outer Hebrides. Before going north I visited Logan. There was no question now of my breaking with him. My spirit was becoming calm; I was capable again of rational judgment concerning him; and I had been happily touched by his attitude to me. He was very excitable, and wisps of delusion still drifted across his mind. But his behaviour to me since we left Iceland had been all kindness and tenderness and contrition. Of the judgments I have since formed about him, not a germ was in my mind then; I have no power of divining the future; Logan, it seemed, was coming back, and with all that had brought into being my friendship for him.

I had spent a lot of my own money in Iceland and, as well, I had borrowed money for our expenses from my eldest brother. (During almost all of his illness Logan wasn't physically—to say nothing of mentally—capable of signing a cheque; only on our last day in Iceland, when I got the hospital bill, had he just enough strength to sign a cheque which I had filled in.) The first time that I visited him after our return, he had bundles of banknotes with him, all of high denomination.

When we had settled up our formal accounts, he said, 'You know you saved my life in Iceland, and I'd like to give you a present. Will you take this?' And he handed me a £100 banknote.

Visions flew into my mind—a car, books, clothes, travel, pictures. But it wouldn't do; to take money like that for services which only friendship had demanded would be to vitiate retrospectively my motives, and would seem to make of natural duties a calculated stroke of business. Logan seemed hurt by my refusal; and I got the impression that he was afraid he had committed a breach of gentlemanly etiquette.

'What will you take, then?' he said, pleadingly. It was obvious that I must take something; I didn't like to accept too much, and it was clear that Logan would be unhappy if I suggested too small a sum.

'I really think I do deserve something,' I said, after a little thought, and explained why I didn't want him to give me the first enormous amount he had offered. 'I'll take thirty pounds.'

Rather grudgingly Logan accepted this reduction of his beneficence. I've never really regretted the odd seventy pounds. Comfort of mind is everything; and, in any case, had a coarser mood been upon me then, it would be a very coarse mood indeed which permitted me to take such advantage of a man not yet perfectly in his right mind. But I have no misgivings about the £30.

That same day I had a long talk with Mrs Russell. We had known each other—though little more than formally—ever since I first came to the house; I think that the friendship which has grown up so happily between us, began over the cable, when I sent bulletins from Iceland: and that it was first certainly established during this conversation.

I told her the doctor's moral verdict on him—'a spoilt old man'.

'Yes,' she said, 'I have spoilt him—but then he has given me a home to share with him for over thirty years. I couldn't help it.'

The details of Logan's madness, unwisely or unfortunately as the event proved, I didn't tell her; to the victim's sister such things, I felt, wouldn't make pretty telling. But I did say this to her: 'If ever such a thing happens again—and we can't ever feel safe now—you must promise me one thing: go away! You'll want to stay, and feel it's your duty to stay; but it's really too painful to bear. So you must promise me *now*, and if ever the time comes, I'll hold you to your promise.'

She promised; and it so fell out that the time did come in the end when I had to remind her of this promise.

The cares of wealth were upon me when I drove off to the bank in a taxi; I had the best part of £200 in notes in my pocket. Idiot fancies of hold-ups and robbery with violence came over me; I have never felt a more foolish sense of relief than I did when, unassailed and with my treasure entire, I handed the notes in across the counter.

That afternoon I went to see my old friend Philip Morrell. About forty years before he had been a close friend of Logan's, who dedicated to him his first book *The Youth of Parnassus*; various happenings of the years between had estranged them.

He asked me how I had got on in Iceland.

'I loved the country,' I said, 'more than I've ever loved a country before. But on the whole I had a dreadful time; Logan got pneumonia, and when he was getting over that, he went mad.'

To my astonishment, 'I'm not in the least surprised,' he answered calmly. 'Mrs Strong,' he went on, 'said years ago in Rome that Logan must be mad, or else with his brains and his power of writing, he'd have been a really great writer.'

Philip had travelled with him as I had, but when Logan was a young man. 'He used,' he told me, 'to be very particular about his conditions for sleeping. Every crack of light had to be kept out. It sometimes took quite a lot of work with the curtains before he was satisfied.'

I had witnessed similar cares. When I first knew Logan, I told him, he used to cover his eyes with a piece of black velvet for his after-dinner sleep; another device of his—supposedly soporific—was to put over his eyes a handkerchief rolled up cornerways and soaked in cold water.

'He never forgave my marrying Ottoline,' said Philip; Logan had disapproved of Philip's marrying out of his class, as he called it, by allying himself with a Duke's sister; to Logan this was evidence of worldliness and ambition; never was a greater mistake, for by this marriage Philip passed, not into Logan's 'Great World', but into that outer world of the eternal rebels.

'He and Percy Feilding and I,' Philip Morrell went on, 'had been the three great friends. Percy was my best man; but Logan went abroad, and wouldn't come to the wedding. He made me send him back all his letters. I often wish I'd refused. They were wonderful letters. He was teaching himself to write, and they were sort of exercises which he sent me in the form of letters.'

Logan's misgivings about the marriage had a certain justification, though not on the grounds which he postulated. It is true, however, that Philip's brilliant and splendid wife put him into the shade, and that many of her friends—I have seen it—treated him in a way that wasn't far short of bad manners. As a boy he had given place in his mother's eyes to a handsome elder brother. Accordingly he had built up for himself a sort of shell, and his sallies into conversation were often marked by a certain unawareness for the feelings of the others.

But any advances of friendship made to Philip were rewarded by the discovery of a sensitive, affectionate character, of exquisite taste, but above all sensitive; Philip, as anybody who knew him well could discover, might be hurt as easily and as deeply and as painfully as a child.

'After we'd been married,' he told me, 'Logan, who had really broken with me, said, "I think I *can* go on seeing you after all. I find Ottoline very interesting, so I shall be able to keep on coming to see you, not as your friend, but as Ottoline's".'

The demon, evidently, was not a companion of later years only. As a writer, Logan carefully and with painful thought, discovered his limitations; in this process he had, I believe, discovered the role he intended to play in life. The character he wished the world to appreciate was as carefully contrived as his prose (though less effectively carried out!)

'Hearts that are delicate and kind and tongues that are neither; these make the finest company in the world.' So Logan had written in

Afterthoughts, and when a friend suggested that this was his own portrait, he took the suggestion complacently, so complacently, in fact, that I am sure he had in mind, when he wrote it, his ideal picture of himself.[1] Wise, friendly, separate, witty, soberly affectionate, kind and cynical—'the sage of Chelsea', monastically devoted to his art: that was the idea; and from all of it, only the last was always true; towards literature he showed at all times a deep-founded and unswerving integrity.

For a period he almost achieved his ideal. In the years before Iceland, while I knew him, he didn't often fall far short of it; that was between the ages of 63 and 73; and from what I have been told by his friends this achievement was not new in 1928. It might roughly be said that his golden years extended from middle age until he had entered his seventies. The vigour of youth and the weakness of age gave equal scope to the misleadings of his demon.

Logan was soon anxious to do something that seemed like work. About a month after we had returned he wrote to me (25.9.38) (A quiver had appeared in his handwriting which, spidery at the best, never recovered its old modicum of firmness):

'I have just been reading a new book on Darwin—I always read everything I can about Darwin—and find that when he was a dull sluggish undergraduate at Cambridge, listlessly preparing to take Holy Orders, he happened to read Humboldt's *Travels in the Equinoctial Regions,* and was excited almost to frenzy by Humboldt's account of his ascent of the Piton in Teneriffe, and when the offer came to him of going on the famous cruise of the *Beagle* he accepted the offer, mainly because they would sail to the south by Teneriffe, and he would really see a volcano. His father, Dr Darwin, had grave misgivings about the long voyage for a boy of 23, on account of something I can't understand—not the danger of volcanoes, but that of "nautical homosexuality". Perhaps you can explain to me what that means. Whether

---

[1] One advantage of growing older is that we may without much impropriety repeat the compliments paid to us in our youth. When *Afterthoughts* came out, Logan said to me, 'Did you find your own portrait?' I thought I had, and quoted 'What's more enchanting than the voices of young people, when you can't hear what they say?' But it wasn't that. He pointed out another aphorism; and I read, not, I must confess, without a little smug satisfaction, "Goodness isn't enough; but what delicate glaze it gives to people who are good as well as charming!" I can the more unblushingly record this since during the years left before this story is ended, such an aphorism about me would rarely, I think, have come to Logan's pen.

There are other little hidden portraits in *Afterthoughts*, but it would perhaps, at least while their subjects are living, be as well to leave them in hiding.

he escaped this danger is not stated, but owing to quarantine they could not land at Teneriffe, but lay becalmed at sea while he gazed with longing at the mountain, no aspect of which he said, "was not unbearably lovely, the cloud-girdled peak seeming of another world, the winds blowing about it the very airs of heaven". He visited many other volcanoes, and wrote learnedly about them (they were a passion with him) but Teneriffe he never saw again, though it haunted him all his life.

'I hope the volcanoes of Iceland haven't put that golden peak out of your mind. My friends, by the way, refuse, some of them, to believe that I didn't die in Iceland, and are talking of getting up a memorial service for me. You will have to come, and mind you wear a top-hat with just the right width of black band about it. The corpse will examine most carefully the costumes of the mourners. Tail coats, of course, will be worn.[1] A notice of the date will be sent you. In the meantime, before I am buried beneath the sod, I should like to revise my *Treasury of Prose*, which Constable's may soon want to re-issue, as they have done my *Aphorisms*. You remember we made a beginning of it. It is the sort of work which isn't work that I could do now, and you could help me greatly. What I should like (if the arrangement suits you) is one day a week (as per protocol—46 days in the year) at the time before your holiday season begins, to have you come up late one afternoon once [a] week, so that we could have the evening for "the feast of reason and flow of soul" (I have just invented this phrase—rather good, don't you think, for one of the deceased?) the following day for work till you returned in the late afternoon as usual.

'We could begin this week if that suits you—all my days are alike, as befits my condition. But next week if you prefer it.

'But dear me this may all be a dream—my bones may be bombed before the week is over and you may be slaughtering Germans. But the general opinion here seems to be that though there will certainly be war *perfide Albion* will keep out. The taste for eating dirt seems to be growing on us.'

Logan was always, in his own phrase, a 'calamity howler'; and on this occasion he managed to visualize a deeper shame even than the shame our Empire sank to at Munich, the crisis of which was upon us. There was, in fact, no great prospect of my slaughtering Germans. Kyrle and I with another friend had volunteered as ground staff at a neighbouring aerodrome; a rather puzzled administrative N.C.O. took our names and addresses down on a piece of paper, and put it in a drawer, where, no doubt, it remained, until the worms or the woodlice ate it.

[1] As I transcribed this I could not help sadly and vividly recalling, with an ironic melancholy, that bleak and all but secret funeral, with only five of us attending.

And so my visits to London started up again. We did very little work. Logan often talked about his madness. This affliction implies no ethical obloquy, and yet its victims—and other people, too—are apt to speak of it as if with shame and moral shrinking. Logan, it seemed to me at the time, felt nothing of this. There was no difficulty in discussing the subject; though when he asked me—as he did from time to time—to tell him some of the things he had said, I always resolutely refused to do so.

I have said that he rarely felt any sense of guiltiness. But on this occasion, for ill deeds which were subject to no ethical blame, he was overwhelmed with penitence; and though he seemed to look on his madness rationally as an uncontrollable accident, yet, for the deeds which that madness had prompted, he experienced the bitterest remorse.

He remembered very little of his time in the hospital at Reykjavík; but he remembered enough to know that he had poured out upon me the most ghastly abuse. One day, when he was ashamedly lamenting this, I pointed out that he needn't blame himself, and that nobody else could blame him, for things uttered under such conditions.

'No,' he replied sadly, 'but it must mean there's a terrible black strain in me somewhere.'

Rather strangely, he remembered one little plan of his craziness, although at the time in Iceland, he had not spoken of it to me.

'Bob,' he said anxiously to me one day in London before he was fully recovered, 'I've been worrying. When I was crazy, did I stop that pittance I pay to you?'

I was able to reassure him. 'That's a relief,' he said, 'I was afraid I had.'

It was evident that in that insanely begotten enmity he had planned to do this; it was also evidence that his wits were still a little astray, or else he would have remembered that it had been, in fact, during his illness quite impossible for him to communicate with his bank.

He tried all he could to make up to me for what I had suffered through him. To everybody he proclaimed that I had, literally, saved his life. This was generous praise, and took away deserved credit from the doctor and nurses. But I do believe that had I not sat by him so often and so long through the painful days when his fever was its worst, he would doubtless have fretted away the last frail fabric of strength which kept him alive. Left alone in the hospital he would almost certainly have died.

He attempted to prove his gratitude and his remorse in more material ways. He was always trying to give me presents which it was not always possible to refuse; and I could never let him know at this time that I'd bought anything without his getting hurt that I'd not asked him for it, or that afterwards I wouldn't let him pay for it himself.

One morning, when I arrived, he said, 'You'll notice a change in me. I've made up my mind, for the rest of my life, to behave like Jesus.'

I suppose the zenith of his golden mood was revealed when he welcomed me one day by saying, during this afterglow which flamed so brightly and beautifully for a while through his penitence and weakness, 'I've been wondering how to describe our relationship. I can't call myself your patron, and I don't like to call you my secretary—but now I've decided how to speak about it. There used to be a definitely accepted relationship in old days. You're my heir.'

I disclaimed this: his literary heir—yes, that I was happy to be, to inherit, as he had so often planned and promised, his works and his papers, and his books, so carefully read and so carefully annotated; and my allowance, which was a settled thing. But as to the rest of his property, I had no desire to make as it were a profit out of his death. Had I been asked then to give a name then for my formal relationship to him, I should, I think, have eventually hit on the phrase I have already used, and called myself his perpetual apprentice.

Such a state of unblemished peaceableness—I should have known it —was too good to last. One day, after a fresh refusal on my part to tell him about his ravings, he said, in a tone that was not without satisfaction, 'I expect I told you some home truths.'

The next relapse was curious. I had spent the night at his house, and the following morning we had got through some sort of work (this mainly involved, at that time, a great deal of talking, and going through fan letters which had been plentifully provoked by the recent publication of *Unforgotten Years*). He was still in a condition of the most pitiable weakness and even such 'work' as this tired him greatly. In the afternoon he lay down, and slept. I had to catch a particular train home. As the time drew near when I would have to go, he was still asleep, nor was he awake when I had stayed long enough to risk missing my train. I thought it best—considering the state of his health—not to disturb him; accordingly, having asked Hammond to give him a message, I left him without waking him.

I had given him the greatest offence where he would never have taken offence before. A faint shadow of his crazed enmity crept into the letter he wrote me, and darkened while he was writing it. The Spanish books he mentions he had given me outright; the time, which he foreshadowed, had come at last when he was to ask for his presents back. Of the two letters he mentions, one was from an American who knew of the Whistler portrait of 'M. de Charlus', for which Logan had sometimes stood in; the other was from the doctor at the Reykjavík hospital, to which Logan wished, out of gratitude, to make a gift. This was the letter (12.10.38):

'As you didn't deign to come to say good-bye on Friday (as you had promised) I must write to you one or two requests I had intended to make. In the first place I should really like to see those two letters which I forwarded to you (if they were what you said they were) the one especially about the Whistler portrait, as I must write to thank its writer, and don't know his name. Also I should like to see the letter from that doctor in Iceland, to whom I sent £30.0.0. I should like also to read again that little book of Miss Philpotts on Icelandic literature. . . . You have other books of mine, Spanish and French, which you have never returned; if I were asked I couldn't say honestly that you had a genius for returning borrowed books. I had intended to say nothing of these as I lay wide-awake, expecting your visit. You know, or ought to know by now, how much I enjoy being kept awake, so you won't be surprised that I was somewhat put out when Hammond came at 4.30 and told me that you had left the house at 4. Altogether, I got the impression that I had got on your nerves and that you weren't as friendly as you used to be. Always remember that according to our protocol you have the absolute right to chuck me over when you want to; and though I may feel grief I shall have no right to a grievance on the sad occasion—I must only remember the happiness your friendship has brought me in the past, which has indeed been great.

'I have just received the American edition of my *Unforgotten Years*[;] they have got it up beautifully, and say that it has been chosen as the Book of the Month in America, which means, before they begin to boom(?) it, a sale of 100,000 copies. To have written a best seller is a cloud on my declining years, but a cloud which has a silver, or rather a golden lining, which will help me to bear the disgrace . . .'

When I first read this letter I nearly sent it back to him with 'Don't send me any more letters like this' written across it. On second thoughts I wrote out and sent him a tenderer form of reproach, a letter which, I hoped, might return his feelings into a more reasonable way. But some reproach, I felt, was necessary, however delicate. A succession of such fantastical attacks would make our relationship impossible.

The next time we met, I told him of my first plan.

'If you'd done that,' he said, 'I'd never have had anything to do with you. You know, I never forgive.'

This was raising an old question that we'd argued over more than once.

I had not yet tried to separate Logan's true character from the personality which prevailed when he was under the directions of his demon. In that proper self of his there was one streak, and one alone, which struck me as actually wicked; this was a proudly proclaimed implacability. During his life he had once or twice altogether failed to pardon a pardonable offence. A reluctant or passionate failure to forgive would have been comprehensible, and something that could itself be understandingly forgiven. But what horrified me—there is no other word for my feelings—was his evident conviction that in such behaviour there was something meritorious. He boasted of it.

This implacability was the gravest fault to be found in his proper character. In excuse, he told me how many years ago he himself had committed an unforgivable sin, by indiscreetly repeating remarks to the wrong people, and so making mischief. 'The friend whose remarks I'd repeated,' he said, 'gave up seeing me. I was very sorry to lose him as a friend, of course, but I didn't blame him. He was quite right not to forgive me.'

'If he found you were sorry,' I said, 'and had apologized, I think it was devilish of him.'

My condemnation of this horrid principle shook him a little, and one day he told me that he had consulted an old friend of his, a lady both wise and charitable. How he questioned her, I don't know; but when he began to quote her in his favour, it became clear to me that what she had given her judgment on was the particular offences of which he most frequently accused my generation; if she gave her opinion on the question of forgiveness, Logan never repeated it.

But I must confess that never except this once, did he include the returning of a foolishly written letter among unforgivable sins.

As he kept on nagging, I tried to joke him back into reasonable behaviour.

'I thought you'd decided to become like Jesus,' I said.

'I've changed my mind!' he answered abruptly, and with perfect seriousness.

This curious little outbreak was like one of the lesser shocks which follow after a disastrous earthquake. Logan was still unbalanced, and he was suffering, as I have said, from an enormous inward remorse. He undoubtedly hated, in the most generous way, the knowledge that he had been, however helplessly, a cause of great pain to me. This sense of remorse and of guilt—so unaccustomed to him—became at times intolerable. At last he devised a means of escape; and, being Logan, his way out was along the path of letters. The work he produced was an odd one, and interesting to consider.

We are told that there is a censor in us which alters and makes palatable all the abominations we actually dream about in our sleep. Logan's illness and madness were like a long sleep to him, and the few faint memories as dreams. When he set about writing these down, a censor intervened; records and chronology were satisfyingly altered, and the result was a narrative not of what happened, but of what Logan would have liked to have happened. How far this falsification was unconscious I have never been able to make up my mind; self deception about our own misdeeds is very easy. I do not think that he wrote anything down which he believed to be false; but I think, at the same time, that he was very ready out of his broken, wraith-like memories, and without much troubling himself as to what the truth may have been, to make a story which showed him up in a better light than the facts would have done.

Inexplicable to me is his first deviation from those facts, a deviation to which he obstinately tried to cling. I have told how he was taken ill in the afternoon at Thingvalla, and how next day Mr Turville-Petre came out to him from Reykjavík. This is what he wrote, 'Rising from my deck-chair I felt a difficulty in walking, whereupon a scholarly-looking Englishman strolled across the garden of the small hotel, and remarked, "I am afraid, sir, that you are ill".' He goes on with a quite imaginary little conversation, and then says 'This exchange of amenities in the interior of Iceland sounds rather odd, but that is what I seem to remember.'

He had first written, 'that is what I remember'. It needed long and persistent persuasion on my part before he added the two words which brought his story more in line with the facts. Nothing at all, however, could persuade him to tell what actually happened at Thingvalla, though this was not in the slightest way to his discredit.

His other alterations of the past are comprehensible, for they enabled him to present an altogether more decorous picture of himself than the truth would allow.

The course of his illness was roughly as follows: for about six days he suffered from a normal and progressively more dangerous attack of pneumonia; then his temperature returned steadily to normal, and for about a fortnight he was violently mad; during the last three or four days in Iceland—and for no longer—he was coming back towards his proper senses. In his account of the matter, taking into consideration the time which actually elapsed, he was, he makes out, ill and delirious for nearly a fortnight, and, while admitting his craziness, he lets it be attributed, as a violent delirium, to his fever. The disease, he says, 'heated my blood up to that fantastic temperature in which the tongue is not in the least controlled by reason, and I began to pour on those who approached my bedside a flood of vile and gross vituperation'. A little later he writes, 'When, on the fall of my temperature, reason was once more seated on her throne, the doctor and I had a good laugh over the mad accusations I had brought against him'; the recollection of some actual conversation may very likely have prompted the picture, but at no time, of course, while we were still in Iceland, was he capable of discussing reasonably and dispassionately his recent condition.

Finally, as a last decorous twist to time gone by, he wrote, 'After my fever and my rage subsided, I lay for two weeks in my hospital bed, believing that life was over'. And he goes on to a reverie about death-beds, and the imminence of death. To an altogether imaginary period he has transferred rational feelings from the first few desperate days of his illness.

On him, it must be granted, the effect was a successful one. I shouldn't really have been surprised at this. His anecdotes, and even some of his memories, as I have realized since, were often the best of fiction. What he told was what appealed to him for its form and its quality; cold facts were not of any great importance. It is perhaps surprising that his written fiction was not more successful.

I was embarrassed when he read out his first draft aloud to me. What should I say about it? I wondered. I resolved not to disturb the happier picture than reality which he had composed; apart from the one correction I have mentioned, I did not discuss the facts with him, although he was able now—having, by so curious and typical a way, got the guilt of it off his chest—to talk more resolutely and sensibly about his madness.

'What I think happened,' he said, 'was that my spirit was quite ready to die, but my body wasn't, and struggled and fought to stay alive.'

I told him now about the deception the doctor and I had practised on him when I was forced to retire.

'I do remember that,' he said, 'I was *awfully* suspicious.'

Rather pathetically he asked my advice about life in general.

'What you must do,' I said, 'is to accept the idea that you were meant to die in Iceland. What's left of your life—and there's no reason why it shouldn't be many years—you must look on as a windfall. Always remember that, and make it as happy a time as you can.'

He professed to see beauty and gold in this, but alas, never, when the help of a golden thought was needful, never, at any time, did he seem to recall it.

Apart from the scarring and disfiguration of his spirit, this illness left, I believe, a tragic legacy; his attitude to death had always been a stoical one, as he so gaily and beautifully proved when he first became ill. But the dangers and torments of the disease had scared him and grafted a terror in his heart. I do not think that he became afraid of death; this was shown by the gay and sometimes uproarious courage with which he endured the bombing of London. But the actual process of dying became, I think, a ghastly prospect to him; and this, as well as the progressive nature of his malady, largely contributed, in my opinion, to his mental disturbance during his last months of life.

He named his small reminiscences *Death in Iceland* (a title which strikes me now with its sadly ironic appropriateness, for something fine and essential had certainly died in him). He became anxious to see it published.

I didn't think it worthy of his best, and dissuaded him with a plan which allowed him to see it in print. I had written a poem about Iceland which pleased him, and I suggested that I should get our two writings printed together, privately, as a single pamphlet; this we could both distribute as a sort of Christmas card. The plan succeeded. I don't know if I was right; but apart from the literary side of it, I didn't relish the thought of my old friend pathetically giving himself away by this writing up of a disintegrated past; and that feeling was not weakened in me by the knowledge that only close friends who had heard the truth from me, would be able to see the falseness of his account.

I have told how, without knowing it, I may have had a clue in my hands to explain, not only certain manifestations of Logan's recent craziness, but as well some others of the irrational outbursts which I had amazedly endured. I must record another blindness. Soon after Logan's death, when the last rupture he had brought about was known to a number of people, one of our mutual friends said to me, 'I think he always associated you with his madness in Iceland.'

Since then it has been pointed out to me that, in the America of Logan's youth, madness was looked upon with more than the natural shrinking which we feel; it was reckoned as an abomination, a disgrace, and something to be most warily concealed. Logan, as I have said, betrayed no such feelings; however—I can see it clearly now—they were evidently lurking dangerously within him.

In speaking of *Death in Iceland*, I have just mentioned his curious twisting of certain seemingly innocent facts; one such perversion I did not mention then, a perversion whose deeply sinister implications had altogether escaped me. He wrote in one place, 'Dying, as I thought, among complete strangers . . .' I remember feeling a little hurt by this phrase when he first read it out to me, and for that reason I had said nothing about its inaccuracy.[1]

What this implied was quite simply that, if Logan lived long enough, our friendship was doomed. He could talk gaily about his madness, fantasticate the story, lighten and make a joke of it; but there was I, the one man in England who had really seen him out of his mind, a witness and the incarnate evidence of that abominable visitation. In the sort of dream-story which, for the peace of his heart, he had put in the place of an actual past—in that story I was already eliminated from the scenes of his life.

I have discussed the irrational enmity which I sometimes had to encounter, and which was due, I believe to an old, unresolved maternal relationship. But these storms, even at their worst, and however painful, had hitherto been transient; when, having accomplished their clinical purpose, they passed away, his friendship for me seemed as strong and faithful as before. Now, in a nook of his hidden character, there was to brood henceforward a sense and a desire that I must be turned right out of his life.

After his attack of madness he never recovered so much integration

[1] I didn't know then that he had just written to an old friend in very similar terms, 'To lie in a tin hut on the shores of the arctic sea among people who only talked Icelandic, looking death in the face for a couple of weeks, was rather a grim experience'. Here, it will be seen, almost all the circumstances of his calamity have been metamorphosed; the hospital at Reykjavík is a large concrete building, on the inland side of the town, which faces, incidentally, not the Arctic Sea, but a bay of the North Atlantic.

of character as he had formerly possessed. His affection for me remained almost until the very end, if, indeed, something of it was not persisting then; when he had work for me to do, I was able to satisfy him as well or even better than before; in my own writing he took as kind and as careful an interest as he had always done. But now and always, even in what might seem the happiest moments of friendship, or the most prosperous intellectual intercourse, he would suddenly contrive a spiritual wound which was the more painful for being quite inexplicable.

Logan himself—blindest of the self-blind—was not aware of his motives. Just as I never divined, nor most evidently did he, that he would be attempting to destroy what he was to speak of as our sweet collaboration. His renouncement of promises and undertakings, his attacks, his little perfidies, some of which I am to record—all of these were, I truly believe, no more to his thinking self than the satisfaction of overpowering whims; of darker causes he allowed himself to see nothing.

Logan felt as bitterly as I did the shame of Munich. I did not always hide my opinions before the supporters of Chamberlain's peace with honour; but Logan, with such people, was liable to transgress too far the bounds of good manners. When dangerous occasions threatened, his sister and I would try and exact promises that he would avoid the subject. After one of these occasions he wrote to me on a postcard (28.10.38):

'My tongue is blistered by the things I *didn't* say to —— on Wednesday. So I will say them to you, "Of course if I were an Austrian Jew today or a Czechoslovak I would commit suicide at once".'

Two days later (30.10.38) he wrote:

'I have received what is almost a love-letter from a bank clerk in the Midlands, aged 25, expressing unbounded enthusiasm for my works, and the exalted determination to be a writer of the kind I approve of. This letter I must answer myself, though I wish I had your help. It is charmingly written, and were I younger, I would answer it in person. But the years, the years and all the accumulation of disillusion! What do you advise me to do?'

Just before Christmas, I sent him his share of our pamphlet. I had decorated it with reproductions of woodcuts from two nineteenth-century books about Icelandic travel. At this time I was working on a book about gardening and botanical journeys, the book I've already alluded to, and in which I described my excursions with Logan to Teneriffe and Iceland. He wrote to me (22.12.38):

'The Icelandic pamphlet has arrived, and I am sending it to my friends. I like the look of it and the illustrations.

'I hope you keep warm, and that you and Kyrle will be merry at Christmas. I have no intention of indulging in merriment—indeed my long-postponed attack of listless melancholy has returned in the last week, and will I suppose hang over me as usual for some time. So I shan't be able to do any work, and you can prolong your holiday and get your book finished. But though I shan't bother you to stay here while I am in this lifeless condition, I hope you will look in if you are in London; and I think I shall have intelligence enough to criticize your MS., if you care to show it to me.'

I was glad of this last invitation, for, since I was mentioning Logan, although under his own pseudonym of 'Anthony Woodhouse', I was very anxious to publish nothing about him which he might object to.

1939

'I can offer neither hospitality nor criticism,' he wrote on a postcard in January (10.1.39). 'But I shall emerge as usual'; and in March (9.3.39) 'I have reached the bottom of my well, I think, so hope I shall soon begin to get my head above water . . . don't dream of coming up on my account—I am too dull for rational society.'

In the spring he became ill with bronchitis, and early in summer, he went to a convalescent home in Westgate—a place with dreary associations for me, since my prep-school days had been passed there. He was still in his gloom. I offered to pay him a visit. He answered (29.6.39) to say that he would probably be leaving in a day or two.

'I hate Westgate,' he went on, 'as much as you must have done. This convalescent home is comfortable enough, however, but the whole place is dreary and unattractive . . . I don't believe in the war, and hope you and Kyrle will get your trip abroad.'

We were able to spend a short holiday in the mountains of Auvergne —a poignant visit, for it semed to our divining hearts as though we should never see France again.

1939

In the middle of August, the advance copies of my book arrived, the book of travel and gardening and botany and village life. Those days of the twilight of peace seem to me now remoter and more strange than my Edwardian childhood. We had no idea of what was coming, except that war was pretty certainly not much more than a fortnight away. Kyrle and I, when Hitler went into Prague, had tried to join the fire-service; instead, after various trifling interludes, we had received a curious letter thanking us for our kind offer to join the First Aid service, which, in our district, was evidently short of men. Since we were apparently wanted in this service, we joined and we were now trained and qualified for the job. It was clear, therefore, if the war came, that I should not be free, as in the past, to visit Logan whenever he wanted me. Other thoughts too were in my mind. Our ideas of air-raiding were based on reports from Spain and China, whence, of course, only the worst raids were described; it seemed to us that any part of southern England might find itself a worse Madrid or Barcelona. Having no foreknowledge of the 'phoney war', it appeared to me not impossible that Logan and I might be quite soon killed by bomb or machine gun. Logan, indeed, during the war, had some narrow escapes; but it so happened that nothing ever went off near enough to me for my life to be in danger.

With the book (which was published unpromisingly on the day that Hitler invaded Poland) I sent a letter mentioning my thoughts, and telling him to remember, if I should happen to get killed, what happy years his friendship had brought me, and what unspeakable gratitude I felt towards him for all his kindnesses and generosity. Acknowledging the book, on August 28, he said:

'I was touched by what you said in your note—I feel immense gratitude to you for your kindness to me, and the pleasure your society has given me. What a lucky meeting ours was! The luckiest thing that ever happened to me.

'War seems almost certain. Most of my friends are fleeing from London, but I shall stay here, and be bombed if heaven wishes it. There is nowhere I want to go, and my life is practically over anyhow.'

There were in existence by this time not a few unpublished manuscripts of works by Logan. The most important was a large collection of letters written to his parents; these, with other notes and MS. he kept in a large red japanned tin box; he also had letters addressed to him by some of his distinguished contemporaries.

A number of journals existed too, in particular one in four volumes covering the years 1895–1905. He had once thought of publishing this, and asked me then to read it through and give him my opinion. It was written during a period when he had not fully discovered what territory of art was to be his; he was heavily under the influence of Pater, and in particular the Pater of *The Child in the House*, and, in his journal he treated himself as the subject of an imaginary portrait by that master of prose. I told him that in my opinion the publishing it of would not increase his reputation.

'I'll throw it away, then,' he had said.

'No, no,' I answered, 'I may well be wrong; and at any rate, it'll be a valuable source of information for your biography.'

'Nobody will take any interest in me after I'm dead,' he declared and though he probably didn't really believe this, he was, I think, trying to speak sincerely at the time.

'I think they very probably will,' I answered.

'Very well, then,' he said, 'I'll give it to you, and you can keep it,' and he inscribed each of the four volumes to me.

I was anxious now, in case London should be bombed, that Logan's manuscripts should be safe. I wrote to him, in September, telling what my duties were, and suggesting that he should send to the bank, for safety, at least the red box (of which more will be heard). Other people more eminent than I had, it will be seen, the same fears.

'I was glad,' he wrote (17.9.39), 'to get news of you—you seem to me fortunate, but I would prepare your mind for a long and grim war, in which we shall probably all be ruined. However, why prepare one's mind? I dare say it is better to live from day to day, and think as little as possible of the future. So I shan't send my red box to my bank—I don't think posterity is likely to interest itself in my life and letters. However, I have received a request from one of the librarians of the Library of Congress in Washington, asking me to send my papers and letters to them—such is now my fame in America! I may perhaps do this before I am bombed.'

Ten days later he sent me an outcry of poverty; grim details he gave, including the supposition that his earnings on *Unforgotten Years* would be completely swallowed up by the Excess Profits Tax; rates would eat up all rents from his house-property; no money was coming from America. Such outcries had been characteristic of his more recent cyclical depressions; on one of these he had told me with unmitigated gloom that he had an enormous overdraft; I forget the exact sum, but it was something from five hundred to seven hundred pounds. When he emerged, he discovered that he had made a simple but important error, by confusing the opposite pages of his bank book; he was actually in credit to the extent of that so dreadfully bemoaned imaginary debt.

'I write to you of my troubles,' he went on, 'in order that you may understand that I may not be able to go on paying you your allowance. I probably shan't have anything to pay it with. I can't tell you how unhappy it makes me to write this—I did so enjoy the thought of your leisure, and the way it enabled you to develop (as you have done) your charming talent. Perhaps, however, I am unduly pessimistic. I am apt to get into these panics, and the skies may clear a little . . .

'Dear Bob, I hate writing this, but I know you wouldn't want to reduce me to miserable poverty.'

After Logan's death I was discussing his malady with a friend who had known him intimately for something like fifty years. This friend said to me that one thing which had particularly shocked him towards the end was Logan's morbid preoccupation over money, since a carefree disregard of such things had been part of his charm. Out of this had flowed the generosity of his spirit.

Of course, we were most of us becoming poorer during the war, but, there being so few things to spend money on, the effect was, as I found, that one could save money on a diminishing income. Logan himself, as events proved, was able to do this, for he died with a large balance in the bank. This letter—though I didn't know it at the time—was the first substantial warning of the disintegration which was finally to be accomplished.

Like the small shiftings and little fissures in a rock which betoken, long before, the disasters of a vast landslide, little actions, out of character, should have warned me of what was coming. But the disruption was gradual—one little break appearing, and another, and then another —until suddenly, at the end, gathering speed, everything seemed to come down in one enormous all-destroying avalanche.

Since in his real character generosity and unworldliness about material things were among the chief marks of his spirit, it was in the reversal of these that his moral dilapidation was chiefly to be noticed. Such affairs are sordid and awkward to write about, and I must make it plain that what Logan was led by his demon to deprive me of were not things of huge commercial value; each material object, however, may have a symbolic value and meaning to our spirits. As relating to things that could have been turned into currency, all these matters were trivial enough; but as vehicles of ill intent they turned into something black and tragical, and appeared to me as more than of mortal importance. I felt a pain as though his occult and cloudy motives had been expressed and made known to both of us. Such timid struggles as I was able to put up had a passion and a fear behind them as though I had realized the truth, namely that I was struggling not for marketable objects, but for his friendship and his very self.

In his golden days Logan would give things away, to anyone, on the smallest impulse; his bounty had nothing of pride in it, but was easy to him and unconsidered as breathing. Objects were like words for him then, to be as happily and gaily bestowed as jokes on a company of people. Now they had become as weapons, for injury. Situations arose which were hardly possible to deal with; we can expostulate with a friend over immaterial injuries; but when the intention to injure is signified by a substantial loss, however insignificant, there is little possibility of decorous reproach, and a comprehending reconciliation.

There was an alert over all the east of England during the first week of the war; our district just came into the area covered by it. After this we were, for a few weeks, expected to be always readily available, but gradually, as I shall tell, the restrictions on our movements were relaxed, and I was once again able to pay regular visits to Logan.

1940

In January of 1940 he sent me a postcard (29.1.40), 'I want your help. I am trying to get at the history of the Fall of Milton—I believed it happened on the banks of the Mississippi where T. S. Eliot spent his youth. I dare say Ezra Pound helped to bring him down.'

There occurred at this time, it may be remembered, huge snowstorms and curious frosts, and we were snowed up, so that I was unable to get to London, or even to telephone. Only the post carried on, and I managed to let Logan know of my predicament. He answered (1.2.40): 'Sorry you were snowed up and untelephoned yesterday. Perhaps

you will be thawed out and able to come to London one day next week
. . . when you come up, you might bring the 4 vols. of my diary, as I
could send them to the Librarian of Congress, who keeps bothering me
for MS.'

About the same time he had written to various old friends asking if
they would send to the Library of Congress such of his letters as they
had kept. They all very naturally refused; and I, as naturally, refused to
surrender the diaries which he had given to me. And, the subject being
thus opened, I ventured to protest about other papers; of these, I reminded him how he had always promised that they were to become
my property.

'They're going to be sent in the diplomatic bag,' he said, in excuse,
'and I like the idea of my papers travelling like that.'

To fight and press him over such things would introduce too
worldly and distasteful a strain into our friendship; I had made my
protest. Logan was just a little touched by it, and the incarnation of his
feeling was the absolute gift to me of some letters from Robert
Bridges, while the others, it was agreed, should go to America.

His Icelandic frenzy had made, I discovered, a complete reversal in
Logan's character. Before that he had, as I have already told, made
virtue out of his vices; and now exactly the opposite was the case. And
this was quite evidently the process.

He had undertaken obligations to me; he was repudiating them; this
repudiation vexed his conscience, and made him uneasy; I was the cause
of this uneasiness; and in his resentment at this, he did me another small,
half-vengeful injury; his conscience became uneasy once more; and so
the sorry process went on; there was no way out of it. His conscience,
in the seat of virtue, was abetting the demoniac wrecker of our friendship. As I have said, the end, if he lived long enough—perhaps I should
have guessed it then—was inevitable as the flow of river water to the
sea. Strangely enough, this flow—if I may safely continue the image—
was over the bedrock of an established friendship. There was never a
time when, as a boulder protrudes here and there above water, the
solid and lasting part of our relationship might not, if only for a
brief instant, be revealed in its enduringness; but at the end this firm
rock was hardly discernible and the waters were very wide.

A cynical reader might say—with an appearance of common sense
—that I was in some degree at fault, that something provocative must
have entered into my behaviour. I suspected this at the time, and care-

fully examined my conduct. I was not aware of anything but the usual faults which Logan had cheerfully put up with for nearly twelve years. It may be objected, however, that few people are aware of their conspicuous failings. True enough; but within a month of his death, Logan produced a list of misdeeds by which he attempted to break to me and to justify the repudiation of all his most solemn agreements; and this catalogue was made up partly of delusions, and in part of things so paltry that, in his normal state, he would have treated them only as occasions for affectionately malicious joking. For all that, my knowledge that he had once been mad, however carefully I hid it, may not, in moments of stress, have been without its alarming effect on me. And yet that no behaviour of mine was likely to have altered his behaviour is, I think, demonstrated by the fact, which I discovered in full only after his death, that at the same time there was growing up in him the same reasonless hostility to other and older friends of his. For some reason, his happy past was becoming for him a sort of trap.

The essay on Milton began half as a joke and a gay air pervades it[1]; but once it was started, he worked with the most scholarly scrupulousness.

The two chief dethroners of Milton appear to have been Ezra Pound and Mr T. S. Eliot, both of them Americans who had settled in Europe. Logan was deflected for a while into a study of other cultivated compatriots of his who had done the same, and at one time he might easily have produced, instead of that gay and brilliant essay on Milton, a satirical 'who's who' of expatriate Americans. He actually, with an unconscious parody of scholarship, began collecting material for some such a purpose. Part of this material he used with great effect for his ridiculous introduction to the essay on Pound:

'I am coming more and more to believe,' he wrote 14.2.40, 'that the great Ezra is the originator of this anti-Milton stunt. In the book you got for me from the London Library, *Make it New* (1934), he writes of his "Year long diatribes" against Milton. He is older

---

[1] The estimate I have implied of this book is not, as I see now, a right one. Logan's work has had a most noticeable effect; even Mr T. S. Eliot has recently, in a lecture, given young writers to understand they may now, and with no fear of harm, read such poems as *Lycidas* and *Il Penseroso*, or even, I believe, *Paradise Lost*. Logan's oblique and scholarly pin-pricks have proved themselves infinitely more effective than the hammer-blows of learned diatribe. A few, to be sure, in spite of Mr Eliot's handsome and scholarly amends, still talk about the 'dislodgment' of Milton. What has happened is that some have stumbled ludicrously against the titan's pedestal, and given us a good laugh in the process.

than T. S. Eliot, who only echoes with feeble squeaks Ezra's full-mouthed denunciations. I should like [to] make certain of this if possible—it would be a fine stunt if the most slipshod and illiterate of published writers should have toppled from his august throne the most finished and scholarly of our poets . . .

'How do you like this new Ice-age which is upon us? Have any glaciers appeared at Stanford Dingley?'

In a postscript he adds, 'I am reading a scholarly clever, witty life of Archbp. Laud by a Merton Don named Trevor-Roper.'

During this odd period of the war—the 'phoney war'—I was able to take more freedom from my duties, and work on Milton continued almost as other work had done in peace-time. It came into his head to suggest an interesting job for me to do on my own. 'The Church of England has a poor shop-window', was a remark which he made more than once. He suggested an anthology showing off the fine Anglican culture: this would chiefly involve work of our favourite period, the early seventeenth century. Logan suggested the name 'Via Media' for it, as expressing the Laudian philosophy held by most of the great Anglican writers. It was a pleasant task, and I brought my discoveries to him. Between this occupation and the compilation of his high-spirited essay on Milton, he was generally in a good frame of mind; nevertheless there was always a faint sense as of a harsh ghost, just outside the door, or walking noiselessly up the staircase.

On the invasion of the Low Countries, we were at once required to be continually on call in case of raids. We did not, under the part-time conditions of country service, keep regular shifts at the depot; but for stated periods we had to be always about the house, or near it, in case of a telephone call; and, until a more satisfactory scheme was arrived at, it was difficult for me to leave the district very often. I wrote to Logan, explaining this. In that new crisis we felt, it will be remembered, not only that we might be quite probably blown to pieces, but also that we could easily find ourselves surrounded and engulfed by German para-chutists. It didn't seem at all unlikely that Logan and I might never see each other again; so I put into my letter all the kindness I had ever felt for him; and, indeed, at that time, I saw for a brief inspired moment his bad behaviour as what it indeed was, a sorry but inescapable intrusion upon his true character, a wound or an infliction, not to be condemned upon moral principles.

Since we had had little 'words' over the papers, and I was anxious that there should be no smallest burden of bad feelings between us, I alluded to the subject. I said, as I remember, something like this, 'I hate anything coming up at all which depends on your death. You know that I would immeasurably prefer to have you than all your papers: I don't want to get them. But I couldn't help being hurt when you altered an arrangement that had stood for so long. But the few trifles that have gone, or are going mean nothing, and we needn't think about it any more.'

'Certainly,' he answered (14.5.40), 'you are right not to desert your post at present. I felt sure you couldn't come. My paper on Milton can wait—there is a more important counter offensive going on—at least I hope so. In the meantime we are denuding ourselves of all our extra furniture for the Belgian, Dutch, and Luxembourg refugees who are pouring into Chelsea. I only hope we shan't have any quartered on us.

'I wonder what you will do if any clerygymen descend in parachutes in your meadows? You mustn't shoot them at sight, I am told, but ring up the police. If botanists drop out of the sky, don't accept any bulbs from them—you can guess what kind of bulbs they will be.

'I went on Friday to see the non-parachuted Dean of Westminster . . . [he] was perfectly charming, and showed us . . . over the abbey, or over the part of it we wanted to see. I gave him your plan for the *Via Media*—he seemed delighted with both the idea and the title . . . I told him that you had given as a child ringworm to —— [a high dignitary of the Church]; and he laughed (rather loudly I thought for the abbey) and said that perfectly qualified you for composing such a book.

'Thanks for your kind words—you know how fervently they are reciprocated. I was made happy to find that you didn't regard me after all as a completely false and ungrateful friend.'

This acquaintance which he mentions had started with a request to Logan from the Dean, who asked him, as a fine prose-writer, to compose the inscription for a chapel restored in memory of the Wilberforces; and it ended when the Dean, shortly before his own untimely death, conducted, in St Margaret's Westminster, a memorial service to Logan.

At this period of danger and anxiety, he returned for a while to the benignity of his proper self. In answer to my news that it was once more difficult for me to say when I should be free to visit him, he wrote a long cheerful letter. I should perhaps explain that there was no reason, out of his playful imagination, for thus referring to the lady he mentions as a murderess. In writing, as he did, of the Henry James volume, he was under a bibliographical delusion; there is much, on the other hand, to be said for his literary judgment of it.

'These are indeed black days,' he wrote gaily (28.5.40), 'though nothing has happened that I hadn't long expected.

'Of course you must stick to your job, and not think of coming up to London on my account, much as I should love to see you. I am finishing off and (I think) improving my Milton . . .

'I have been going over masses of old family papers, and renewing my memory of the past with old photographs and letters. Here is a sentence from one of my mother's letters written when she was about my present age—"I hope you enjoy as much as I do to see the earthly life beginning to fade away a little. It is so delicious to get done with this world, and to have the beautiful prospect of the next world draw nearer and nearer day by day." All but the last clause expresses what I am feeling—I do rather enjoy "seeing the earthly life beginning to fade a little". And yet it has never shone so prettily in my eyes, as in its (presumed) fading in this sea of woe. And I have charming adventures—a new bookshop has just been opened round the corner by one of the succession of foolish bookish youths who open bookshops in Chelsea, and then soon have to close them. I have just been there and have bought for 3d. one of the rarest, and to my mind, the most delightful of Henry James's books, *Terminations*.

'I sit out in the gardens opposite every afternoon. Do you remember the gaunt, aristocratic, spinster murderess we talked with there one afternoon? As you know, I have that delicious so-called affliction of age, that softening of the brain which makes everything I write and say seem delicious; so that, as we sit on what Desmond calls my "bench of desolation", I can tell over and over to the spinster my favourite stories, and enjoy them more and more each time I tell them, while she who is suffering, she says, from the same loss of memory, declares that they are all perfectly new and fresh to her each time I tell them. So there we sit telling each other stories of old scandal, each sunny afternoon.

'Your cousin, Mrs ——, stalks past now and then giving us the unglad eye of her aristocratic disapproval.

'I am tending to see everyone as a parachutist, which adds to life a not unpleasant excitement. Desmond was here for hours yesterday, and I eyed him with great suspicion. I am expecting Marjorie Madan this afternoon, and if she arrives out of a parachute, I shan't be in the least surprised.'

Our times of duty were however soon reorganized, so that on three consecutive days out of every nine I was free; and I continued my visits and work with Logan. Just after he wrote the last letter, indeed, I was able to see him; I took with me some trout which Kyrle had caught. Kyrle, as well, had sent him a letter, mentioning, among other things, his enjoyment of *Trivia*. Logan wrote back to him (31.5.40):

'I am glad you find comfort in my *Trivia*—it was kind of you to write. I don't know whether I have ever mentioned it, but I have loved you—it must be for years now—and I am not a person who knows how to change.

'I must read *Trivia* myself, as the only comfort I have been able to find lately has been in reading the Astrologer who writes a page every week in *The People*—a kitchen paper which Hammond (who wishes to be remembered to you) brings up on Sunday mornings. She says this astrologer has so far been always right in his prophecies. . . . So do look at the stars—don't go peering down for the nests of warblers in the grass.

'I am glad you have made friends with the warblers. The advent of these birds with their delicate voices was, when I was happy and un-worldly and lived in the country, among the most exquisite of my pure and solitary pleasures. How I wish you had known me then! You would I think have liked me.

'I like the cheerful chiff-chaff, which is the first to arrive of these travellers, but the Willow-warbler, with his sweetest of tinkling songs, is perhaps my favourite. The Wood-warbler is exquisite too, and rare and mysterious—I have only heard his two-fold song once, when staying on Boar's Hill. You have heard, I suppose, the grasshopper warbler, but I'm sure you have never seen it. If you tell me that you have seen the Dartford Warbler, I shall tell you that you are a liar, and that I suppose will end our friendship. That I think would be a pity.'

About a week later he wrote to me (7.6.40):

'I must say that I miss your company awfully—your sympathy and mockery and all the rest. But of course you are tied to your post, especially at this crisis, which seems to me even blacker than most people will admit. The evacuation of the B.E.F. caused a moment of wild exultation here, even in very high quarters, but Winston soon stopped that.

'However, why speak of this wretched war? We must suffer what we must, and there is nothing to be said about it.

'I have been meaning to go to Bath next week, to be out of the way of that sacred rite, spring cleaning, which stirs the female heart with Dionysic fervour, but that is all postponed now, and I stay in London for the present anyhow.

'I had a visit this week from the author of that excellent life of Laud —Hugh Trevor-Roper, who is in London in khaki, on some mysterious job connected with the war. He loves letters, and what pleased me, he loves my writing, and knows a good deal of *Trivia* by heart. He doesn't however love Laud or the church of England. He won't admit that Laud had any taste[1]; the only mention Laud makes of contemporary literature is an attempt he made to have Donne's *Paradoxes* suppressed (T-R said Dunne), and the improvements he made in the church services had no aesthetic meaning, and would seem very plain and low to modern Anglo-Catholics. A charming erudite young man, all the same, and he told me one thing that I didn't know, which is that Milton's *Elegia Tertia* was written as a lament on Lancelot Andrewes. The boy Milton weeps himself to sleep, and finds himself in a dream amid the flowers of [a] lovely meadow, and suddenly (Cowper's translation):

> The seer of Winton stood before my face,
> His snowy vesture's hem descending low
> His golden sandals swept, and pure as snow
> New-fallen, shone the mitre on his brow
> . . . Attending angels clap their starry wings

and Milton awakes and Lancelot Andrewes does a fade-out. Trevor-Roper wants to bring out an edition of Corbett's poems. Do you know them?

'I have made another friend—a young corporal of literary tastes who is in charge of the big temperamental balloon opposite, which misbehaves itself now and then. I hope the corporal is better behaved! I lend him good books, which he reads with avidity.'

In my answer I gave him the melancholy news that Kyrle was seriously ill.

'I am so sorry,' he wrote (13.6.40), 'to hear . . . of Kyrle's illness. Give him my love . . . We are all probably doomed creatures, seated on volcanoes that may burst into flame at any moment; or are floating,

---

[1] I had criticized this admirable book on the grounds that no mention was made in it of Laud's aesthetic sensibility. I still maintain this criticism, and have personally maintained it in the face of Mr Trevor-Roper. To assert that the patron of Jeremy Taylor, and the builder of the Second Court of St John's at Oxford, had no sense of art, seems to me just fantastic.

shipwrecked, on rafts amid stormy seas. All we can do is to shout vain words, or wave wan white towels or handkerchiefs to each other in the distance. No, that isn't the full truth, since I at least do other things, leading a quite pleasant existence; polishing phrases as I lie in bed in the morning, or watching charming youths play cricket or tennis all the afternoon. Above them floats the silvery crescent of the new moon, looking inconceivably icy and remote and lovely and unconcerned, as I gaze at it through my field-glasses, floating in the azure sky above me, a picture of the serene desolation which is the ultimate fate of this bloody planet.'

The rest of this letter was full of information I had asked for; it was drawn from the D.N.B. concerning Nahum Tate's father, Faithful Teate, a minor poet and charming discovery of mine. A follower of Herbert, he strangely anticipates later poets; Shelley, for instance, in

> Why, friends, when winter's over spring comes on

or Hopkins in

> All dapled like the time of day

and this might almost be Blake's

> But th'other day I saw a Lamb take wing
> And flie to Heaven from an hill;
> I watcht to see if anything
> Would fall from him in flight, and found a quill
> Of which I made a pen, and fell to write.

But this passage is all his own

> When Love that, ev'ry Ev'ning, makes my bed
> Had not whereon to lay his head:
> Except you'll call that bloody Cross and bitter
> A Love-sick Saviour's bed and litter . . .

I sent a little collection of extracts to Logan, including this,

> Faith makes man's heart
> That dark, low ruin'd thing
> By its rare art
> A pallace for a king.

He answered (19.6.40):

'Thanks for your letter—your voice sounded very ghostly on the telephone—but it is well-known that I am the one who is dead. If people come to see me I have to communicate with them by table rapping . . .

'The little verse you quote from Faithful Teate is delicious—

Faith makes men's heart, etc.

and might do on the title page of your book.

'Or as a motto I should choose Section 5 of the *Religio Medici*— "There is no church whose every part so squares unto my conscience", etc.

'I enclose . . . Raymond's [Mortimer] review of David Cecil's Anthology [The Oxford Book of Christian Verse] . . .

'I wrote to Raymond about the sentence "Shakespeare's poetry is, I fear, conspicuously unchristian", to ask him if he had found Jesus. He replied that he hadn't; that the sentence was as ironic as if he had written "Gibbon was I fear conspicuously unchristian". It's all this Xtianity that is losing the war for us. We had [a] Sunday of Prayer, and the next Tuesday Belgium gave in. Last Sunday we prayed for France, and on Monday it surrendered. Now they are praying for Roosevelt and I hear his health is breaking up. So will you and Kyrle please stop your praying!

'I sadly miss our sweet collaboration.'

A month later he wrote (17.7.40):

'I am just finishing off my paper on Milton, and want a little information and confirmation from you . . . [these were requests to confirm and locate some quotations]. An odd thing has been happening to me which is gratifying, but ought to be more gratifying than it actually is. While I have (as I thought) been airing my dark prejudices and gratifying my ancient grudges, it would appear that sentences of glittering wit and golden music have been flowing from my pen, the Clarendon Press are enthusiastic about my diatribe and want to print it, not as an S.P.E. Tract, as I had intended, but a pretty little book by itself . . .

'I enclose a fine passage—at least I think it a fine passage—from Carlyle about Iceland[1]. I wonder if you will like it?'

I was able to visit him once or twice during July. I had found some pleasant passages of prose in Henry Vaughan's *Mount of Olives*, an ob-

---

[1] 'In that strange island Iceland, burst-up, the geologists say, by fire from the bottom of the sea; a wild land of barrenness and lava, many months every year in black tempests, yet with a wild gleaming beauty in summer-time; towering up there, stern and grim in the North Ocean; with the snow jokuls, roaring geysirs, sulphur-pools and horrid volcanic chasms, like the vast chaotic battle-field of Frost and Fire;—where of all places we least looked for literature or written memorials, the record of these was written down. On the

scure book, published in 1652, the year after Jeremy Taylor's *Holy
Dying*. One was a long set-piece on the deaths of great men and mer-
chants. These are two shorter passages:

He that sets forth at *midnight*, will sooner meet the *Sunne*, than he
that sleeps it out betwixt his curtains.

Suddenly do the high things of this world come to an end, and their
delectable things pass away, for when they seem to be in their *flowers*
and full strength, they perish to astonishment; And sure the ruine of
the most goodly peeces seems to tell, that the dissolution of the whole is
not far off.

On July 31st he wrote to me:

'I have just been reading Lancelot Andrewes' *Devotions*, in a translation which seems to preserve, or to possess, some of what must be the
beautiful diction of the original Greek.

"O thou that walkest in the midst of the Golden Candlesticks—"
"Thou art the hope of all the ends of the earth and of them that
remain on the broad sea—"
"We do all fade as a leaf and our iniquities like the wind do take
us away—"
"Thy areopagetic nocturnal examination—"
"The evermemorable conversation of the Saints", etc., etc.

'Your extracts from Vaughan sounded wonderful as you read them,
but alas, as I read them in type-script their glories have rather faded, and
the diction seems on the commonplace side . . .

'For the *Via Media* you must avoid the *fureur de l'inédit*, which makes
one anxious to publish new discoveries; or at least one must put such
discoveries by to read again, and see if they retain their lustre.

'I am distressed by reading that awful book *Guilty Men*, which shows
by what incompetent and complacent old men we have been governed,
and are still being more or less governed, I fear.'

'Distressed' was not the perfect word for describing his state; Logan
at this time seemed to revel in disaster. For the first time since I knew
him, he took comfort in his American blood. 'I've suddenly discovered an American eagle in me,' he would say; but from this, I am

seaboard of this wild land is a rim of grassy country, where cattle can subsist, and men by
means of them and what the sea yields; and it seems they were poetic men these, and had
deep thoughts in them, and uttered musically their thoughts. Much would be lost, had
Iceland not been burst-up from the sea, not been discovered by the Northmen.'
CARLYLE, *Heroes and Hero-Worship*. Lecture I.

afraid, American patriots cannot claim that he was returning, piously, to the bosom of his native land; for that land he had found no fresh love; it was only against his adopted country that he loosed this bird of prey. To me, being British, he used to pour out a gloating prognostication of defeat and catastrophe; a diatribe against British Generals, and politicians, and fighting men, and the British nation in general. 'I think we're beaten, and we deserve to be beaten,' he said to me with fury one day. To agree was impossible; and at silence—my instinctive refuge—he tore and extorted comments from me, pouring venomous contempt upon the remotest optimism. His sister told me that he was—as we all were—miserable and worried about the war; I suppose he was unthinkingly following his instinct, when inwardly distressed, for throwing personal blame on to his nearest companion.

Another part of this letter, where he mentions my reading of passages from Vaughan, needs some comment. I am a very bad reader—I say this without false modesty—yet Logan, so acute was his feeling for beauty in words, could suck from the poorest presentation of a work, the utmost of beauty in it. (I once mentioned this to a mutual friend. He said, 'Logan couldn't very well complain about bad reading; he was the worst reader I've ever known.' I had to agree, and recalled a time when Logan drawled wearisomely with drooping voice, and false dialect quantities, through William Barnes's *Woke Hill*.)

When we came back from Iceland we turned, very naturally, to William Morris. We had both read with enchantment his Icelandic journals; but Logan, I felt, did not grant him his full worth as a poet. I reminded him of the vague but lovely poem, *A Garden by the Sea*, beginning 'I know a little garden-close'.

'Read it to me,' he said.

I went ahead, humbly, and as best I could. At the middle passage I noticed that he was very still—

> 'There comes a murmur from the shore,
> And in the close two fair streams are,
> Drawn from the purple hills afar,
> Drawn down unto the restless sea:
> Dark hills whose heath-bloom feeds no bee,
> Dark shore no ship has ever seen,
> Tormented by the billows green,
> Whose murmur comes unceasingly
> Unto the place for which I cry.

nd I read on to the concluding passage:

> Yet tottering as I am and weak
> Still have I left a little breath
> To seek within the jaws of death
> An entrance to that happy place,
> To seek the unforgotten face,
> Once seen, once kissed, once reft from me
> Anigh the murmuring of the sea.'

I looked up at him when I'd finished, and tears were running out of his eyes.

At this time the war over England had begun. For a few weeks desultory bombs were being dropped round about us in the country, and for that short period we were able to boast of our adventures to people living in London (a boast that was soon sered and swept overwhelmingly away). However, my times of duty were now so arranged that I was still able to pay occasional visits to Logan, even when the day-raids over London had started. (I bear a dully-charmed life; only once on these occasions did I hear a bomb fall; and later, during the heavy blitzes, whenever I spent a night there, it was always a quiet one.)

Logan and his sister, with Hammond, and the cook, Mary, stayed boldly at home. He told me that he rather enjoyed the raids, and that at any rate, he would rather be bombed in his own house than spend the rest of the war in another.

However, in war-time, such arrangements are often beyond control. In September (22.9.40) Mrs Russell sent me the following postcard from a Sloane Street hotel:

'We hoped to stick in London, in spite of the many (harmless) bombs in the Terrace and Square, but are beaten by the Time Bombs. Twice we have had to leave at 5 min. notice, and this last exile is not ended yet after 8 days. And even if we can return soon, a hasty exit may come again, and it is too much for Logan not knowing where to go ('tis very expensive here and no safer nor quieter). So we move tomorrow to. . . Bishop's Stortford, hoping it will be safe? and quiet?'

From his temporary refuge Logan sent me a long wail of anguish.

'Thanks so much for your kind letter,' he wrote (28.9.40) . . . . 'I have been too harried and ill, and so driven from pillar to post to be able to write a line: We were turned out of our house two weeks ago at two minutes' notice, and have gone from refuge to refuge, each worse than the last. At present we are in an icily uncomfortable hotel at this place, but my sister has gone to town today to see if our house is still standing, and if it is, I think we shall go back there on Monday—we prefer the risk of bombs to the kind of life we are leading, which is really no sort of life at all. But perhaps we can't live on in our house, even if unbombed, as the destruction in Chelsea has so affected my house-property that my tenants are all leaving, and the principal source of my income has vanished . . .' (There followed a warning that he might not be able to pay my allowance.) 'Altogether everything is too wretched for words, and the charming civilized world I have lived in so long seems to be crashing to pieces.

'I hope at least that you are paid for your war services which you certainly ought to be.

'I write with miserable feelings, and all sorts of regret and sorrow. 'But I send you my best love all the same.'

Never until near the end of his life did I know him to betray another mood so utterly drained of all moral strength.

I cannot remember if it was now, or earlier, that I persuaded him to let me take the red box, with his papers in it; at any rate by the summer of 1940, it was down in the greater security of my home.

After a fortnight Logan decided that an hotel room, even in the comparative safety of an East Anglian town, was worse than bombs and barrage, and home he went to Chelsea.

One reason for Logan's anguish over this flight into Essex was the influence of his melancholy. In the early days of his cyclical moods, and before he understood their nature, he had gone for an Italian tour with his sister Mrs Berenson. She was in poor health, and Logan, in his still uncomprehended condition of gloom, had to look after her. Later, he described the misery of it all to me; I should guess that he felt as one would feel if kept awake by force in the extremity of drowsiness.

During the first onset of this particular melancholic mood, he corrected a copy, for American publication, of *Milton and his Modern Critics*.

In much the same condition, he had gone through some of the proofs of *Reperusals and Re-collections*; among these was his essay on Jane Austen. He had put into this at first, as a note, a facetious but entertaining letter, once written to the *New Statesman*, attacking Emma Woodhouse in order to exalt Fanny Price; this letter, he moodily expunged from the proofs—and, when gaiety returned, cheerfully blamed me for allowing it. In a similar state of mind he now toned down his attack on Ezra Pound, and Logan's public in still neutral America beheld a less lively onslaught than was put in front of the English at war.

1941

Gaiety returned with the spring. Once, apart from the awkward transitional period, I had looked forward whole-heartedly to these times, save only for a little humorous apprehension as to how far Logan was going to get himself into trouble. But now and henceforth a poison might be mingled with the glory of his happy moods. An aspect of his case that had surprised me in Iceland was the association of misery with great vigour; such a thing I had never before seen in him during his full exuberance. But in the last phases of his life the association was frequent; his 'interlunaries' were none the more happy for it, but his 'happies' very much less so.

There were periods and occasions—oases—of pleasure; the old Logan, gay and wise and friendly was there; mocking good-naturedly, or paying where he thought it merited, ironic respect. In the keep and stronghold of his spirit sat in almost entire security the writer and artist. But too often there materialized a pale demoniac whose wit and intellect armed with a deadly precision his zest for giving pain.

To an old friend of his whose wife was Dutch—that friend from whom he had learned in imagination the criminal status of my Dutch acquaintance—to him he retailed with immense and unbearable gusto stories of German atrocities in the Netherlands.

To me he would pour forth, never-endingly, supposed details of British incompetence, and forebodings of utter defeat. The mildest expostulation provoked a contemptuous fury, or furious contempt— it's hard to say which. If I listened silently, biting my tongue, he would demand a comment.

This impotent indignation would sometimes burn into his letters: I will only quote one such passage, his curious comment on the speech broadcast by Mr Winston Churchill when Russia was invaded, that brilliant and statesmanlike oration with which he satisfied or silenced all the anti-Bolsheviks of Britain—

'Winston's broadcast last night,' he wrote (23.6.41), 'convinces me that he is crazy, as he once attacked the Bolsheviks in just the same fashion.'

Psychologists tell us that slips of the pen or of speech are really intentional, and that in them we give away our genuine though hidden opinions. Just such a significant slip of the pen Logan made in the sentence immediately following:

'I hear from sources of the highest unreliability that this is the opinion in America, who won't come into the war on this account. They know they've got to fight Hitler before long, but prefer to keep their armaments for this conflict, rather than hand them over to a madman who, in his strategic withdrawals will give them to Hitler——' the rest of the paragraph is indignantly illegible.

This passage, curiously enough, follows careful instructions for the writing of an anonymous letter.

His attacks on the Prime Minister—whom he incidentally admired both as a writer and as a man of action—were sometimes more humorous. When Mr Churchill's son-in-law, Mr Duncan Sandys, was given an important post, Logan said, 'People are very unfair to Churchill, but *I* defend him. I keep on telling people there's no truth in the rumour that he's going to make Vic Oliver foreign secretary.'

About this time he evolved a very strange grievance. In the course of a special savings drive—this one was called War Weapons Week— it was suggested that patriotic citizens might give some money to their country, instead of merely lending it. Logan, impelled by his good self, did give outright a sum of money, not enormous, nor yet by any means inconsiderable. He was the only person in Chelsea to do so, and his contribution appeared publicly on the balance sheet. Though I was not present to witness the whole growth of his indignation, it may be easily deduced. 'I suppose I'm the laughing stock of Chelsea,' he must have said jokingly to somebody—most likely to Hammond—who probably answered, in the same tone, that, of course, everyone was laughing at him. This, almost certainly passed off as a joke. Then that strange and sad metamorphosis took place; the joke became earnest.

'I'm the laughing stock of Chelsea,' he said loudly and with complete seriousness when he told me about it. 'We were asked to *give* some money, so I thought it was my duty to do it. Instead of being grateful, they look on me as a *fool*. "Ho! Ho! look at him!" they say. "He's *given* some of his money." They've stuck it up, and everyone can see what a fool I've made of myself.' (The 'Ho! Ho!' I should perhaps emphasize was the expression he actually used; 'Pooh!' was another incredible ejaculation which he often introduced into reported speech.)

Logan, it may be noticed, had, in some of his letters, spoken more kindly than it deserved of the work I was doing. Now, however, in the distinguished company of the Prime Minister, I began to be abused by him for that work and in a manner which was, I think, even less deserved than the praise. Peevish criticism is not, unfortunately, an odd manifestation of the human spirit; but with Logan it was regrettably evident that he was becoming more and more the slave of his moods. This had always been true of him—to some extent; formerly, however, he would criticize and often correct in sober mood what unreason had led him into; but now his violently conceived plans and opinions were tending to remain fixed. He was liable, when least sound of judgment, to commit irrevocable acts, or come to decisions which could never be reversed.

I do not think he was the least aware that his character was altering. I have spoken of his unpredictable behaviour according to his different moods. When he was a baby his mother had written, "It really seems as if the fellow was composed of two individuals." The different persons he was made up of, were becoming more and more separate. In old days, when this was less conspicuously the case, the finer self, the true self, had been dominant; now the demon-directed person was setting out to become master.

If there was any struggle this was not in itself apparent, yet the fact remains that while his correspondence was now liable to betray an unkindness I had not hitherto—save in his Icelandic frenzies—experienced from him, that same correspondence was written in tones and terms more affectionate than ever. Was this, I have sometimes wondered, his good angel struggling within, fighting with those weapons which Logan could most deftly use, the weapons of words and phrases? But alas, whatever the truth of that, the struggle if struggle there was, proved in the end to be a losing one.

He discovered about this time, or it would be truer to say rediscovered, an exquisite little anthology, the long-out-of-print *Words* *and Days* compiled by Bowyer Nichols, and originally published in 1895. He took such a fancy to this that he resolved to write a new preface for it and get the book reprinted.

I have told about Logan's method of taking help from other people —phrases, words, or ideas—and so heightening and contriving them that they became altogether his own. An illuminating example occurs in this preface. When he was planning the little work, he gave me a copy of *Words and Days*, in the first edition. After reading it through I told him—whether in a letter, or during our talk, I cannot remember —that it might be called an inspired anthology; I meant by this, I explained, that one had the feeling that passages had been taken, not only for their intrinsic beauty, but also because they chimed in some personal harmony with the compiler's spirit; he had not chosen them only as a collector might gather together objects for a particular exhibition, but as a writer seeks out and selects—as Logan himself sought out— phrases and words and ideas appropriate to his context. The anthology thus became a personal and original work.

He liked my comment, and made use of it. He paraphrased a letter from 'a lover of the book'; but it was not the letter which I wrote to him—if indeed I did make this particular comment in a letter. He added a beautiful conceit of his own, using the etymological meaning of the word 'inspiration'; he introduced its meaning of a breath or a wind wafting the extracts into the compiler's mind, a wind stirred by the turning of pages: 'The extracts . . . were whirled in the little eddies of the compiler's thought-full garden: or awakened as he listened in his library to the rustling of a thousand books.'

He finished this preface full of gaiety, though hardly a night went through undisturbed by the sound of bombs. And then, on April 16, he informed me on a postcard:

'I am "gone with the bombs" so to speak—a grandiose experience but it has left the house uninhabitable. Your books however are safe for the present. I will let you know the address of my new refuge, if I can find such a thing on this unsafe planet.'

Five days later, he wrote:

'I haven't left London after all. We have each found a habitable corner where we can live without too much discomfort—and here we shall stay till we are blitzed to heaven. So if you ever revisit this City of the Plain do come and see me. You can help me hurling the Oxford

Dictionary, as I am writing again on words. But don't put yourself out,—I think it better that you should work for your country than for me.

'I tried to find accommodation out of London, but the way you country people try to rook us is a perfect scandal.'

I visited him soon after this. Logan was at the crest of his euphoria and seemed glad rather than otherwise of his misadventure. A parachute mine had hit a block of flats on the west side of Burton Court, barely two hundred yards away: this I could see for myself. The windows of Logan's house had almost all been blown in, and were now filled up with black-out material and white oil-silk; the front door was cracked and askew; inside, plaster had fallen down from walls and ceilings; Logan's bookshelves were some of them crooked (to the end one was always liable to come upon small pieces of glass among the volumes). But no one in the house had been injured; Mrs Russell had the narrowest escape, for the door of her room had been blown on to the bed, and she had been unable to move until it was taken off her. Very heavy gunfire had warned Hammond that a severe raid was probable, and she had got Logan out of his bed and safely downstairs when it happened.

'It was tremendously impressive,' he kept on saying to me. 'Like the day of judgment. I wouldn't have missed it for worlds.'

It wasn't long before glass was fixed into most of the windows again; and Logan put up cheerfully with the rest of the damage, hardly noticing, it seemed, those pieces of plaster-board, which for a long time were all that covered the patches in the walls.

Not long before this incident, he had written to me in a letter (6.4.41):

'Henry James now overshadows me like a giant Jinn from a bottle.'

From this bout of re-reading, he made what he looked on as a great discovery; he began to examine Henry James's use of adverbs, and from this he fell to considering the importance in prose of these parts of speech. This investigation lasted intermittently for the rest of his life, and he asked me to report any interesting use of adverbs which I noticed in my reading in any language.

I tried to put on him a kindred subject, namely the adverbial use of prepositions, 'play up', 'take in', and so on, a characteristic idiomatic usage in ours and other northern languages. However, he didn't bite. Indeed, I think that he found the whole matter too large for his strength;

and he did little more than write of the subject as it applied to Henry James. It must be regretted that he did not make this discovery earlier; we have lost such a linguistic essay as he alone could have written.

I may here lament another unwritten work. I often pressed him to write a portrait of Henry James, as he had so admirably done of Walt Whitman. He liked the idea, but something stopped him. The failure would have appealed to Henry James himself who planted most of his friends into phantasmagorical predicaments. 'Ah yes, poor dear Logan,' he would say whenever Logan's name was mentioned (of whom he had said, when they first met, that he was 'monstrously, indecently, young'), a fact of which Logan himself was aware.

The essay I so earnestly proposed never, in my experience, got beyond the immediate telling of three anecdotes, which are perhaps worth recording. (He did in the end write a very short sketch of his great fellow-expatriate.)

Once the two of them were walking together in the wide-horizoned interior of Romney Marsh: Logan, as is often customary with expatriates, was attacking his native land of America. Henry James protested; how could he speak so of his own country and countrymen? It was altogether shocking. He stopped, and turning full circle, surveyed the entire unpeopled landscape. Then, reassured that they were quite alone, 'My dear boy,' he said, putting his hand upon Logan's shoulder, 'I can't tell you how passionately I agree with you.'

The other two concerned Henry James's naturalization, when Logan was one of his sponsors. (Logan had for some time been suggesting this action to him, and Henry James had always resiled with professions of horror. Then one day the telephone rang; it was Henry James. 'Logan,' he said, 'how do you do it?') 'You will find out,' said Logan, beforehand, 'that as soon as you become an Englishman you will get a taste for water-closet stories. You can't escape; it happens to all naturalized Americans.'

'But Logan,' replied Henry James, throwing up his hands despairingly. 'I don't know any!'

After the formality was over, they were walking past Buckingham Palace. 'Isn't it strange,' said Logan, pointing to the Victoria Memorial, 'to think of that old lodging-house keeper sitting on top of the British Empire?'

'Logan,' replied Henry James, very solemnly, 'you forget who you're talking to.' Then he turned towards that huge white ugly agglomeration of marble, and took off his hat. 'I salute my sovereign,' he said.

I happened, early this summer, to bring Logan some trout. They had been caught in our river by Kyrle, to whom he wrote (8.6.41):

'I have been meaning to write to you before to thank you for the trout you sent me; they were delicious, and were much enjoyed. Here in London we talk of nothing but bombs and food; we loot food in secret, and then meet to boast of our losses by what the papers politely call "enemy action". I have a bill of £700 to pay on my house; but Miss —— outboasts me, as she lost everything, books, manuscripts, clothes and cosmetics—her All, except, we must hope, her virginity, and a pot of marmalade. She is thinking of starting life in an entirely new line, and has asked me what line I advise her to take. I have several suggestions, but she says she is too old to be a streetwalker, too patriotic to become a spy; and having lost all her jewels, feels inadequately equipped to be a Mayfair Jezebel, as I suggested. In the meantime she goes about with a lorry so conspicuously inscribed, *Pity a Poor Bookless Woman*, and makes such hauls from all our libraries, that we begin to suspect that it is all a racket, and that she hasn't been bombed at all. We all toy with the idea of trying this stunt ourselves. However, if you and Bob wish to be kind to Miss —— you might send a book (or a trout) to the denuded lady at her new address.

'I too am going to change my life, for having lived for 75 years on the world, but unspotted from it, I have now after being nearly bombed from its kindly surface, emerged from under a shower of broken glass and plaster, as world-loving, as mundane as the most pushful social climber. All I want is titles and social glory, and I have just succeeded in having the title, His Excellency, bestowed on me by an aunt of the Prime Minister and the friend for 50 years of H.R.H. the Duke of Connaught.

'So tell Bob to put H.E. before my name if he has the honour of writing to me. Ladies must curtsey to me and men not dare to sit down in my presence; and I shall pinch their bottoms if they break these rules of etiquette.'

Etiquette was the seasonable joke. In addressing his envelopes to me, he carefully broke all those little rules whose obedience is looked upon by the correct as an essential test of birth and proper up-bringing. In June a letter arrived for me addressed to 'The Hon. Gathorne-Hardy', omitting any Christian name or initial ('The Horrible' had been a more robust variation which he once used at Hammond's suggestion). The name of my house was between inverted commas, for, as he said in a note on the back of the envelope, 'If you want to be really lower-middle, you ought to have notepaper with "The Mill House" on it printed within quotation marks.'

The occasion of this particular letter was my eventual answer to a challenge thrown out in a letter which Logan had written during March of this year.

'After having three of my songs sung on the wireless yesterday afternoon,' he had written (13.3.41), 'I had a look at my little book of verse. I like the translations from the Chinese, and there is a song on p. 23 which I rather like. But, dear me, it is all written in the dead language of 30 or 40 years ago, which your generation has got rid of, though the diction you have instead doesn't convey much to me. What Tennyson said of Browning, that he "lacked the glory of words" seems to apply to most younger poets.

'So just possibly there may be a return to the old stuff, and just conceivably someone may glance at my little book with a kindly eye. After all, I could write a sonnet, which none of you can do. I am therefore sending you a corrected copy of my little book—put it with my other MSS. for the dust of oblivion to fall softly on it.

'I can't find the Bridges letters, which is a pity, as we are peppered with bombs every night and I expect that all my books and MSS. will be destroyed.'

In a postscript he added 'You promised to copy out and send me Eliot's *Boston Evening Transcript*'—his favourite poem by Mr T. S. Eliot, excepting perhaps number four in the *Ash Wednesday* sequence. This latter poem he used to describe as meaningless but of incomparable beauty.

In answer, I think, to a repetition of his challenge, I wrote a sonnet, and, some three months later, as will be seen, I sent him a draft of it. I make no particular claim for its merit as poetry or that it was as finished in diction as it ought to have been; but I do claim that in matters of rhyming scheme, and of structure, both formal and emotional, it was perfectly correct; and I think it was no worse than many which Logan himself had written and published.

Other paragraphs of the following letter need elucidation. The second arose from some allusion—I have altogether forgotten now what it was—to that quite imaginary sex-life with which Logan so plentifully and playfully endowed me. The third involves a curious story.

Some friend of Logan's had discovered, during the course of alterations to their house, which had once belonged to an eighteenth-century jeweller, a concealed safe, locked-up and long ago forgotten, They invited him to be present when they were having it opened. 'Don't touch it!' he implored them. 'You can imagine all sorts of treasures in there. Whatever you find can never be as good as what you can imagine. Just think; if you leave it, you can always feel that you have the most exquisite possession.' He made this a test for the state of people's souls. When he asked me what I would have done, I had to admit that I would probably have opened that safe; but, I added, there was just so much of grace in my heart that I would have known I was doing wrong. William Plantagenet was a pseudonym which Logan had got me to use for some anonymous letters.

As to the last paragraph: once, during the period of the heavy raids, I was spending the night at Logan's, and, much as he had asked if I felt sea-sick on the Bay of Biscay, he asked me if I was frightened; I answered, quite truthfully, that I wasn't. But I jokingly suggested that he should make out a document so that, if we both got killed, whatever he intended for me should go to Kyrle. He professed to take this as indisputable evidence of terror.

'I like your sonnet,' he answered (23.6.41), 'which proves that you, as Dryden puts

> Dare with the mummies of the Muses play
> And make love to them in the Egyptian way.

But I fear that the Muses, though mummified, would remember having heard the adjective "proud" applied to the hawk more than once before; and their feet in their mummy dance would stumble a little at the succession of hyphened adjectives . . .

'I have been reading a most interesting article in the *Encyclopaedia Britannica* on *Paranoia*. Paranoia, as you no doubt know, [is] an incurable form of insanity which usually develops in middle age which you have now attained. It generally begins with persecution mania, with the belief that there is a conspiracy against one, or a hidden hand that prevents the recognition of one's literary or other merit; this is succeeded by the delusions of grandeur, and also by amatory paranoia, which takes two forms, one of love reciprocated by some person of eminence, but hindered by an enemy; or secondly (and to this I would call your attention) the hallucination that improper liberties have been taken with one's person. The subjects of such hallucinations are the most dangerous of paranoiacs and have "most frequently to be secluded in the interests of the social order". Seclusion is the only thing; recovery from this form of paranoia never occurs.

'I had a visit from George Plank yesterday, and found that he was, as I knew he must be, one of the Redeemed, who would never have, save at the threat of starvation, opened that safe at Richmond. Of such are the Kingdom of Heaven; George and I shall be there, and Henry James and Santayana; but not you, nor the English Rose, nor indeed any woman. W. Plantagenet perhaps? It will, I fear, be a by no means overcrowded Paradise, but none the worse for that.

'If you are going to your mother, do inquire if there is an hotel at Aldeburgh in which I could find refuge, if bombed out of Chelsea. But we have made a bomb-proof room, guaranteed safe even if the house is demolished, so when you appear, as I hope you will, on Tuesday, you need not shake and shiver and vomit with the terror, as you did last time.'

For a year and a half now, being free from my duties on three days out of nine I had, when he required me, been working with Logan, much as in the old days. A change was coming. On one important job only was I now destined to give him more than casual help. Never again was I to do regular work with him. For the next four years it would be impossible. During the last few months of his life, when I was free once again, he didn't want me.

In August of 1941 I became a member of the full-time first-aid service in Reading. I was told, when I joined up, that I must never, even when off duty, go outside the borough without permission, for we were always required, whenever the siren was heard, to report at the depot. As it happened, the heavy inland raids had ended; and I found in time that this restriction was not so stringently applied as I had expected. However the first letters I wrote to Logan from my lodgings in Reading were written on the assumption that many months might go by before we saw one another again.

In the early days of our friendship Logan had sometimes been abroad without me, and I from time to time without him. Except for these few occasions, hardly a fortnight had gone by from 1928 until the outbreak of war without our meeting one another. A different scheme was to rule the last period of our mutual life, and my narrative, accordingly, must undergo a small alteration of form and method.

I have mentioned in this book from time to time—too often, perhaps, it may seem—my own works. This was done with no desire of vaunting or of self-advertisement. 'Writers,' Logan had written, 'should split hairs together, and sit side by side, like friendly apes, to pick fleas from each other's fur.' (Eventually, in the last edition, he altered the last word, at my suggestion, to 'prose'.) 'Flea-picking', as he called it, was a chief pleasure in his life. He seemed to enjoy himself just as much going over my work, as he did when we went through and talked into order the more considerable products of his own pen. The submission of anything I might have attempted, for the castigation of his immaculate sensibility, was an important part of our relationship. To leave such things out would have involved a disfiguring deletion in the history of my friendship with him.

For the rest of his life Logan was to attempt no long-sustained writings. He produced from time to time essays, sketches and even one or two reviews; if, when I was able to visit him, he was at work on one of these, he would read it aloud to me, or let me read the typescript for myself, and I would pick out what fleas I could find.

My own works I would send to him—that is, if I didn't think them too long. Never, unless he pressed me to do so, did I give him any full-sized book to criticize; he would, I think, unless in one of his inter-lunaries, have cheerfully undertaken the job; but I always felt that to do so uninvited would be too much of an imposition.

On his encouragement I had tried from time to time to compose little aphorisms. In one of the first letters I wrote to him from Reading I sent him a specimen or two, together with a collection of brisk and improper phrases which I had picked up from my new friends, in particular from a mouthy old soldier, a proper humbug, but an exuberant and unfailing source of picturesque expressions. I suggested to Logan that he might come down to Reading for a short visit when I should be on night-duty, and thus free to be with him during the day. He himself, it will be seen, had been making a similar collection mainly from the crew who managed the balloon anchored in the open space of Burton Court.

'You are certainly,' he answered, 18.8.41, 'learning to speak with strange terms—I think low life is a more profitable region than the peaks of High Life to which I used to aspire. I do however get a little low life from my association with the soldiers and airmen across the road; they know all the terms you mention; and in some respects I think the vocabulary of the metropolis is richer than that of Reading. [The etymological reason he gives for this assertion cannot, unfortunately, be printed; the meaning of the expression quoted by him would, he suggested, be beyond the obscenest mind in Reading.] . . . "Tuffs" and "Whitehats" they probably know. If not, you can teach them. I should love to come to this fountain of impurity, and to see how you are getting on. But I am afraid I couldn't manage the railway journey—at any rate in my present state of health . . .

'I . . . hope you aren't too much bored at Reading, and find a little time for the Muses. I liked your aphorism very much, but should word it "If Tamerlane is dust, there is dust that *was* Tamerlane"—not *is*. I am busy with various jobs, but nothing of great interest.'

One day some of us had to carry a man, unconscious after a fit, to his home, and up to his bedroom. I noticed that his wife was moving agitatedly about with something in her hand; when we left this proved to be a little money which she gratefully wanted us to accept. It struck me that this incident was the plan if not the theme of a short story; all the story, and all her feelings were congealed into a single gesture, and a single member, one hand with two florins in it. I thought of attempting something in this form, and asked Logan for advice as to models. In the same letter I had to confess that I had been stumped by that metropolitan impropriety.

He began his answer with the details of the most magnificent of all misprints, and one which for a while took the sting out of those lighter errors which so vexatiously troubled him in his own books.

'Gilbert Murray's misprint,' he wrote (29.8.41), 'was "Aegospotamoi" for "Kynoskephalæ", in a book published by the Oxford Press, which went through three editions before it was noticed. I wonder if he ever forgave the person who pointed it out? I always bear a grudge against a person who points out a misprint in one of my books, though I try to be grateful, as I know I ought to be. But such things make a writer's path a stony one. However, I get two pounds of golden butter every week from an Irish admirer, which smooths and softens and oils my path.

'I was much amused by your innocent attempts to get at the meaning of xxxxxxxx. Really Reading must be a Sunday School! xxxxxxxxs are . . . imported from abroad and always confiscated by the police if they can find them . . . But of such things provincials know nothing!

'As to short stories, I can recommend no model. I used to swear by Guy de Maupassant, but can't read him now. Katherine Mansfield is a wash-out, and Chekof had no art. I found for myself a model in extreme brevity—in *Silvia Doria* in *Trivia*, in *The Vicar of Lynch* and *Sir*

Eustace Carr. But Henry James's "dreadful little question, 'How to do it'," everyone must solve for himself.

'I wish we could meet and talk of these things.'

I was to see him return to his old opinion about Maupassant; nor did he quarrel, when I repudiated his views on Chekof. Of Katherine Mansfield, whether it was the last aroma of some personal or social prejudice which led him to this harsh judgment is perhaps, to use his favourite quotation, a question too sad to insist on.

About this time there was printed a poem of mine which I called "*The Silver Swan*". He wrote (19.9.41):

'What a pretty silvery splash your swan makes in today's *New Statesman*! My congratulations—I wish you would do more of this sort of thing.

'I should like very much [to know] how you are getting on in Reading. Is low life becoming more interesting, or is it as hollow as the High Life I used to frequent, and does one's foot sink through a muddy crust as it does through a gilded one, into platitude and boredom?

'I am taking rather gloomy views now of life and the war and things in general, as my period of euphoria is over, and I am descending like Persephone into my winter melancholy quarters beneath the surface of the earth. But I am used to these interlunaries, and have infinite time for reading.

'Come to see me if you are ever in London; you will find me very dull, but you have seen me before in these eclipses. They are the mild misfortunes of a life which is otherwise happy enough, considering my years.

'I have been cheered lately by fan letters, especially a long one, received this morning, written in the Arctic seas by a most intelligent young seaman, who carries my books with him as he cruises in those remote regions. He likes my book on Milton as does a Paulist priest who writes from the shores of the Pacific Ocean. These are my boasts. What are yours?'

The gloom increased upon him, and about a month later he wrote (19.10.41), after mentioning his condition again, 'I hope . . . that your low life at Caversham remains amusing. I went into High Life (my predeliction) last week, but found it so flat and boring that I had to sneak away'—a consequence anyone might have predicted who had seen him in his glooms.

At the nadir of his melancholy, financial troubles began to worry him again; he warned me once more (28.11.41) that he might have to withdraw the allowance he had been paying me. 'However,' he ended the warning, 'I won't make any change until I come out of my tunnel again, and can look into my affairs. At present, I think I am living on my capital.' The implication of doubt was significant and characteristic. 'I hope you are getting on all right,' he continued, 'and have been given promotion, and that you have time as well for the lovely art of writing. As for me, I read and read, and the days pass not unpleasantly. But do send me a line.'

He didn't wait. In about three weeks from the date of that letter, he wrote to say that he had stopped my allowance.

I could not validly complain of this, however unfortunate the results might be; it was done with my permission. He had once said to me, 'You wouldn't want me to keep on paying you if it made me so poor that I had to leave this house, would you?' Naturally, as I told him, I had no desire to be the cause of such a catastrophe.

1942

These last six months of 1941 show a sort of patternless pattern to which, until 1944, our relationship was to accommodate itself. We corresponded with fair regularity between intermittent encounters. The sharper outlines have gone which used to define some excursion or the preparation of a particular book. Over all, colouring and staining, in huge vague shapes, were the shadows of Logan's moods.

I have told how he had just stopped the payment of my allowance. This blow he modified to the extent of allowing monthly to me what had formerly been paid weekly. Harder to pardon than the injuries we receive, are those we inflict. For this injury, however inevitable, and however reluctantly brought about, Logan never, I think, altogether forgave me. One day when he was talking about it, I told him not to worry—no more, at least, than I was worrying myself.

'I can't help worrying,' he said; he was obviously very unhappy about it. But there turned out to be more in this case than a sympathetic anxiety, or the vexation of his conscience. The payment and support of me had meant something potent to him; at its large curtailment there had been for him—and not, I must emphatically declare, for me—the weakening of a link, and some virtue had gone out of his attachment. After that the obligations he had imposed on himself became somehow less binding.

The saving of rather more than £200 a year didn't seem of any great comfort to him. He hinted—but once only—of cutting the small remnant; he did this in a melancholy letter with which, he said, he could only 'send you my regrets, and my unchanged affection'. An obsession of impending ruin troubled a greater part of his few remaining years, and he was always planning little means of salvation from penury. I began to empty the red box of various unpublished works which he thought might bring him money. Chief among these was the Shakespeare anthology—which would have brought him more than all the rest put together; for some reason or other he never used it.

At times he asked me to bring or send him papers which I hadn't got, and once for a selection of his own letters which had by then gone to America. The material I had brought to safety was in some confusion, and on one occasion I failed at first to find something he wanted. In every case, however, he used to accuse me of having lost the documents which were, he would say, indispensable to the remunerative work he was undertaking. There was always, delicately in the offing, the ugly sense that somewhere in his troubled spirit was a not quite materialized suspicion that I might be tricking him. In one instance these undeserved and unworthy ideas monstrously embodied themselves and he came, in the end, as near as he dared to charging me with theft.

Among other things with the papers, was a sealed up envelope in which he had put loose the Greek coins bought in my company some years before. To the original purchase he had added a few facsimiles. He decided that the sale of these coins might postpone his entry into the poor-house, but since they had cost him little more than £5, the postponement, I felt, wasn't likely to be more than a short one. However, at his request I got the coins, took them out of the envelope, and carefully packed them in cotton-wool. This, as it turned out, was a disastrous piece of carefulness. Had I left them to damage themselves in the closed envelope, one trouble might have been averted.

After he had got the coins, he expressed disappointment; he had thought there were more of them; why, I have never been able to guess, unless it was that I had bought for myself a few more and had often shown them to him. I wrote and told him what we had bought to-gether, and what he should have; my list tallied and he wrote (2.9.42): 'I thought I had had some more, but your memory is no doubt better than my decaying wits.'

Five months later he brought the subject up again:

'I thought I had more,' he wrote (5.2.43), 'but perhaps I hadn't. If there were more, and you have stolen them, it's all right. Like Charles Lamb, I don't very much care for good people.'

This—need I say it?—was a joke; but it was the joke which first brought the delusion of my robbery into his mind. As in Iceland, though far more slowly now, a joke was transforming itself into an hallucination.

His depression lasted well into the summer. I visited him from time to time, when my duties allowed it. I had started a new work, on which he gave me a good deal of advice. I had been speculating about the origins of art, and it occurred to me that our aesthetic, like our other activities, could be traced back to an animal origin, that they were, in fact, relics of the animal capacity for display. In July (20.7.42) he wrote giving me a list of books likely to be useful.

'I am glad,' he ended, 'that you keep your intellectual interests alive in these distressing times. Binyon has written some very fine poems, one of which on *The Burning of the Leaves* is his masterpiece. . . . I am still in my black-out, so I can't write much.'

In August he began to emerge and on the first of that month he sent me a postcard in answer to a letter 'Delighted to see you Friday after-noon—you will find me in my dotage—a condition pleasant enough for oneself, though boring to others.'

He passed into that dangerous state I have spoken of, intermediate between gloom and glory; he had lent me a copy of Binyon's poem, and almost immediately wrote a little angrily asking for its return. I had not known that this was his only copy. I tried, when I wrote returning the poem, to console him about his money worries, pointing out that such worries were a regular symptom of his cyclical depression. He didn't like this and revenged himself by sending back my letter with his answer (an act, as I have told, which he once stigmatized as un-pardonable), and he asked in a peevish tone, for the return of some books he had just lent me; on my letter he had pencilled 'borrowed books'. His answer is curious evidence for the mixed condition of his spirit.

'Thanks for returning Binyon's poem,' he wrote 26.8.42. 'The demand for it had been so urgent that I had been left without a copy and was unable to supply demands. Binyon has promised it to Cyril [Connolly] for the *Observer*, of which Cyril is now the very successful literary editor. . . . I saw Max at the dismal celebration of his 71st birthday last Monday—a most horrible performance in his dishonour.'

This letter was a long one, trying to detail his impoverished circumstances; after two and a half pages of financial outcries he continued:

'Don't think I am unduly depressed about money—I have just sold another American mortgage, and the proceeds will keep me going for a few months yet; and who knows what then will happen? We are all in the same boat, which now seems to be leaking badly. . . . It's a great thing to be old and to have no children, and to be fated to leave this disastrous planet soon.

'By the way, I came on your *Swan* poem lately, and find it *lovely*. You ought to write this sort of thing more often.'

In a postscript, he added:

'You will be glad to read in the paper I enclose that the blur or blot on the wings of the Swan of Avon has been finally washed off by learned scrubbery, and a Glasgow engineer has proved it to have been a pen! You will share my delight in this great discovery.'

The paper he referred to was the prospectus for a book of curious Shakespearean theory. This undertook to prove that the works of Shakespeare, together with Spenser's *Faerie Queene*, his *Amoretti* and Marlowe's *Hero and Leander*, had all been written by the daughter of an Elizabethan merchant-adventurer named Captain Antony Jenkinson; being born unluckily out of wedlock, she took her mother's name, and was called Anne Whateley. Owing to this discovery, declared the prospectus, 'the taint of perversion, so odious to all lovers of Shakespeare, has been dissipated'. These lines were appreciatively underlined by Logan, who had filled up the order form for 12 copies, over my name.

A postcard followed (31.8.42):

'Can you put me wise about Paul Sudley, and give me the low-down on him? My article on Max has brought a few pilgrims to my alabaster tower among others the author of *William*, who was most astonished to hear that it was remembered. He hasn't read it since it was published

and doesn't possess a copy. You couldn't lend me one I suppose? . . .
'Here is a good Sussex dialect word for you, "Coloury"—a coloury
cow, etc. Price 1d.'

Financial worries we most of us had during the war; but Logan's
were very largely obsessional. He was never, and had never been during
his life, within measurable distance of anything approaching poverty,
or even of having to leave his home. I was pretty sure of this, but the
thought that he might really find himself in need was not a pleasant
one. During the early part of the war I had saved some money, and I
wrote to say that if at any time a hundred pounds would be of real service to him, I would gladly lend it him for an indefinite period. The
offer was an honest one; though I dare say there was an element in it
of turning the other cheek, 'the dirtiest trick', as Logan used to say,
'which Our Saviour ever invented'.

'Thanks for your letter,' he answered, 'and most kind offer. I may
avail myself of it some day, when the wolf is actually at the door. But
he only howls faintly in the distance just now, as I have sold an American mortgage, which was derelict, and brought me in no money. . . . I
sent your Swan to Ethel Sands at Fyfield—she liked it very much (her
taste is impeccable) and took it to read to your aunt and uncle, who are
her nearest neighbours. Can you guess the word they shouted at her —it
was TOSH!! So put that in your pipe and smoke it. . . .
'Cyril has maliciously turned a spot of limelight on me, and the door-
steps of my alabaster tower are beset by readers of my article on Max
in the Observer. There seems to [be a] writer in my belly yet; but I was
inspired by the subject. Max and Binyon are our createst contemporaries, but Max knows his limitations which Binyon doesn't. The Leaves
was an inspiration; the other poems he has just written lack that fire—
as, if I may say so, do your other verses you send me, though they have
merits.'

A lecture on the vice of book-borrowing took up parts of this letter
in which, with an inconsistency which he himself admitted, he asked
for the loan of my copy of William, by my old friend Lord Sudley.
Logan knew of three copies only, Sir Max Beerbohm's, Mr George
Plank's, and my own. When I brought it up, I found that he had Mr
Plank's.

Sometime during 1942 Logan enclosed in a letter to me what pur-
ported to be a prospectus of Smith's Temperance Hotel—his own house
in fact. He had always welcomed friends who wanted a bed when they

came to London; and now, it appeared, he was proposing to make a small charge. I give some extracts from the prospectus:

'Owing to loss of income Mr L. P. Smith has made his refined home into a lodging-house or hotel (for gents only). He has a comfortable room, centrally heated, slightly bombed, but watertight, with a V-spring bed, which in former days was occupied now and then by non-paying guests, such as Robert Bridges, Sir Walter Raleigh, R. C. Trevelyan, and others. They said they found decent accommodation in it. . . . A latchkey is provided; if the P.G. finds it difficult to manipulate, the Home Guards, who are always on duty, will assist him.'

Among four rules, these two were peculiar:

'2. P.G.s may return at any time of the night or morning, but must not yell on the stairs or dance horn-pipes in their rooms after one o'clock a.m.

3. Should they not like to spend the nights alone, any companions they may bring home for the night must be out of the house by eight o'clock in the morning.'

Though I stayed there not infrequently for single nights, I never found that I was expected to pay for accommodation.

1943

1943 was, I think, the happiest year for us in this last epoch of our friendship—the epoch which succeeded his attack of madness in Iceland, in 1938.

In January (17.1.43) he sent me a letter—half-worried and half-peevish—asking for some papers from which he hoped to make money. He was planning, he said, a book, to be called *Saved from the Salvage*, and which was to be a miscellany of letters he had received and small unpublished essays of his own. He had asked me to send the red box, and the method I suggested for transporting it did not satisfy him. It was characteristic that, to a querulous letter, he added this postscript:

'I'm haunted by an aphorism of yours, "If Tamerlane is dust, there is dust which was Tamerlane." What will you sell this for? Or will you change it for this of my own: "Old age brings golden gifts—only one drawback, the poverty of its improper dreams"?'

I had time, now and then, to give him help over this projected volume; however, the first piece of 'work' we did was with other material. Logan decided to go in for a *New Statesman* competition—a short collection of aphorisms on the English Character. For this he borrowed two of my own, and adapted them to the subject. He also took what he believed to be an original remark of Hammond's, 'Don't do what I do; you do what I tell you.' Living in a closed universe, he didn't know that this, in certain classes, is a popular and almost proverbial expression; he was particularly struck by the idiomatic emphasis of the initial 'you' in the second part of it.

When the result was announced—he had won a prize—he wrote to me (5.2.43):

'It was certainly pleasant working with you again, as of old; and if you have seen the *New Statesman* this week, you will notice that our labours were profitable. They print two or three of your sayings, and one of Hammond's, and you both must have a rake-off on the prize-money.

'I have sent you an interesting, crude, powerful new novel—the Cambridge School has produced it, and though I don't love the Cambridge School, I read the book ... with interest. I should like to know what you think of it. It is written in Pansy, a Cambridge impure dialectical variety of Oxfordian, Paterian pure Pansy, but Pansy, like Romany and Lesbian, has different forms, but they are all at bottom the same.'

It was in this letter that he made the black-omened, jocular suggestion of my having, perhaps, stolen some of his coins.

During February, four bombs were dropped on Reading one afternoon. One of these fell into the middle of a crowded restaurant, killing about sixty people, many of whose bodies were blown to pieces. I found myself involved in the grisly duty of digging out their bodies and the fragments of them. In one case I helped in the recovery of a body, no more of which had been left than the trunk with a single arm joined on to it. As I helped to load this on to the mortuary van it occurred to me that here was something less horrible than bodies that had been less deformed; it appeared so dead, that it seemed as if there had never been any life in it at all. It was impossible to impute, with melancholy and commiseration, a breathing human life to this cold and heavy mass.

With such scenes, and their aftermath, I was taken up for a fortnight or three weeks; after bodies, and fragments of bodies had been cleared away, there was a great deal of débris and rubble to be shifted.

In the middle of these preoccupations Logan sent me a long letter about his projects; an essay which he called *Donna Violante* was just being published in *Horizon*, with a facsimile of a drawing by Mrs Morrell, and of some beautiful calligraphy.

'Cyril,' he wrote (28.2.43), 'says he wants to print more of my Salvage in later numbers—of course he would be glad to reproduce some of the handwriting of Bridges and Virginia [Woolf.] What a beautiful thing a letter from Binyon is! It makes the world seem a better place. He has given me a list of the verses of mine he thinks worth preserving —I hope you will do the same, as you promised.'

Almost as Logan was writing this Laurence Binyon had died unexpectedly. Logan contributed a short notice to *The Times*, of which he sent me a cutting.

'I am sending you,' he wrote (17.3.43), 'a copy of my tribute to Binyon (with several misprints as usual) in yesterday's *Times*. No one sends proofs any longer, though Cyril has done so for my story in this month's *Horizon*, which will be out in a few days.
'. . . The last sentence [in the obituary] is stolen of course (as usual) from you. So the debt mounts up.'

For once, in my opinion, Logan had degraded a thought of mine by borrowing it. I had remarked that a visit to the Binyons—a sanctuary of unworldly achievement, of kindliness, and beauty, and integrity—always left me with the realization that man, after all, could be a fine and friendly and noble animal, a thought very consoling in modern times. Logan had transmuted this to the true though commonplace statement that the contemplation of Binyon's life 'made England, made indeed the whole world, seem a better place to live in'.

He ended this letter with a pseudo-botanical query, in connection with a story which he was polishing up; 'Can you suggest better names for my two Thibetan shrubs, *Viburnum Farreri Fragrans*, and *Reginalda Obstans*. The latter has large blue flowers (gentian blue). How about *Reginalda Cerulea Obstans?*'

I happen to know about the principles of botanical nomenclature, and both by letter, and by word of mouth, I explained these to him, carefully, and, I flatter myself, lucidly: I told him how the generic and the specific names are applied, so that as a rule a flower has only a double name; I also expounded the rules which govern the use, in these circumstances, of capital initials.

George Moore once burst rudely out at Logan, so the latter informed me, with the complaint that he ruined conversation by repeated and meaningless interjections of 'Yes'. I never found this myself; but Logan had a 'Yes' which could bring a sense of frustration. He would ask a serious question and then as it were pull down the blind and put up the shutters. A 'Yes' would come out; but that particular affirmative, although it had acquired by long use the sound and expression of a meaningful response, denoted, in fact, a mind momentarily blank. Such a blank met all my attempts at explanation of this botanical problem. I suggested *Orbis tecta* ('roof of the world'), as a fanciful and unlikely, but not impossible specific name. Logan, inverting it somewhat unclassically to *Tecta Orbis*, employed it as an infinitely improbable generic name.

But he was not a story-writer, and I have never looked on this tale, 'Ivanhoe', as anything but one of his failures, in which, with the whole of it, such small pedantic slips may be cheerfully lost and forgotten.

The infinitely dead air-raid casualty I have mentioned, turned itself into the occasion for a poem. I sent a draft of this to Logan who curiously, as I found out after his death, copied it out at the foot of one of the essays which he never lived to publish.

His comical and not altogether charitable allusions in the following letter to aspects of what he called my aristocratic origin got mixed with his feelings towards other members of that class for which he held a sort of admiring romantic contempt. Recalling grand people who have written vapid memoirs, and others with talents which they have wasted, giving up precious time to smart visits and gay trivialities, he composed the aphorism 'All aristocrats are amateurs'. Once a prejudice had been crystallized into words, it became a fixed part of his outlook; for the rest of his life he endowed me with an innate incapacity for serious work. This, however, did not impede his most serious appraisement of anything I submitted to him; on such occasions he altogether forgot the fantasticated splendours of my origin.

This onslaught was particularly strange, in that Logan had often suggested as an interesting subject for study the aristocratic authors of England. He hadn't got in mind an undiscriminating peerage of letters, like Horace Walpole's *Catalogue of the Royal and Noble Authors of England*; he was thinking rather of such fine or splendid writers as Sir

Philip Sidney and his friend Lord Brooke, Rochester, Halifax, Shaftesbury, and Bolingbroke, Chesterfield and Horace Walpole, and Byron.
From modern times he would have added Sir Osbert Sitwell (who
incidentally appealed to his predeliction for the baronetcy); after the
appearance, in 1929 of *The Man Who Lost Himself*, he was continually
saying, 'I back Osbert as a great prose-writer.'

As to his loss of talents through age—he never, I think, believed in
this. When he mentioned the subject he would bring up the old story
of Gil Blas and the archbishop. I, of course, was supposed to be in the
position of Gil. (Towards the end, when I was undergoing a not altogether dissimilar experience, I once, as a melancholy joke, signed myself in a letter 'Bob Blas, brother to Gil'. This produced no response.)
To console him, I would bring to his memory artists of all kinds whose
talents had improved with age—the old Titian, Verdi producing Fal-
staff in his eighties, and Bridges *The Testament of Beauty*. Sub observations pleased him; but the joy of consolation was, I think, no greater
than his fear.

'I ought to have written to you before,' he wrote (4.4.43), 'to thank
you for your casualty poem, which I think a success and like a great deal.
I have shown it to Cyril, who liked it, but didn't jump at it for *Horizon*,
as he should have done. . . . Besides my *Donna Violante* (which I myself
think will do), I liked in the current number Philip Toynbee's funeral,
and the letter he prints from that American manufacturer of barbed
wire for the great concentration camp—vast beyond imagination—in
which America will imprison the "Spirit of Man". That is the ultimate
fate of this planet—to become an immense sanitary concentration
camp, wisely regulated and run by hygienic Americans—a great
Sahara of dreary dust like the Moon—that awful unheeded warning
and forecast of our ultimate fate.

'But to return to your poem . . . [and he goes on to say how he had
put it, with the *Swan*, under an American editor's nose 'to sniff at'].

'. . . I of course didn't and couldn't give them permission to print it.
But in this world it is worth while to give a squint now and then at the
Main Chance, as they call it; even Bridges and Binyon gave a dignified
glance now and then in that direction, though they didn't spend their
lives, of course, with eyeballs fixed on that object of attention, whatever it is in its idiomatic origin.

'Better of course to gaze on the Star of Perfection; and here I think
your eye wanders now and then. Take off the coroneted ring from your
finger when you take up your pen, and grasp the file, and forget for a

few moments (if you can) what Henry James calls the "luckless title" which is tied to your tail. I often feel in your work that the exquisite word or epithet has escaped the gaze of your Dundreary eye-glass. You seem satisfied with a word that will "do" instead of spending a sleepless night, like Flaubert, in an agonized search for the epithet which will enrich and magically enhance your meaning. Thus for instance in your "Casualty poem".[1] I hesitate at "dull" though it may be right. "Dusty" bed is wrong, I am sure, and I suggest for the last two lines—

> 'No, not in the thought that quite soon I might be
> So cold so crushed so utterly dead as he.'

['Utterly' he had underlined, writing a question mark and 'so dead' above it.] 'Quite soon' has a spark of idiomatic idiom in it that makes it more alive than 'some day'.

'But then, as you have often said, I am no poet.

'Trevor-Roper tells me that I have reached that slope on the decline of my years when I ought to lay down the pen that has grown feeble in my palsied fist. I wrote *Donna Violante* to confound him. Don't you think I have proved my point? Anyhow Cyril grabbed with avidity and carried off with him yesterday another story I have recently written and says he will publish it in the May *Horizon*. For the next number he has secured Binyon's beautiful Swan-song which I think I showed you.

'I miss Binyon more and more. His last stay in this Temperance Hotel was a perfect occasion. You must come to the hotel soon. Towards the end of the month R. W. Chapman has engaged a room, and the Passionate Pilgrim [Mr Stuart Preston] has also promised to come.

---

[1] So typical and interesting an example of Logan's castigation is incomprehensible without the original poem; perhaps, therefore, I may be acquitted of egotism for printing here, in the modesty of a footnote, the verses requisite for understanding his letter:

> Headless, dislimbed, and cold, and crushed, and grey,
> Under the crumpled wall and roof he lay
> So dead, we thought, 'Can such flesh ever have lived at all?'
> So grey that flesh, so heavy, so dispirited
> That even in its terrible and dusty bed
> It lay less terribly than drear and dull,
> And stirred no dread,
> No, not in the thought that we ourselves might be
> Some day so cold, so crushed, so dead, so utterly dead as he.

Were I printing these verses for their own sake I should, following Logan's advice, delete 'and dusty' from the fifth line, and, in the last substitute 'quite soon' for 'some day'. 'Dull' in the sixth line and 'utterly' in the last, I eventually accepted. 'Dusty' I gave up with some reluctance, for the body did in fact lie amid bricks and rubble and timber in a bed of the finest driest dust, and it seemed pleasant to echo so truthfully a Shakespearean epithet. When I put this to Logan he merely answered as if inattentively, 'People *always* fight for their fleas.' He was right, of course; in a case like this the material facts are of no importance.

The fish still floats in these waters—it turns the nose scornfully from all the worms and coarse flies cast before it.'

I sent him a revised version of the poem, and five days later he wrote (9.4.43):

'You have certainly improved your poem and I agree that "utterly" is needed. Try putting your ring and your monocle where you suggested that my austere mentor should put his suggestion. . . .

'The muse has visited me again, and I have written a quatrain to the Thrush—

'O fret not after knowledge—I have none,
And yet my song comes native with the warmth,
O fret not after knowledge—I have none
And yet the evening listens.'

'—— says these lines turn the stomach. Other lines of mine make him furious

'Wherein lies happiness? In that which beckons
Our ready minds to fellowship divine,
A fellowship with essence—'

(You will hate them too!) . . .

'Which do you think the best of Henry James's novels? A great boom is beginning, Cyril and Raymond blowing trumpets. Shall I join them, or hold aloof?'

This was the occasion which I anticipated, giving my response, when I described, how eight years earlier, in Teneriffe, reading Keats, I came upon, and recalled to him, those lines about the thrush. The other lines are, of course, from *Endymion* (Book I, 1, 778–780).

In the endless preparation for his book he decided to use some letters of his own; from time to time, when he was particularly pleased with a letter he had written, he would make a copy of it. A bundle of these selected letters he had sent to the Library of Congress. This he denied, and failing to discover them in the red box—which he now always referred to as the box of Pandora—he began to insinuate that I had lost or made away with them. He claimed to have collateral grounds for this accusation.

When bombs first began to be dropped about in the country, I collected all my irreplaceable and most treasured possessions into a single room so that they could be easily rescued. Buried among the heap of these things was a box containing the letters of Robert Bridges which Logan had given to me. He asked for these letters, and, having entirely forgotten what I had done with them, I thought at first that he had them. It was then, and for the only time, that, in all Logan's worries about his papers, I had to admit myself in the wrong.

His intermittent work on *Saved from the Salvage*, was diverted for a short time into the region of his older researches. He had found an old note which suggested an earlier date than he had yet known for the use of the word 'romantick'; it was on the title-page of an obscure allegorical romance of the seventeenth century, *Herba Parietis or The Wall Flower*, by Thomas Bayley. The first edition was published in 1651. He asked me to verify this in the British Museum. I did so; but it happened that I already possessed a slightly later edition of the same book, an edition printed in 1679. I sent him this, as a present, with a letter saying that since it was spiritually already his rather than mine, he had better have the complete ownership of it.

The next time I saw him we had a wrangle, quite amicably so far as I can recall, in which, however, I protested rather vigorously against his insinuations about my treatment of his papers.

To make myself quite clear—for he was apt to be inattentive when he might have been putting himself in the wrong—I afterwards put down in a letter the situation of the various papers he had been worrying himself about. In the same letter I sent him a few specimens from a collection of aphorisms which I had been composing.

The Librarian of Congress, if Logan wrote to him, must have confirmed the presence in his library of the letters alluded to. If he did so, Logan never mentioned it to me; nor alas, did he bottle up suspicion and allegations.

He answered (3.5.43):

'The way you go on about that box of Pandora seems curious to me, and tends to make me believe in my outrageous accusations. You must admit that there was a certain hocus-pocus about the Robert Bridges letters—however, I have written to the Librarian of Congress, and if, as you allege, I did send him that packet of chosen letters, I will withdraw my accusation, and bottle up all suspicions and insinuations. Your gift of the "Wall Flower" certainly is evidence of an exquisite sense of the true principles of private possession and ownership. I have stolen phrases and even ideas from you, but as I have put them to the best uses, I have not felt unduly guilty. If we could find a Christ—but where can we find one?—we might hang on either side of him as unrepentant thieves.

'I look forward to your aphorisms and like the foretaste of them that you give me.

'I'm so bedevilled and bejinned by the brooding apparition I have evoked that I can think and write of nothing but Henry James.'

He had got back on to the adverbs in Henry James.

Encouraged by his observation I sent him my aphorisms typed out. He answered (15.6.43):

'I am returning your aphorisms, which I read with much interest. You certainly have the gift of aphoristic thought, and not infrequently of sharp and pointed expression. I have marked // those I thought successes; others I have amused myself recasting. My general feeling will be found in these pencil notes; or read fragment XXV in Leopardi's poems—

Musa, la lima ov'e? Disse la Dea:
La lima è consumata; or faciam senza.

'But you do use the file, but not for the final polish. You know how I preach this, but to vain ears, aristocratic or other. Many of your aphorisms need to be shortened and sharpened, and every bit of superfluity filed away. The bittersweet agony of that exquisite and desperate occupation is a draught of oxymel of which your generation inadequately taste. It has been the delight and misery of my life; but, as the Muse said to Leopardi, when he asked whether the file oughtn't to be sharpened, "hassi a refar, ma il tempo manca". "Oh yes, she said, but we've no time to bother." That's the answer I always get when aspirants to literary success come to see me or send me their MSS. for criticism.

'If I were you I would resift and repolish these aphorisms, more than once, for they are certainly worth it. I don't think you would be doing [yourself] much credit to print a good number as they stand.

'My publisher likes my Salvage book, and is eager to print it as soon as possible. If you could come up for a day next week, you could help me greatly.'

When I read over this letter before copying it out, I became stirred by that crazy vanity which can possess the humblest and most reasonable of authors: Logan, I felt, had been captious. And then I looked at the typescript which he had gone over and corrected so carefully. A nobler feeling took hold of me. Logan's criticisms had been all of them exquisitely correct. I will allow myself two illustrations.

'Practise a pretended anger'; I had written, 'it's far pleasanter than losing your temper, and, if ever the need arises, just as effective.'

Logan had first bracketed off 'if ever the need arises', and then, underneath, re-written the whole thing, 'Pretended anger is pleasanter than real fury, and just as effective.'

Another, which he had marked with approval, was 'Modern man is an atheist, harried by ghosts'. The first half he altered into 'We moderns are atheists', etc. The introduction of a personal pronoun brings new life into the sentence.

At intervals with unavoidable interruptions I went up and helped him with *Saved from the Salvage*; but our progression seemed to be circular, and the work never any nearer towards completion. At his request I made out a tentative arrangement of the contents, which he accepted; but he never got the book ready for publication. I have always been glad of this; some of the contents were not of a quality to satisfy one; he was including trifles which were amusing enough as private jokes, but not worthy of a place in one of his serious books.

And so the summer went by until, early in the autumn, I had a letter from him (28.9.43):

'I have been meaning to write to you, but have been, and am still, in one of my usual eclipses—the "interlunar caves"—into which I periodically retire after a period of activity and work. You have seen me in these dull periods before—they are dull, but I am not to be pitied as I always eventually emerge.'

1944

I think I saw less of Logan during 1944 than in any other year during the whole of our friendship. His interlunary lasted well into the summer (he mentioned it in a postcard which I received in June).

As the time drew near for the invasion of the Continent, it was naturally anticipated that towns such as Portsmouth and Southampton would be very heavily bombed. In consequence large reinforcements of the Civil Defence were sent down to the south coast, and I spent May, June, and the first half of July in the little seaside village of Highcliffe, about four miles from Christchurch.

I have told how, on occasions when it seemed possible that my life might be in danger, I had written such a letter to Logan as would please him if I should happen to be killed. Each time I had been fooled—I don't mean of death but of any likelihood of it.

The south coast at a time of invasion—though we didn't know the date, we all knew it was coming—really did look like a dangerous assignment. As usual, I wrote appropriately to Logan. He answered (28.4.44), 'Thanks so much for your kind letter. Being still in my tunnel, I find it difficult to write and can only say that I fully reciprocate all you write. Let us hope for better days!'

As usual, I was fooled. For the month before D-Day, there was a certain amount of excitement. We saw convoys far out at sea fighting off air attacks; most nights sporadic aircraft came over, and gunfire and searchlights made the darkness spectacular. One German, indeed, unloaded all his bombs in a lump together between four and five hunded yards from us, but only two of them went off, and I was never in the slightest danger. In the six weeks after D-Day a serenity as of peacetime settled down on what our officers, with rather pathetic self-importance, kept on trying to call the front line.

During his period of gloom I had visited Logan from time to time. In fine weather he would spend the afternoon sitting, privileged, in the enclosure of Burton Court (the use of this open space was allowed to a number of local residents). 'If you come in the afternoon,' he would say, 'and the weather's fine, you'll find me on my bench of desolation.'

These afternoons became an almost adventurous part of his life. He would sit down and get into conversation with strangers—soldiers, neighbours, all sorts of people.

Logan could not be called a humanist as that term is defined in the exquisite phrasing of Walter Pater in his essay on Pico della Mirandola: 'the essence of humanism is that one belief that nothing which has ever interested living men and women can wholly lose its vitality—no language they have spoken, no oracle by which they have hushed their voices, no dream which has once been entertained by actual human minds, nothing about which they have ever been passionate or expended time and zeal'.

Their language fascinated him all right: but their dreams and passions and oracles, into these he could rarely insinuate his spirit. He liked odd facts, and was delighted when, for instance, on one of his sunlit afternoons, he encountered a man who worked in the sewers of London. But it was only the narratable facts which he liked, the phrases and anecdotes which he could recognize from his reading as the typical substance of a good story: the man's heart—if I may use that word—was nothing to him. The inner feelings of other people were for him a dead world; and naturally enough, when his own fiercer emotions were a forbidden and fearful territory.

The oddities he encountered were often not very odd. 'Something extraordinary,' he said to me once when I was going with him into that timbered square, 'always happens to me whenever I go in here.' His evidence for this was that he had happened to sit down beside a man who was reading Proust. I felt I had capped his phenomenal experience when I told him that I had lately seen a man reading Lucretius on the top of a bus. On that particular occasion, however, his assertion was justified. We got into conversation with a man with a dog. After some anecdotes about his younger days he went on to inform us that he was the friend of a man well known to the public (his name and profession, since he is still alive, I must not reveal). We both happened to be slightly acquainted with the gentleman concerned, and were convinced of the man's story by the sight of a letter on which we recognized the handwriting. And then we found ourselves in the middle of a story—a chronicle of horrors and squalor, of drink and drugs and seduction, and entanglements into marriage—a tale whose exaggerated improbability would altogether have ruled it out as—to borrow a useful Spanish word—a novelable subject. Truth isn't only stranger than fiction: it's often less probable as well.

Burton Court might certainly be held to have had an odd effect on Logan. Once, when I came up to his room he said, 'I'm going to get myself into the most dreadful trouble from these raging, implacable dog-lovers.' It turned out that he was composing a letter to the necessary official asking that dogs might not be allowed into Burton Court. His reason was that children were liable to fall over and dirty themselves in the muck deposited by dogs. I couldn't help pointing out to him pleasantly the humbug of this, since he was accustomed to proclaiming himself a child-hater. ('Once,' he used to tell me, 'I went to luncheon with a friend who told her children that a child-hater was coming to the house. When I arrived I saw faces peering at me out of one of the upper windows. It was the children. They thought I must be some kind of ogre, and they wanted to see what I looked like.') He evaded this by declaring passionately that dogs were, in his opinion, the filthiest behaved of all animals. 'Oh, I shall get into trouble!' he kept saying hopefully, 'these dog-lovers will want to tear me limb from limb.'

To his letter, which he did send, he received a polite but, to him, unsatisfactory response. After his death, I was somewhat surprised to read in his mother's letters that in a household which already included two monkeys, he had, as a boy, been the loving master of a St Bernard which smelt and had fleas; and that in addition, from a trip to the West, he had tried to bring back, apart from some stuffed birds, three prairie dogs.

But that happened before 1944, and when Logan was not in one of his interlunaries. In the year I am writing of he would sit quietly on a bench, not trying to make conversation with strangers. In such periods, he was not merely quiet or unhappy; he was a different person. A stranger who had seen him only during a cyclical depression, would not have taken him for the same man when the height of euphoria was upon him.

I, as intimate as any of all his intimate friends, was received then with a quiet sort of old-fashioned politeness. He would, with an air of formal good manners, ask me what I was doing, and then, with a conventional but seemingly genuine interest, put a few questions; the rules of intercourse, he might have been saying to himself, demand such queries; in fact he behaved exactly like a quiet well-behaved fellow-guest to a stranger at a correct, dull, dinner-party.

In one respect only did he not conform with the practices of etiquette. I would watch carefully the sad, heavy droop of his eyelids, and, when he seemed to be tiring, I would get up and go. But often enough he forestalled me. 'Bob!' he would say, rather hurriedly, 'I'm afraid I must ask you to go! I'm getting tired. You've seen me in this state before. Come again when you're in London.' He hardly seemed to enjoy one's company at all. And yet he was pleased, I know, to see me; or rather it would be truer perhaps to say he was pleased that I came to see him. At the nadir of his interlunary he could scarcely put up with so much as fifteen minutes' conversation.

In all the decrepitude of his glooms he had unrestricted energy for reading. (During the last interlunary of all, he read straight ahead through a large part of the Dictionary of National Biography.) When I visited him in these periods he would almost always have a book open on his lap, and he would only look up when I was close beside him, and would be reading again before I had left the room. On these occasions he accomplished the most prodigious tasks; as I have mentioned, he read through all Hazlitt during an early spell of gloom, and when I knew him, he read as if it were a single work, the whole of Carlyle, including his correspondence. Towards the end of his life it was usually historical books. He was gestating a companion to his essay on Shakespeare; it was to be called *On Reading History*. Of this work, alas, nothing seems to have been accomplished.

1944

While I was on the south coast I was finishing off—in odd moments —a work which interested Logan. I had made a book out of my theory about art. When it was finished I found myself dissatisfied, not only with chunks and details of the work, but with my finished presentaton of the theory. Accordingly I set about re-writing it on a smaller scale. The result—in the form of a letter to a painter—was published in a periodical in October of that year.

With the exception perhaps of three or four poems, Logan was better pleased with this than with anything else I had written. Since I have printed strong criticisms of my work, I may perhaps, without impropriety, quote some of Logan's praise. In October, he emerged propitiously from his gloom to read my work in print. 'Everybody writes prose for the eye nowadays,' he said, 'and it's quite dead. Except you. Yours is written for the ear.'

A part of my hypothesis which particularly appealed to him was the suggestion, supported by medical opinion, that speech and gesture are, as physiological activities, closely allied; they are, indeed, controlled by corresponding lobes on either side of the brain. This fact was an important part of my hypothesis; and in developing it, I had borrowed a theory of Logan's. He had suggested that our national reticence of gesture is connected with those vigorous idioms of ours which are founded on images of bodily motion, these idioms being, he believed, a direct substitute for gesture.

He accepted my theory, and his interest in that particular aspect of it undoubtedly affected his attitude towards the writing of prose. (An aphorism of mine which he had marked with approval was 'Poetry is a song; prose is gesture'.)

On October 10th he sent me a postcard:

'Constable wants to reprint *Trivia* and ask for my revisions—Could you come up for the day as soon as convenient to help me amend the Sacred Text . . . If you have a copy do see if you can suggest amendments.'

An unsettled problem of English usage is the inflexion of verbs governed by collective nouns. It is said that Robert Bridges once compromised by writing some such sentence as 'The University Press in their wisdom has decided . . .' Logan, it will be seen, in the first sentence of his postcard, made, perhaps unintentionally, a similar compromise.

This was the last big work that I helped him with. He had become, through his revived study of Henry James, fascinated with adverbs, and the main thing he now did with *Trivia* was to interlard it with these exciting parts of speech. It was enthralling work and I soon began to share his intoxication; he was delighted when he was able to use 'abracadabracally'—'abracadabracally inscribed in letters of menace on my bath-room floor'.

Getting carried away, I tried to persuade him to use 'antidisestablishmentarianly'.

'But how could you use it?' he asked, doubtful but not uneager.

'A high-church bishop antidisestablishmentarianly perambulating his diocese,' was all I could think of. No possible niche could be found in *Trivia;* otherwise I really believe he would have put in my monstrous invention.

Not only had he discovered the cabalistic potency of adverbs; he had also conceived a great esteem for colloquial language.

'I'm beginning to believe,' he said to me, 'that one shouldn't use any words or constructions in writing that one wouldn't use in speaking.'

This I thought was going rather too far; it precluded the rich revival of antique words, the coining of new words, and the proper introduction of neologisms—three activities he had been enthusiastically preaching up for many a year. But I was ready enough to acknowledge the value of a principle which I had accepted for my own guidance. After the introduction of potent adverbs, the main work he did on *Trivia* now was the colloquializing of passages which had seemed to read too formally.

I have said, some way back, that I found it hard to tell in a finished work how many suggestions of mine Logan had made use of. In this particular case I am able to call in the precise science of statistics. I now possess the copy of *All Trivia* which he lent me to mark down the fleas I had found, and my suggestions for changes.

I read this through, as usual in such cases, captiously, noting anything at all which might possibly be susceptible of improvement. I made about a hundred and fifty marks and notes; of my proposed alterations he used a hundred and eight, and in sixteen cases he thought out for himself a change in the questionable passage.

There was one word the use of which worried him. 'Lytton,' he said, 'used to criticize me for using "around". He said it was an Americanism.'

'Well, why not?' I replied. 'After all, you *are* an American. Why get rid of every drop of your native blood? Besides,' I added—it was a matter I had already thought about—'it seems to me that there's a use for it, as distinguished from "round". "Around" can be used for position, and "round" for direction. You might say that you went *round* the house which was *around* the corner.'

'I think there's something in what you say,' he acknowledged; but a little doubtfully, for, in the case we were discussing, he accepted the posthumous criticism of Lytton Strachey, and 'around' became 'round'.

It was fair, indeed, that he should accept some of Strachey's strictures, since, for that writer, Logan had great admiration, and in particular for his critical writings; and yet it was not quite reasonable, for Logan would say hard things about the style of them. On this occasion he happened to recall a fine but far from perfect passage in Strachey's *Landmarks in French Literature*, a passage describing the Versailles of Louis XIV. He looked it up, and, as he read, his admiration wilted a little, 'What intolerable clichés,' he said, 'let's re-write the passage.' And, interrupting work, we started together removing the objectionable, worn-out expressions; in a few minutes, he decided that the task was too large a one, and gave it up.

This work with him was altogether delightful; a halcyon had appeared as though from the untarnished and irreproachable past. His little crazed irritabilities seemed to heal in the intensity of his application. He thought over and talked over every one of my suggestions. Only in the case of the longer pieces, the little stories, did he feel there was less necessity for minute correction. He showed himself properly grateful for the help I had so much enjoyed giving him.

One morning, when we were at work on *Trivia*, the house was rattled and shaken by a crash which was followed by a long reverberating echoing as of thunder.

'That's one of these rockets,' said Logan, imperturbably and without looking up. He was taking the V2's more calmly than he did the V1's.

It is a matter of history that during the late summer and early autumn of 1944 London was assaulted with flying bombs. The height of this attack came when Logan was in his deepest gloom, and before the revision of *Trivia*. He had come triumphantly, I might almost say uproariously, through the blitz; but the flying bombs distressed and frightened him. This, I think, was largely due to their coincidence with his interlunary.

One fell close to Lower Sloane Street, farther off than his parachute mine, but with much the same effect. Once again his windows were smashed, his roof partially stripped, and his front door blown in. Repairs took longer, and he had to pass the winter with opaque fillings in many of his windows.

I saw a good deal of him during the winter of early 1945, when a curious chapter in my life was opened.

With the almost complete cessation of piloted raids, and greater control of flying bombs, the Civil Defence services were being cut down. I found myself looking for a job. I had made a number of very good friends, and I was anxious, if it was possible, to end the war in their company. Two of my particular friends were plasterers. With one of them I volunteered for Civil Defence work in liberated territory; since he was highly skilled, and I had the qualification—curiously rare in the circumstances—of speaking French, there was, of course, no response to this.

The labour exchange officials were completely flummoxed when I put down my profession as 'author'. They couldn't even advise. And then the two friends I have spoken of got jobs working on bomb damage in London. I thought of joining them. At the labour exchange in Reading I was told that there were no openings for unskilled labour. My friends, however, immediately discovered that it was just this unskilled labour which was desperately short in London. On their advice I went to the surprised but sympathetic manager of the firm they were working for; within less than twenty-four hours I was engaged; and on January 1st, 1945, I started work, as labourer to my two friends, on bomb damage, in Hampstead.

1945

All the time I was working, I lodged with a friend less than twenty minutes walk from Logan, and I often went round to see him in the evenings.

In the latter pages of this record I have largely suppressed many little faults which appeared in Logan's conduct and correspondence. The fusses and insinuations which occurred over his papers would be wearisome and almost endless in the telling; and in many—too many—of his letters were little hints as to domestic troubles.

Logan had never, I think, at any time of his life, undertaken the management of a house. In the few years, perhaps a decade or a little more, that he lived alone, he had a housekeeper. For the rest of the time, first his mother, and then his sister took all such troubles out of his hands. He once said to his mother, 'If the house is on fire, don't tell me.' The news of such a catastrophe it never became necessary to withhold from him; but he lived to the end blissfully, wantonly, unaware of scarcity in the larder, or the difficulty of getting servants.

The three women in his household, Mrs Russell, his sister, Mary, the cook, and Hammond, sacrificed themselves continually to him. If eggs came to the house, he had them all. Admirers from overseas sent him a steady succession of food parcels. Only leavings went to the others. He took these things as a right.

In peacetime, I had often brought him game—pheasants or partridges, shot by Kyrle. During the war these resources became scarce and trout failed when our river dried up in 1944. One day he seriously complained that I had been keeping him short of such delicacies.

He liked entertaining friends. As everybody knew, such pleasures were hard to indulge in war-time—everybody, that is, but himself; when this was explained to him, he took it for a vexation and an insult. He began to think that he was being thwarted, and the thought stole crazily into his head that if he were to live on his own he could lead a life of high spirits and continual entertainment.

I knew that he was fussing about domestic difficulties, but I did not realize until a year later that the enmity—for such it was becoming— which had shown itself intermittently towards me, was also manifesting itself towards his sister. We hid our troubles until they became too large and conspicuous for concealment.

He seemed to be deliberately estranging himself from the two he had most depended on—from his sister who for well over thirty years had seen after his well-being, and from me who had been for more than fifteen years the chief aid and companion of his intellectual work. It was at this time that I conceived a definite theory as to his condition, namely that he was the victim of a 'mother-fixation'. With age and the increase of his manic-depression, the power of moral resistance was becoming feeble in him. The demon was in his heart and gave no assistance.

He had lately become interested in Miss Mitford; one week-end, I fetched from my home and lent him a three-volume edition of her letters. I have often wondered if any thought or feeling was stirred in him when he read a particular passage. She was speaking of her father's behaviour in the decrepitude of his age. 'Once a week,' she wrote, 'he goes into Reading to the bench, and *then* he rallies; and nobody seeing him then could imagine what the trial is at home.'

Logan's mother had taught as her dearest belief that religion is a matter of the will and not of the feelings. Had her son but recalled that teaching now! He *could* pull himself together, and to strangers, or friends not known for long, he would present a tolerably decent front. To me indeed he frequently appeared the sage and artist I had known for so long. Of the friend I was less easy. He was often appreciative and still respected my judgment. Asking one day for my assistance with a piece of writing he said, 'I wish you would help me with this; you're so good at this sort of thing.' He still, most of the time, treated me as his literary heir. But always in his company I felt as it were like the keeper of some animal not quite tamed. I was for ever watching my step. I never felt, and was never to feel again, the security which had been, and ought still to have been the crown of our old friendship, so tested and tried, and that once had seemed altogether unshakable.

It was as though his spirit had been a crystal, many-faceted and filled with fluid, so that it appeared as a full and perfect thing; now the fluid had run out and the facets had become separated; each was entire still, but distinct altogether from the others. Whichever of his moods he revealed, it was complete; but there was little connection between each of them. His personality was disintegrating into its discreet components.

I'd not been long in bed after my first day's work—it was New Year's Day—when I heard a rocket. These explosions began to become more frequent. One evening the friend I was lodging with said to me, 'I'm afraid you've come to London just as a new kind of air attack is developing.'

'I'm rather glad than otherwise,' I said. 'I don't mean I want it to happen. But if it does happen, I want to know what it's like.'

It was a very curious sensation, living under that languid, slow-motion bombardment (the largest number of explosions I remember counting was eighteen in twenty-four hours). The feeling came back to me when I read the other day about the large meteors which may at any time hurtle themselves directly upon us out of space. I used sometimes to try and make myself believe that a rocket might, at the moment of my thought, be actually coming down through the roof of the house I was in. I couldn't do it.

One day Logan said to me, 'How do you enjoy the idea that you might be blown to eternity, without warning, at any moment?'

'Funnily enough,' I answered, 'I do actually rather enjoy it. I find I miss the explosions after we've had a quiet period. The point is, the only thing it's like is the Day of Judgment. As I don't believe in that, I'm not conditioned to be frightened of this sort of danger. Except at night when I've been woken up by one. Then, in that short, bewildered moment before one's reason has taken charge, I do sometimes wonder if one is just coming through the ceiling, and feel a moment of terror.'

'I suppose,' he answered, 'according to your theory that all our feelings are due to our being animals, it would be to an animal's advantage if it could enjoy danger. I feel the same as you do about these rockets.'

But he was still frightened by flying bombs, although very few of these were now falling on London. One evening when I was with him, we heard the siren; since piloted raids had ceased, this could only mean that a flying bomb was on the way. It was getting late, but he so anxiously insisted on my staying until we heard the 'All Clear', that I was forced to comply.

I told him also that I found the noise of explosions seemed to give a stimulus and purpose to my work. The cracks on a wall, or the defects in a ceiling, had an interest, an excitement about them so long as the bombardment was continuing. But to this observation he made no response. My daily, strenuous life was something beyond his imagination or comprehension. It wasn't just that he couldn't quite make out what I had to do. My work was not for him a palpable fact.

'Bob,' he said to me one day, 'do you *really* work like a workman?'

I assured him that this was exactly the case. He didn't answer, and began talking about something else. It was a sort of inverted delusion. With a touch of craziness he refused all cognizance of a demonstrable fact. Only for the purpose of indulging his furies did he accept my experience, and my status of a working man.

One morning, while I was at work in a district of shattered and scalped and blinded houses (an unfortunately falling rocket could do the most prodigious damage) I heard the familiar bang, with its long following reverberation of fading echoes. We were working in Hampstead and the noise came from the south of us. In the evening, after I had got home, I discovered that this particular rocket had hit a wing of the Royal Hospital at Chelsea, just across the open square from Logan. For the third time plaster was shaken from his walls and glass from his windows, and his front door was split and blown in.

Gone was the exuberance with which, in 1941, he had savoured the experience of disaster and melodrama. Destruction was widespread, and though the first patching up was usually done with speed, the final repairs began to be long delayed. During my work I discovered at times what seemed like favouritism in the choice of houses to be repaired. I was once sent with another man to clear some rubble out of a garden; the house that went with it was patched up; and then, for many weeks, empty and habitable it stood, among damaged and uninhabitable dwellings, and with a notice on it 'To Let'. Since the clearing out of the garden had been requested by a member of the borough council, it was not unnatural that the word 'racket' passed my lips when I spoke about it. I insinuated this word into an article which was published anonymously. I also used it—God forgive me!—in front of Logan.

His immediate response was a joke in his proper and particular vein of irony. 'If you find a racket,' he said, 'try and get in on it. If you can't, expose it.'

An awkward symptom of his craziness—and one that I have already called attention to—was his faculty for transmuting a joke into something serious. A humorously invented anecdote would turn, for him, into fact, and facetious principles became serious guides of conduct.

Repairs to his house were delayed. Of all the innumerable grievances which made him cry out so tediously during the last months of his life, this was the only reasonable one. Temporary fillings of windows let in the cold and made his sister ill; his own room was left dark and chill and draughty. One day he rang up the town hall, according to his own account, and, after a little argument about his repairs, he said, 'The whole thing's a racket!'

'You've no right to say such a thing; there's not a word of truth in it!'

'Oh yes there is,' said Logan. 'I've heard all about it from somebody who's in the know,'

'Who is he?' came the indignant question.

'You'd better let him alone,' said Logan—and mentioned threateningly some relations of mine whose names might impress the general public. Next day, he affirmed, some workmen were sent round.

That my information and my connections had been of apparent service to him had no influence in my favour. Accepting one fact of my life, that I was for the time being a workman, he laid himself out, most times that I visited him, to attack my temporary comrades. The matter, on the surface, was trivial; however it is not the weapon a friend uses which hurts, but the fact that he is making an assault. Unhearingly, unceasingly, he would pour forth his petulant attacks, in a voice whose angry flow I despairingly began to recognize, the voice I had heard in the hospital at Reykjavík.

The threat of his hostility became a settled part of our relationship. Now, and for the rest of his life, I knew that his friendship and faith were things I could not depend upon again. I resolved, in a mood that was almost pedantic, never, so far as it lay with me, to quarrel finally with him. My memories were happy, my gratitude to him immense; and I set myself the rule that I must always, where it was possible, keep these happier strains in mind.

There were golden, transient halcyons; these were usually founded upon literature. I used to borrow his volumes of Maupassant. It was 26 years or more since I had read this author, and I feared to look at him again, lest I should ruin a beautiful illusion of my youth. My middle-aged judgment supported the boy's, and Logan, catching my enthusiasm, shared this re-reading with me. He made me index his volumes, marking the passages and stories which I particularly admired, and, in these calms of appreciation, while we compared our finds, the old life returned for a little while; even the shortcomings of British workmen were forgotten.

Occasionally he would vent a normal grumble, which, from the healthiness of it, was refreshing. 'I'm altogether bored with the war,' he said one day, during that period when the result was assured, and only the time of it uncertain, 'aren't you? Or do you feel an overwhelming sense of joy at the defeat of Germany?'

'No,' I said. 'What I feel is an immense impending relief that soon no more people will be being killed; I'm not expecting any particular comforts when the war is over. We'll find just as much to grumble about.'

'I just feel bored with the whole thing,' he said.

One evening he rang me up. 'Will you come round as soon as you can,' he said, and I heard over the telephone the excited accents of his highest euphoria, 'I want your help. I've just found out how to write. You have to use gestures.'

He had taken up again his essay on Henry James, and when I arrived he began to read it out, beginning with the title.

'The *Adverbosity* of Henry James,' he read, nodding his head violently at the accented syllables. 'That's a good title, don't you think?'

He was never quite satisfied with this essay, and was continually altering and re-writing it; he never published it.

The altogether happy occasions were few. More often he was indulging his propensity for 'sticking pins'; only the weapons he stuck into me now, were larger, and more vicious in effect than mere pins. A curious subject kept creeping, with perfid significance, into his talk. He kept asking me about my financial prospects, and what legacies I might have to expect. Since I could tell him of none but a small settlement which, I devotely hope, is not likely to fall due till my old age, these questions were easily answered. Nevertheless he persisted with them.

The links were almost broken; the benefits involved and promised were becoming for him irksome drags to a relationship from which he desired to escape. I write this in the clearness of retrospective vision. At the time I saw only that I was becoming the victim of a craziness which I still hoped might vanish again, as he had seemed to recover from his Icelandic frenzy.

The questions as to my prospects were evidence that his conscience was still alive; and this was also illustrated, I think, by a piece of work he tried to put on me now.

There had been a rather eccentric American named Jonathan Sturges, an expatriate, living in England, and a friend of Henry James. Under the title of The Odd Number he published, in 1889, a not very good translation of thirteen stories by Maupassant; this book had appeared with a preface by Henry James. He also wrote a few original short stories, of which two were quite good. Logan had borrowed the letters which Sturges had sent to Mr R. C. Trevelyan, and he wanted me to write a portrait of him.

I do not think that I could have made a good job of this at any time. Beyond an admiration for his two praiseworthy tales, I felt no stirring and no creative impulse. The letters did not appear to me as of any greatly noticeable merit. All I could have managed, at the best, would have been hack-work of the sort which Logan so properly despised. Apart from all this I was too tired most evenings from my labouring to set about an uncongenial, or even a congenial task.

When Logan handed me over the letters, he said, 'You might make some money out of this, and it would be very useful to you by getting your name known in America. You could make lots of money then.'

He was planning—if so orderly a word may be used for so wild and disordered an impulse—to turn me adrift, with the pension of a lucrative American reputation. Though whether the most brilliantly drawn portrait of Jonathan Sturges would have earned so prosperous a fame is a matter for very considerable doubt.

This suspicion is not vitiated, in my mind, by the fact that he was often suggesting to other people special subjects for work.

'All my life,' he used to say, 'I've been handing people golden keys for golden locks. But they never use them.'

He never explained why he didn't use them himself. The subjects I remember his most often suggesting were lives of Antichrist and of St Teresa. But he didn't put these forward—as he did in my case with Jonathan Sturges—as money-making plans, or as anything else but the possible subjects of delightful books.

I warned him that I could not manage the job, and eventually he asked me to give him back the letters, which I did willingly enough. I think he attributed my failure to what he called my 'aristocratic laziness', instead of to its prime cause, an entirely proletarian fatigue.

When he took the bundle of letters, he said, 'That's all right. I'm getting somebody else to do my work now.'

What he meant by this, I didn't care to inquire. If he was getting temporary help because my time was taken up, well, there was no harm or injury in that. And I didn't want to hear what I half suspected might be the case. I didn't feel there was anything to be said or done about it; I had realized that he was on the way to losing his wits again; if he had become obsessed by some fixed idea, neither protest nor pleading nor argument would shame or shake him out of it now.

When the rocket bombardment ended—I think it was during Easter week—the zest, I found, began to go out of my work. While destruction was continuing, a wrecked house had for me an air of excitement and history: it was a memento of continuing danger. But once the danger was quite evidently over, the wreckage seemed nothing but a mess. When I had been working for about nine months altogether, I was told that if I kept on in my job for a year, I should find myself classed as a permanent building operative, and therefore subject, for an indefinite period, to the Essential Work Order. I decided, if I could, to get away from my employment.

I visited the publishers to whom I was already under contract for an unspecified book, and asked them to write me a letter suggesting that I should now settle down to work on it. From another publisher, and from friends well known as writers, I extracted testimonials, and took the whole lot down to the labour exchange, and made an application for my release; it would be hard to tell whether the surprise caused by my bundle of letters was greater, or the bewilderment.

To my own surprise, I found myself, within a fortnight, a free man again.

'Well, Bob,' said the foreman when I showed him my release, 'if you want your job back again, I'll sign you on tomorrow,' so I suppose I hadn't done too badly. It must be added, however, that unskilled labour was still very scarce.

During the summer Logan had retired for the last time to his inter-lunar cave. He still, as in other glooms, refused to see most visitors; he was still glad to receive me for short periods; and yet——

It is hard to describe the melancholy impression I received. It seemed to me as if he were, in contrived spite of our friendship, trying to re-pulse me. His emotions at these times were always languid and quiet; but in his continual asking me to revisit him, there was a sign that he still regarded our long friendship as an undoubtedly existing fact. And yet, as I have said, and yet—equally undoubted was the cold slow growth of a deliberate enmity.

His glooms were recuperative, and with such hoarded energy he was able, even to the end of his old age, to get through, during the period of euphoria, almost as much creative work as would, in his full working years, a more normal writer of equal fastidiousness. In his glooms he was drinking, it seemed, of a dark elixir, which raised and inspired the fully awakened spirit. Such drams and drugs cannot for ever be imbibed with impunity. The goblet, which seemed once to have held the purest waters of Hippocrene, contained now a sabbatical draught, crazing and envenomed.

He had likened his descents to those of Proserpine. This pretty image deviated now from appropriateness, yet so as to remain, in a way, hideously appropriate. What he brought up with him at his last ascent were not the bounty and strength of spring, but fruits of hell—fury, bedevilment, madness.

His gloom lasted until close to the end of the year. On November 9th, in answer to a letter of mine, he wrote on a postcard, 'I'm glad

223

you are getting on with your book. I'm still deep in my tunnel and see nobody. When I begin to emerge I'll let you know.'

As this peculiar malady increased, his emergences became more and more startling and suddenly marked. He had in fact, so his sister told me later, emerged on November 5th, four days earlier. The force which separated us was gathering strength; the avalanche had started. He first asked for my help over a trivial matter. During the war when such things were scarce, I had got hold of a watch for him in Reading. This needed repairing, and, when at his invitation, I went to see him, he asked me to take it to the jewellers I had bought it from. He gave me to show them a little record of the watch's behaviour. In his dates he mistook the century, and referred to its vagaries during the 1840's. (Nearly half his life, it must be remembered, was passed in the last century.)

The year ended with what was for me the last afterglow of his true self. He made a collection of words privately invented by some groups and families; to these he had added a few expressions which needed words to describe them. He proposed to get this list printed, and to circulate it among his friends.

The watch arrived, duly repaired, and in letting me know he said, on a postcard, that I had, by this service, 'perhaps unwisely, saved his life'. The only thing requisite now to his perfect content, he added, was to have his catalogue of words printed. When I next saw him, however, there was some catch; we should have to wait a bit. At the same time, as a Christmas present, he gave me a copy of the lately revised *All Trivia*.

I read it through, marked a few misprints, and noted a few phrases which still seemed to me capable of improvement. I sent him a list of these, saying, at the same time, that I felt his destiny was to survive until he had finished with *All Trivia*: that he would go on through his eighties and nineties, now altering a word, now re-writing a phrase, until eventually, when he was altogether tired with life, he would leave a book that was perfect. and not susceptible of any improvement.

To this I got in answer a postcard (31.12.45):

'Thanks and unthanks—for the corrections of *Trivia*—I accept some and gnash my false teeth over the others.

'S.O.S. I much want your help—can you come up one day soon—*I can give you lunch* if you send notice a day or two before.'

1946

I went up soon after this summons, wondering a little what he wanted my help over: something literary, in all probability, I thought. As usual, when I arrived, I stopped downstairs for a short talk with Mrs Russell. On these occasions, during Logan's euphoria, we would discuss his latest extravagances.

'He's becoming awful,' she said this time, 'he wants me to leave the house and go and live somewhere else.'

'You mustn't go,' I said, and I must confess that I was thinking less of her than of Logan. He was old and frail; I did not at all relish the thought of his being left in the house with nobody responsible there in case he should become seriously ill. I went upstairs determined to do what I could about it.

Logan was sitting in his room, in a dressing gown.

'Those corrections for *Trivia* you sent me,' he said. 'Some of them are good. But such things cause resentment which it's unsafe to bottle up; so I must bite you in return.'

This was a joke in his old manner; but it wasn't a joke which followed. I ought, he said, to have all my teeth pulled out; they were, he went on, a disfigurement which made people shudder when I came into the room. He ended his unexpected advice in a tone of venomous anger.

'Now there's something else I want to talk to you about,' and he suddenly launched out into a list of grave offences which I had committed in the past. Among them were my failure to find at once in the British Museum the catalogue slip of Duppa's aphorisms: the ancient escape, when my housekeeper had nearly made away with those cuttings of Mr MacCarthy's: the occasion when some proofs arrived during my visit to Scotland: my narrating of his accidental intoxication in my house: and the missing coins.

I was angry (I had not yet realized the extent of his mental disintegration), 'If that's all you can bring up against me after nearly eighteen years,' I said, 'I must have been a pretty good friend to you. But I can see that you're planning to do the dirty on me in some way.' I went on to point out the triviality or falseness of his charges. He took up the comic story of his drunkenness.

'Why did you do it?' he was shouting now, 'Why did you do it? You could see I didn't like it!'

'No one blamed you for it,' I answered.

'Why did you do it?' he shouted, louder than ever.

• 'You usually like having your leg harmlessly pulled,' I said. 'And I never told the story in front of you after I found you didn't like it.'

'And then,' he said, 'there's the mystery of the coins. I don't know what you did with them.'

'The only mystery there,' I said, 'is how you came to imagine that you ever had any others. You bought five pounds' worth——'

'*Five* pounds' worth!' he interrupted angrily, 'it was more like fifty pounds!'

I began to discover a sort of blankness in his eyes; it seemed that only at moments was he taking notice of what I said. He passed from my theft of the coins—he'd evidently determined to make that of it now —to the other offences, ending with the affair of the Duppa aphorisms. When I pointed out that I could hardly be blamed for a seemingly mis-placed catalogue slip, he said, with an air of finality, just as though I'd been on trial for a few weeks, and hadn't suited, 'Well then. We were unlucky.'

He meant, it was clear, to be shot of me; the end had come, and for ever, to what he had called—how few years ago!—our sweet collab-oration. How many times, I thought, had he said that his coming into the shop that day, when we first talked together about Jeremy Taylor, had been the luckiest moment of his life. I didn't say it, however. I was possessed with more than anger; a horrible realization was coming upon me.

He moved to his sofa, where he now spent most of his days, and Hammond made him comfortable; then he started on the meaning of his SOS. He put down all troubles to the presence of women in a house—an ungrateful sentiment since, for almost his whole life his com-fort had depended on women. 'I had forty years of comfortable bache-lor life on my own,' he said to me a number of times. He was born in 1865; he did not set up house on his own until after he had left Oxford, and he did not go to that university until he had been for a time at Harvard, and spent a year of business slavery in New York. In 1905 or 1906 he settled into a house with his mother, and ever since her death he had lived with his sister. To fit that forty years into his history is a problem beyond the complexities of relativity, and a question for mystical mathematics—but not of the city of heaven.

As he became fired with the subject I realized that Mrs Russell would be well advised to leave the house. The time had come for her to redeem that promise I imposed when I first came back from Iceland. This was the full voice of his old frenzy; I recognized it too horribly well.

The memory of nightmares becomes mercifully confused. I have a recollection of trivialities monstrously enlarged; and the utterance of a voice which ran on and on like a terrible and outrageous storm. I remember the feeling that Logan himself had receded, gulf after gulf, to a distance that was almost beyond infinity. The demon had altogether taken possession of his body. If this was his perpetual state, I felt, there would be nothing for it but to have him certified.

His present attack differed noticeably in one way from his more acute attack in Iceland. Then his rage increased during the day, so that by the evening his company was unendurable; now, as the continual talking fatigued him, he became quieter in the afternoon.

He did not become any more rational; that is, he held, without dignity, to his preposterous and unjustifiable complaints. The dictates of his rage governed his less frenzied moods. But the expressions of his unreason were quieter; the voice was more like his own.

'After all,' he said, 'I'm not a difficult person to get on with. When I had my yacht, and my skipper arranged to meet me, and some of his friends tried to persuade him not to go, he said, "I wouldn't disappoint the boss for a fish as big as a frying-pan." That must mean I'm an easy sort of person to get on with.'

But that, I didn't answer him, was when you were altogether a different person from what you are now.

I went home shaken with trouble and dismay, but having promised to visit him the next week. I had not been able to see Mrs Russell before I left, and when I wrote I did no more than advise her not to see him in the morning. An afternoon interview, I suggested, might be less unbearable. When I next saw her, however, I reminded her of that old promise. Daily encounters with him, I felt, could not be borne.

'Be selfish for once in your life,' I said. 'You'll make yourself ill if you stay. I know what it's like.'

It was then that we each discovered how, in late years, he had been slowly turning against the other. To me—and I think to her—the discovery had much of consolation in it. Although I had been pretty sure, for some little while, that Logan was gradually going out of his mind again, all the time there was the cruel question. 'Is it my fault? Is it something that I've done?' The answer should have been easy. For many years Logan had put up cheerfully and affectionately with all my faults. Now I knew for certain that something was happening beyond my control or my responsibility, something, nevertheless, that was more tragic and horrible than bereavement or a deserved unfriendliness.

Throughout January and up to the beginning of February I visited him at regular intervals. Each time he tormented me with a wit and verbal precision that was diabolical; each time when I left, he asked me to come again soon; and each time I went home to the anguish of an almost sleepless night. I entered his door during that period with the same reluctance and effort which I had felt at the hospital doors in Reykjavík. (Indeed, since Mrs Russell left, I have never dared pass his door again; the place has retained for me all the defilement and unconquerable terror of a haunted house.)

'Why do you keep on going to see him?' said Kyrle. 'He only asks you up to torment you.'

'Why do you still come and see him,' asked Mrs Russell, 'when he treats you so cruelly?'

'I owe him so much,' was the substance of my answer in each case; 'I've got so much to be grateful for that, whatever happens, I'm not going to quarrel with him.'

This was true. I was—I am—indebted to Logan for much, much more than can be expressed in words, or measured in terms of currency. I set this strictly to myself as the grounds of an unquestionable rule. But there was more to it than that, and deeper.

I once had a series of recurring dreams. The setting of each was different, but in every case I found myself involved in a mystery of which the solution was just appearing when I awoke. Never did I learn the answer to those nocturnal problems. I felt now that I was involved in a problem and an experience which I must see out to the end.

Looking back I have realized that there was something else I was searching for; I was searching, quite simply, for Logan. How could I woo and win him back, his old and true and estimable self, to that body which was now so dreadfully possessed? 'It wasn't my old friend lying there,' was said to me after his death by one who had known him many years longer than I, 'it was a screaming devil.' When, unbidden and unwelcome, the image comes back to me now of Logan in his sharpest outcries, it is the image of a spirit crying out on the fringe and verge of damnation.

Among the principal objects of his mania was the desire to get out of the house that sister who had devotedly and unselfishly seen after his well-being for more than 35 years; with her was to go the cook, Mary, who had stayed on without any thought of running away through all the dangers of bombardment in London. In this and other plans of his crazed spirit he expected my blind obedience.

Had Mrs Russell and I not been friends, and had there been, as there was not, any justification for his plan, I should still have felt strongly disinclined to concern myself with the affair. To appear as a sympathizing partner in the iniquity he proposed, was impossible. In that household then it was not feasible for Mrs Russell and me to have long conversations. Our interviews were snatched and furtive like forbidden assignations, and I didn't know that she had already made plans for her future. In an evil moment I asked Logan if somewhere among his house property there might be a pleasant flat where she could live comfortably.

He pounced on to this idea, like a cat on to a bird. He had no vacant flats, and he suggested that I should go that moment round to some decent apartments of his, with a cheque in my hands for £100, and offer it to the tenants as an inducement to leave.

'If you offer people cash down,' he said, 'they'll do anything.'

He evidently imagined that they would quit immediately, and that within two days his sister would have moved in. He wasn't in the least troubled as to what would happen to the people concerned, in the unlikely event of their succumbing to the temptation of his offer. Not unnaturally I refused to carry out so distasteful a task, but eventually I agreed to go to his house agents, and put the plan before them, and see if anything could be done about it.

On the way out, I stopped for a moment to talk with Mrs Russell. 'I've been trying to find a home for you,' I said, and told her what I was doing.

'I won't want to go there,' she said, and she told me how a friend had arranged to lease her a flat, when the present tenant left in April. We decided that I should reveal, in confidence, the whole situation to the house agent, and see to it that Logan's own flat should not become available for her. Even this was hardly necessary, for, the house agents, being a respectable and decent firm, declared very firmly that they did not wish to do this sort of business, which was, in any case, apart from all moral considerations, of doubtful legality.

Logan soon learnt of Mrs Russell's plans, but it became a fixed idea with him that he must get possession of those apartments. Any thwarting of this aroused a turbulent fury in him. He tried to revenge himself on his sister for making other arrangements by saying that her friend did not really want to let her have the flat when it was available. He sent me back to the house agents, insisting that I should talk to the head of the firm. Within a short time, as will be seen, he conceived the delusion that this gentleman, whom I had sought out only at Logan's request, was a particular friend of my own choosing.

Turgidly compounded with all this were the object and purposes of another mania. About this time the Minister of Health had made an appeal that people should put their empty rooms to the use of the homeless; if this appeal failed, it was hinted, compulsory billeting powers might be taken. I happened to be well informed on this subject, for it had been brought up and long discussed on the local district council of which I was a member.

On the top floor of Logan's house were three rooms: a largish one occupied by Hammond, and two smaller rooms, of which one had been used for visitors. For these Logan conceived enormous and profitable plans, and it was now that the word 'racket' which I had so unfortunately brought to his ken, returned intolerably upon us. His iteration of it became as exasperating as the perpetual slamming of a door or shutter on a windy night.

'There's a *racket* in all this,' he said (he always raised his voice loudly when he pronounced the word) 'and I'm going to get in on it.'

His plan concerning this was to offer the two small rooms—they were little more than attics—to the borough council, get them done up at public expense, and let them at five pounds a week, preferably to a friend who used to come up to London about once a month; or he might have them occupied by well-paying strangers. To make these rooms separately habitable, it would have been necessary to install a cooking stove, and extend the plumbing from the floor below. When I pointed this out to him, he failed altogether to comprehend the difficulties, and said, 'Ring up the town hall; tell them the whole thing's a *racket* and that you'll expose the whole lot of them if they don't get the work done.'

I managed to whittle this line of approach down to a request for information (which I already knew) to be sent to me at my own address. I had already explained the situation to him, if that expression may be used for an exposition of which he took in no more than if I had been talking in a secret language. His response was, in tones of surly sarcasm, 'Oh, *you* know *all* about it!'

When the papers came, I marked the significant passages, and explained them all in writing, and sent them off to him; I pointed out how little likelihood there was of rooms being requisitioned in a not very large house where lived two elderly people, and two servants, and a lodger. I had the salutary malice to warn him that if his sister left, with Mary, the situation might be different.

The last affair which troubled his bewildered and angry spirit was one over which I could honestly support and sympathize with him. I knew something now about bomb damage, and the ways of local authorities; Logan's house had been neglected, and obvious effects of bombs and blast were being left for repair at his own expense. I put myself to great trouble over this, interviewing officials and expressing myself strongly. It was refreshing to fight a battle for him which I believed in.

In all these affairs, he ranked me as one of his enemies. So hopelessly had his power of reasoning faded that even in the matter of his bomb damage he came to class me—I suppose through my mere association with the business—with those who thwarted him. As will shortly be seen he blamed me, not for failing to get things done, but as a cause of that failure.

The increase of his malady was illustrated by a return of that faculty which turned jokes into his serious beliefs. Throughout the war Hammond had charitably amused herself by getting bottles of drink for some of Logan's friends (I came high among that fortunate number). One morning, he began, as a joke, to accuse Hammond of carrying on a business in intoxicants, without a licence. He then insisted that I should ring up his solicitor, and ask what the law was. As the minutes passed he began to get serious. The solicitor, when I unwillingly questioned him, said that, very strictly speaking, any exchange of liquor for money without a licence was, in fact, against the law, but in the case given there was no danger of any action being taken. Logan had now worked himself into a fury, and when I gave him, in milder terms, the mild opinion of the lawyer, he said that Hammond's benevolent traffic was illegal and disgraceful, and must stop.

His attacks on me developed as inconsequently. He had had a party. While he was cheerfully telling me about it, a look of wild anger— that look which was becoming miserably familiar to me—appeared in his face. 'You noticed,' he said, 'that I didn't ask you,' and he went on to viciously explain why. I was not a suitably-mannered person to be asked to one of those parties; the chief reason, it seemed, was that I did not treat him with proper respect. As I had to give up work at home to visit him, and he knew this, I had not thought anything of his omission. I doubt, even now, if he had originally meant anything by it. At the time he spoke to me, however, he had brought himself to believe that he had been injured by the irony and jokes which had once, to his great enjoyment, passed so pleasantly between us.

As might be expected, his obsession of ruin loomed hugely now. Fifteen or sixteen years before, when he gave up his house in Hampshire, he had made a present to Kyrle of some pictures. 'The only condition I make,' he had said, 'is that you don't sell them while I'm alive. I'll never want them back, and after I'm dead, you can sell them if you want to: but not till then.'

He now began to ask for them back. It wasn't a subject to quarrel over, and when he requested it, I brought him a piece of Italian tapestry. At the same time Kyrle wrote him a conciliatory letter.

When I brought it up he said, 'Well, now I've been so successful with this, I think I'll try and get back a Chinese picture I let——have.'

'Why do you want to get it back?' I asked.

'Just to spite him,' he answered.

A little later he said, 'Kyrle sent me a most charming letter.' Then the darkness returned to his face. 'Did you help him with it?' he asked in a tone of suspicion.

These anecdotes may appear trivial, and it might, perhaps, be suggested that I myself have betrayed a peevishness, though milder than Logan's, in recounting them. Trivial enough, indeed, they may seem; to one intimately acquainted with Logan each was an occasion for horror and despair. In each is revealed a complete reversal of his natural behaviour. His behaviour to his sister and to me, the straightforward ill-manners, the humourless resentment towards good-humoured teasing, the niggardly reclaiming of presents—these, ten years before, would have been things beyond all conjecture.

I have said that I had undertaken the search, the spiritual search in a wood darker than Dante's, for the soul of my old friend.

When we were in Iceland I had hung out in vain the lure of a linguistic question; now I tried the revelation of some small literary discoveries. I told him one morning of some beautiful passages I had found and copied out from the works of the seventeenth-century divine, Thomas Fuller.

This was one passage which I read to him,

'Music is sweetest near, or over rivers, where the echo thereof is best rebounded by the water. Praise for pensiveness, thanks for tears, and blessing God over the floods of affliction makes the most melodious music in the ear of heaven';

and this was another,

'When we behold violets and primrose fairly to flourish, we conclude the dead of the winter is past, though, as yet, no roses, and July flowers appear, which, long after, lye hid in their leaves, or lurk in their roots; but in due time will discover themselves.'

Not as once, like the moth to the lantern, did his spirit fly out at the lure of bright phrases; no tears came to his eyes now as visible homage to the beauty of words; dead, dead, altogether dead seemed his dull response, 'Yes, that's good. I once copied out some phrases of Thomas Fuller's.' And then no more was heard of Thomas Fuller.

Early in February I went up to London to visit him. He was in bed when I arrived.

'People have been saying,' he said, 'that the time has come for me to give up writing. To disprove what they say I've been writing a series of essays on the pleasures of old age. I think you'll agree that I've succeeded.'

He began reading aloud.

I will say no more of what I heard than that I feared the advice he mentioned had been only too wisely given.

He was at least good-tempered while he went through his reading. But when he got up and settled for the day on his sofa, his demon took absolute charge of him.

After Logan's death a friend of mine observed that madness is like one of those diseases which distort the face. The acquaintance is entirely recognizable, and yet a hideous and immense difference has come upon him. Since his death I have realized that Logan's actions, at this period of his life, were not susceptible of moral condemnation; at the time, however, it was undeniably Logan who was there, and whatever cool judgment the intellect might arrive at, the heart could not assent to it. It was still my friend, my old friend, once so dearly loved, who was boiling with diabolical cruelty; mingled with a huge sorrow, I realized that I was coming to hate him. My affection was there, warm and faithful, ready in all its strength should Logan present himself again, but now it had no possible object for attachment.

He seemed to be under the influence of a malignant drug, like a man who has drunk himself angry and cruel and vituperative. And all the time I had that feeling as though I were communicating with a soul at some incalculable distance. Where was he, I seemed to be wondering? Where else, came suddenly the monstrous reply, where else but in hell!

Relief came only in moments of humour; the great joke was about his death-bed. He talked about this in the highest spirits, and with obviously no apprehension of that actual death which was now but a few weeks off.

I have said that he was no longer susceptible of moral judgment, and yet there was a moral to be drawn from a part at least of his anguish. The Icelandic doctor had, to a certain extent, been correct in speaking of Logan as a selfish old man. In complete devotion to his art he had taken for granted all the ease and comfort which the world, and his companions, gave him. Those companions had gradually become for him no more than the sources of all that made his life smooth and easy; as separate live beings they were ceasing to exist for him. The punishment for selfishness is to turn the world into a solitude. Into such a solitude Logan had strayed, a vast and terrifying desert where he could discover no companionship, or affection, or sympathy. At times, as his talk flowed dreadfully and incessantly on, he seemed to be talking to himself in a room empty of people. I felt that he was hardly aware of my presence. Only in the surprise and unfamiliarity of new friendship did he now feel the sense of companionship which he needed.

'. . . just beneath everywhere I walked or sat, six inches under every floor, or pavement or plot of grass on which I played, there seethed the flames of Hell into which I might be sucked down at any moment.' I have quoted already this sentence of Logan's. The menace which darkened his childhood, was tormenting, inscrutably transformed, his latest days. It came over me as I watched and listened that this was the spectacle old writers had tried to represent when they described the perishing of damned souls. At times I could easily have fancied in his eyes the reflection of satanic flames. Was it some warp of the spirit, bequeathed from childhood, tormenting him now, so that, as a dog

in a trap bites its rescuers, he railed and snarled against those best able
to comfort him? His mind must have been running on his early years,
for the task which he had lately set himself was to edit a selection from
his mother's letters (Those letters which he had been studying not long
before his attack of madness in Iceland).

On that February day, a large part of the afternoon was spent in the
not altogether uncongenial occupation of having indignant interviews
with local authorities about Logan's bomb damage. For this he insisted
on arming me with a letter, in which he described me as his secretary
(the position he had lately abolished), and the relative of some titled
people, whose names he gave; fortunately this letter was almost
entirely illegible. The report of my interviews made him angry.

'You should have told them it was all a *racket*,' he shouted, 'and that
you were going to *expose* them. But *you* know best,' he added; 'you
will do things your own way.'

I managed to calm him a little with the information that I had
arranged to meet an official in the house itself, and to point out to him
the unrepaired damage.

He wanted more out of me than this task, namely to interview the
house agents again. Since no time was left for this, I agreed, when he
asked me to stay up for the night.

He had spent some eight full hours of the day in unmitigated talking,
and the resulting exhaustion calmed his rage a little. I slept on the sofa
where he had passed the day. He asked me to leave open the door into
his bedroom in case he wanted Hammond and she didn't hear his bell.
'She sleeps like a *dog*,' he said rather peevishly. When the night was
over, I didn't find this surprising.

Sore and in anguish from the day, I didn't find sleep easy. When I
dropped off, I was woken up soon by Logan's thunderous coughing. It
struck me that he had difficulty in clearing his lungs; this failure was
eventually one cause of his death. Three times he rang for Hammond;
twice I had to go up to her room. The third time she came down of her
own accord. Logan, finding himself unable to sleep, wanted one
particular book to read. He couldn't lay his hands on it, and, instead
of taking another from the shelf above his bed, he woke her up to look
for it. Even for the devoted, unselfish, patient Hammond, this was too
much. Not finding the book at once, she told him he'd have to do
without it for the time being, and went back to bed.

In the morning I had to encounter his frenzies again. I have told about a dear friend of mine whom Logan disliked, and how, when he tried to talk about her, I would stop him. On that morning he twisted the conversation round to her, and then suddenly, like a gramophone record running much too fast, he hurried out his invective, anxious, evidently, to accomplish his attack, before I stopped him. I thought of leaving the room, but decided that my best course was to stay quite silent and expressionless. This vexed him.

'You don't like hearing this,' he said.

'I've often told you,' I said wearily, 'that this should be a forbidden subject between us.' I think he felt that his malice had fallen a little flat; to give a wound seemed to be most of the time the only communication of feeling he was capable of. I sometimes regret that I didn't show him then a wise aphorism of his own. 'Since few things—as we know —more annoy other people, why do we delight in crabbing their friends?'

Such regrets often troubled me then, and, indeed, have not infrequently troubled me since that time. It has been impossible not to imagine potent turns of conversation which might have brought him to himself. Futile imaginings! I knew then, and since, by the strength of memory, I can be certain that he was beyond the reach of all expostulation. No appeals to affection or honour or morality, no argument, however logical could shake him, alone as he progressed along the undeviating and solitary course of his increasing mania.

He sent me off to the house agents with another betitled letter, and orders for an impudent course of behaviour, which I had no intention of following. I managed to bring back a placating and reasonably convincing story.

As usual on these occasions my lunch was brought up, like Logan's, on a tray, and we ate in his room. He seemed capable for the time being of gaiety, and I made him laugh with bawdy stories I had picked up a few months back from my fellow workmen.

In the afternoon he lay on his bed. I sat beside him. He was quiet, partly, I think, from a sedative, and partly from the bad night he had spent. The evening before, when he was tired, his talk, though feeble in sound, had flowed forth as fervidly as in the morning. Now, as by a miracle, quietness of demeanour seemed to be not far off.

'You always give me wise advice,' he said at one moment. 'What do you advise me to do now?'

'Don't do anything now,' I said. 'Your sister has made her arrangements. Don't interfere. She's going to go. Let there be a truce. Everything's settled. Don't do anything to quarrel with her. It'll make you unhappy if you do. Be friends now.'

'Oh, we're quite friendly now,' he said. 'I've just sent her down a very friendly letter.'

Mrs Russell's interviews with Logan had been so painful as—no wonder!—to spoil her sleep and threaten her health, and her doctor had forbidden them. The brother and sister had accordingly done their business together by notes. The note which he had sent down this day had been conspicuous for a peculiarly vicious and quite unfounded piece of vituperation.

The thought of this evidently roused him. 'Do you know what she's planning to do?' he said suddenly, 'she's going to fetch a van and take *all* the bed linen away so that I shall have none left! I don't know what else she may take! While I'm up here she may take all the furniture away and leave nothing for me!'

This delusion grew, apparently, until he had an image in his mind of all the lower part of the house denuded of furniture. After he was dead I discovered the cause of it. Mrs Russell had pointed out that half the bed-linen was hers, and that not unreasonably, she would need this when she went. What was left, she warned him, might well not be enough for his purpose. (He had fantastic dreams of parties and paying guests.) From such rational seed arose the monstrous growth of his delusion.

He fell to grumbling quietly. Why couldn't he be let alone? All he asked was to live in peace, with no domestic troubles, and see his friends when he wanted to.

'I want,' he said dreamily, 'to be old and gay and obscene.'

He lay weak and quiet for a while. Then he began speaking again, moving his jaw as though to do so were a heavy task.

'I lie here,' he said, 'thinking that they may get me certified. It does happen to old people, you know. And I shall be left here all alone for the rest of my life, and none of my friends will be able to come and see me.'

Now I saw him as infinitely pathetic, and I found myself forgiving him all his injuries and malice. Indeed, the danger was a real one. The very way he expressed it was evidence of this. Here, though in a milder form, was the same claustrophobic delusion which had troubled his madness in Iceland, when he thought that I had kidnapped him, and had shut him up, and was holding him to ransom. I have sometimes thought that part of his crazy rage against his sister arose from the fact that she was living on the ground floor, between him and the street. I think, too, that since she had lately endured the worst of his frenzy, she was now sharing my role, as a witness and living testimony to his growing mania.

When the time came for me to go he said, 'Give me some good advice. Write me some wise moral advice in a letter.'

I never saw him again, except in his coffin.

Associating with my thoughts about Logan there was then something nearer to comfort than I had known for some time. Had I—it seemed possible—glimpsed a hope of returning friendliness? Vain hope, and false interpretation! As drink is said to paralyse at first the higher senses, something, fatigue of a particular extent, or the physical effects of a sedative, had dulled down for a while the outward heat of his frenzy. I had witnessed not the reversal, not even the short arrest, but only a fleeting palliation of his mental decline.

Having made a number of corrections and additions in my bibliography of Jeremy Taylor, I wrote and asked him about the proper person to write to at the Oxford Press in connection with it. At the same time, I told him that I would not be able to come and see him in the following week. I ended 'I'll be sending you some moral observations, and general advice, wordly and unworldly, soon.' He answered (28.1.46) on the back of my letter (this practice, as I have already shown, he had adopted as a form of insult). The letter is almost illegible. After giving me the name of my requisite correspondent, Mr Kenneth Sisam, words follow which are indecipherable: then he goes on—

'I tried to put you into touch with him once, but you didn't feel like doing what I suggested. You might have been of the greatest help to this man, all of gold, but you didn't feel like it. He would have paid really well for your help.

'I'm writing crossly I'm afraid, but all your struggles last week have failed. The men have been taken off the job here as I expected; your new friend Mr —— of ——'s [the manager of the house agents] completely got round you. I've gone into palpitations over the telephone this morning, so if I saw you just now I should *bite* you.'

As to the first part of the letter, I am quite uncertain as to the lucrative help which I might have given to Mr Sisam; I am still farther from certain that he would ever have needed my help. I think the train of thought came zigzag from the memory that I had been making from time to time a collection of vernacular names for flowers; Logan had suggested that I might use these one day in an essay to be submitted to the Society for Pure English.

I thought this a good occasion for moral advice. In answering his letter, I pointed out that biting old friends was not a process likely to bring happiness. And I quoted his desire to be 'old and gay and obscene'. These three adjectives together, I suggested, did call up a jolly picture, but that of the three qualities implied, gaiety was the chief requisite. Age and obscenity alone were not a merry association. I put in some generalities, into which he might read, if he would, my determination never to quarrel with him and to guard for ever all that I had ever felt towards him of gratitude and affection. I added that I would visit him the following week, bringing two more of Kyrle's pictures which he had asked for.

The result was a very strange letter, with its curious misnumbering of points. It was written on sheets from a packet of unlikely paper which was never meant for writing letters or anything else on[1]. This was the letter he sent (9.2.46):

'I'm afraid I shan't have even time enough to bite you next week. All your efforts last week have made the muddle here worse than ever.

'(1) Town Hall has stopped all war repairs, though obviously needed.

'(2) I have offered to do them at my *own expense*, but this can't be done without permission from Town Hall.

'(3) Your friend at ——'s Mr —— has turned out to be deeper than anyone in the racket and a person of a shady reputation.

'(4) In chatting with my sister you have said that I have told you in the strictest confidence that Julia doesn't want her and Mary in the flat beneath her. So at least my sister alleges, and has commanded Julia to write me to say that she is wanted. The fact that what I tell you in confidence is repeated to others has upset me more than anything. On Wednesday next I have to arrange—

'(1) aiding (?) J—— to write her lying letter.

'(2) Drafting a new will with my solicitor and signing the same.

---

[1] His last note to Mrs Russell, to parallel this, his last letter to me, was written on the backs of seven little pieces of paper, consisting of five used pay-in slips from the bank, and two cancelled cheques.

'(3) Seeing Sir —— M.P. to explain to him that he has come to live in the most corrupt borough of London.

'(5) Arranging to transfer my property from ——'s to other hands.

'So you see I shan't have time even to bite, but if you will leave at the house the two Chinese pictures it will be some comfort.'

In the quivering and barely legible script of this and the preceding letter, I recognized the handwriting I had seen on another epistle of his. This he had given to me in the hospital at Reykjavík. It announced his kidnapping, and was addressed to the King of Sweden.

I don't know if the allusions to other people need any comment. Perhaps it would be proper to say that the vague accusations in his third paragraph were less than without foundation; he had curiously confused the stigma which had at times and in some places justifiably attached itself to repair of bomb-damage, with the business of an entirely respectable house-agent. His accusation against me had no truth in it, and his evidence for it was due to his own perversion of other facts. As for the plans which were to prevent my visit, those that he carried out were already completed before that day.

For the last few years, it seems evident now, Logan had been trying many devices to estrange me, so that I myself might break up our friendship; or failing that, to discover some grounds to justify a breach on his own part. The rule I had in all honesty set myself, to remember old joys and benefits, and never to quarrel, had proved an all but impregnable defence in that blind and shapeless struggle. Now, as though desperate with the foreboding imminence of death, he had pounced, snatching at a false extenuation to accomplish the reckless and urgent breaking of our friendship.

After much thought, I wrote to him as follows about his untrue accusations:

'A moment's quiet reflection should have told you that such behaviour on my part was utterly out of character. As far as it has been in my power through all this unhappy affair, I've done my best to make things go as little unhappily as possible for everyone. And it has always been my practice to avoid, when it's possible, saying or passing anything on that gives pain. For these reasons alone I should never have said anything so cruel to your sister.

'Mrs Russell did tell me in conversation that you were saying that J—— didn't want her. I assumed it was you that had told her this. If it didn't come from you, I don't know who told her. All I know is that it wasn't from me she heard it.

'What I said in general at the end of my last letter, I might as well now repeat more particularly. No quarrel between us shall ever come from my side. I shall never forget our many years of happy friendship, of such profit and pleasure to both of us: books and travelling and talking and working—for all this, whatever may happen, I shall always be immeasurably grateful.

'I'll bring up the two Chinese pictures, and drop them in on you on Wednesday morning. If you find you've more leisure than you expected, leave a message, and I'll pay you a short visit.

'You once wrote, "For souls in growth, great quarrels are great emancipations." But, believe me, for souls done growing, great quarrels bring nothing but desolation.'

I went up to London on that Wednesday. I saw Hammond; no message had been left for me. As I heard afterwards, she had besought him, with tears, to see me. Was it that, by this time, he had already injured me too deeply to endure my company? Mrs Russell advised me to go up in spite of him. This might have been wise. Who can say? All I know is that I was too sore at heart and sick of spirit to accomplish so strenuous a gesture.

I stayed for a while talking to Mrs Russell, and the good friend, who was providing her with a home. I told them for the first time some details of Logan's Icelandic madness. But it hadn't needed this to convince them that he was now out of his mind again. We all knew that there was nothing to be done. The great quarrels of his life were accomplished. His sister and I had been thrown brutally and violently out of his demoniac life.

The week after this an old friend of Logan's visited him. Among his complaints he suddenly said, 'When Bob Gathorne-Hardy comes to see me, I'm not even allowed to give him some lunch on a tray.'

One small contact remained. Kyrle wrote to him, taking as his occasion the return of his Chinese pictures. He pretended that he knew little of what was going on, that I had not told him, but that he had seen how depressed I was after each visit. Under the guise of defending my character, he pleaded for me; as to the pictures he said, 'If you really need the money, I gladly return them; but if you are doing this to hurt Bob, it's not worthy of you.'

Logan received this letter, and answered it, after he must have known that his accusation against me was not true.

'Thank you,' he wrote (13.2.46), 'for writing and returning the pictures. I didn't ask for them back for any lower motive than greed—

certainly not with the notion of annoying Bob. I'm hard up, to tell the truth, and hope I have found a way of selling profitably some of my possessions—I have debts to pay and my illness is very expensive. I live on capital, as all Americans have to do now. I have never for a moment doubted Bob's loyalty and complete goodwill—his prudence and wisdom I have doubted, as I think he likes to do things his own way, and sometimes—I am sure with the best will in the world—he has repeated things I have said that have made trouble. But let that all be forgotten and I hope that he will forgive me for being more irritable than I should have been. But I am dosed with M & B and if you know that drug you will know the effect it has on one's temper. Give Bob my love.'

I am not writing with any intention of defending myself. My purpose has been to describe Logan's character, and, where I can, attempt to explain it. But I may be pardoned for saying that only once had he complained of my repeating things—recently, for the first time, and falsely. It is a curious fact that he was not, at this period, being dosed with M and B.

This letter, it will be noticed, was more temperately written than those which I had just received. Where any formality of relationship was requisite, he was able to exert a little control upon himself. His second madness had not yet taken such entire possession of him as did the first. It is probable that only in the presence of old, familiar friends did he betray the full and furious extent of his craziness. There was a race now between utter insanity, and death.

March had hardly come in when, one morning, the telephone rang. Mrs Russell was asking for me. 'It's over,' she said; 'Logan died early this morning.'

I set out at once for London, and when I arrived I said to Mrs Russell, 'I wept for Logan when I thought he was dying in Iceland; but I can't weep now.' It seemed to me as if he had been dead for a long, long time, a period to be measured, not in weeks or months, but in years. I may borrow once more that saying of one who had known him for half a century; it wasn't my old friend who had just died.

Quite soon after his actual death a friend urged me to write down my memories of him. Slowly, as I set about this recovery of time past, I found that I was also recovering my friend to whom I had given for many years so large a part of my affection.

I have fallen short, no doubt—though adhering as closely as I could —from the austere principles of art so assiduously preached to me by Logan; but to one of his earnestly prescribed rules, I have been entirely faithful; I have told the truth. I would not kill him again after his death, nor pay him the false tribute of flattering distortion. Yet, as I observed at the outset, the truth itself can mislead. To close my history now might be to leave in front of the reader that chill and obscure cloud which for some time darkened and blinded my own spirit whenever I looked into the past. Logan was not the creature I have described in the latter pages of this book.

Among his favourite poems, written by a poet from a younger generation, was, as I have said, Mr T. S. Eliot's *The Boston Evening Transcript*. In it these lines occur:

'turning
Wearily, as one would turn to nod good-bye to Rochefoucauld,
If the street were time, and he at the end of the street.'

Where is the end of the street I must look to, if I am to see him, undarkened by cloudy vistas, standing in his brightness and proper selfhood? I needn't look to the 'end of time' or anything like it—not so far even as to the beginning of our friendship. From my search, both in the heart, and among recoverable facts of the past, the object and goal seems to have been achieved some ten years back, before our disastrously-ending journey to Iceland. Now, when I call back Logan to my thoughts, reason and the affections present his image to me as he was about the years 1935 to 1937. Of him, then, the companion whose friendship meant so much to me, and of whose affection I could so reasonably be proud, let me, in Hume's words when he wrote his own life, conclude, historically, with his character.

EPILOGUE

His proper height must have been about six foot, but his bulk and his stoop made him stand apparently shorter than my own equivalent stature. At the times I am thinking of, he was sluggish, but the weakness of ankles had not yet made him incapable of reasonable walking. He rarely 'went for a walk', but if need be, he would go on foot for more than a very short distance. Once, in Teneriffe, when I was taking a bus with the intention of coming back, botanizing, by a circuitous route of a few miles, he actually came a little of the way with me, before walking home by the direct, short course to our hotel. This was so unusual, that I began worrying as to whether he could manage it, and whether, should he fail, he would be able to ask the way, or explain where he was staying. I was so careful in giving him some short Spanish sentences, in making sure that he knew the way, fussing in fact, that he said with good-natured impatience, 'You needn't worry about me; I can look after myself; after all, I *have* travelled and been for walks before.'

He had the faintest vestige of an American accent, which, with familiarity, very soon became quite imperceptible to me. All that I could notice of it afterwards (apart from his use of 'around') was his way of saying 'gas', which he pronounced, transatlantically, as 'gaz'.

In formal matters, he liked to think he was very formal and correct; when he was having a luncheon party, for instance, he used to open windows, in order, he said, to get rid of the smell of cooking, that enticing, aerial antepast which greets one inevitably, and by no means unpleasantly, in most houses that are not very large. He did this with the preoccupied manner of a very correct host. The smell rarely faded quite away, but he had soon forgotten his cares on the subject, and didn't trouble. This formality of behaviour was, in truth, the thinnest of thin shells. One day I came in and found him wearing a medal, an unglorious Belgian medal, given to him for work among refugees in the 1914–18 war. It was meant to outshine some imagined glory of my own. When the joke was over, the medal remained, forgotten; some people, not intimate friends, were coming to lunch. He greeted them, and entertained them, all the time still wearing the medal. Almost exactly the same thing happened on another occasion when he decided to wear a Guards tie, because, as he truly pointed out, this was an adornment which I myself was not entitled to.

244

In congenial company, and when his spirits were high, he was exceedingly gay—too gay, it might sometimes have been said, and I have known him talk down a whole tableful of his guests. His conversation was not artificial; or perhaps it would be truer to say that it showed artifices which were all his own. When once he was excited by good company or a good subject the trammels of conventional manners proved themselves to be as the silk of spiders; they clung about him, but in shreds; and although he might reveal now and then a momentary, flickering awareness, as of something faintly clinging, this hardly affected the movement of his talk.

Once, in the irresponsibility of his euphoria, he asked a small party, of which I was one, to—of all things—a birth-control luncheon. The meal itself went off all right, as in the general noise the conversation at our table couldn't be overheard; but, with the speeches, trouble began.

'I have always felt,' the first speaker proclaimed, rather irrelevantly as we thought, for the public character referred to had died a bachelor, 'that the character of the perfect father was to be found in the late ——'

'——!' said Logan, loud enough to be heard several tables away, 'but —— was impotent.'

This youthful speaker was followed by another.

'Oh, my God,' said Logan; 'this is the greatest bore in the world.'

We tried to hush him.

'But I *know* him,' he said.

The speech, it is true, was a very long and very tedious one. Logan evidently tried to behave himself. It got too much for him.

'Bob,' he said to me and not in a whisper, 'stop him! Hit him on the head with this bottle,' and he brandished the proffered weapon.

We didn't stay to the end. Our conspicuous exit, which might have been so embarrassing, was, to his guests at least, nothing but a relief and a release.

He was not like the man in Sassoon's poem 'Who talked of serious things at Lady Lucre's table'. His public conversation was light and ironic—when it wasn't verging on the outrageous. I do not mean that he became rude to his guests; but he would trounce, downrightly, though with good nature, an opinion he didn't hold, or the praise of an author he didn't think much of. Even in matters of literature, though he would be vehement in condemnation, he was rarely, on public occasions, vehement in praise; when he did give high praise, it was most often uttered dictatorially, though not without fun, or in the tone and wording of a paradox.

When Miss Lehmann's novel *The Ballad and the Source* appeared, he was enthusiastic and discriminating in its praise. Some people came to tea with him, and he introduced this subject by daringly announcing 'It's the best English novel since *The Golden Bowl*.' Miss Lehmann herself, however, humanly delighted by the praise of a fine writer, would, I am certain, be a little uneasy at finding herself planted so assuredly on so ticklish and, for all its eminence, so slender a pedestal. (This incident took place, it is true, in the decline of his years; but the moment was one of afterglow, as not infrequently appeared, when for awhile his old self would re-emerge in all its regular brightness.)

An innocent snobbishness might creep into his conversation; and he was not averse to letting slip the names of distinguished or titled people he was acquainted with. His own social weaknesses he has acutely and revealingly pictured in *All Trivia*; nevertheless, by an odd paradox, he was a great deal less than often aware of them himself. Occasionally, however, he glimpsed the mild philosophical infamy he had been guilty of.

Once he was asked, as a lion (it was during what he called a 'swim-gloat', when he was being pleasantly talked about), to a week-end at a country house—a house whose name, I must say, sounded more glorious overtones in his imagination than in mine. (I'd never been there myself, but many of my friends had.) 'I'm afraid I was guilty of a snobbish weakness yesterday,' he said to me, 'I was at Lady ——'s, and I couldn't help letting it slip out, as though quite casually, when we were arranging to meet again some time, "I shall be down at —— for the week-end."'

Such endearing and unobjectionable little displays of weakness detracted in no way from the pleasantness of his company; furthermore, in effusions of a similar mode were crystallized, gem-like, small anecdotes of a more enduring worth. 'I can't believe——' he would start, and then, almost invariably, after a pause, he would say, 'As Henry James used to say, "When I say 'I can't believe anything', what I mean is that I do believe it".'[1]

Almost as frequently, when he started a disquisition on the need for care and art in the writing of prose, he would recall the time when

---

[1] Concealing its origin, Logan had made an aphorism out of this, 'When we say we are certain So-and-so can't possibly have done it, what we mean is that we think he did.'

Robert Bridges and Bernard Shaw had lunch together with him. Shaw, holding forth, said, 'If anyone finds that he takes more than ten seconds to think of the word he wants, he should give up writing,' upon which Bridges, grumbling into his beard, muttered, unheard by his fellow guest, 'What nonsense the man's talking!'

He had a large circle of friends whom he met on terms of lightness and jest and irony. Just as, in making his anthologies, he would beautifully discard the longueurs and dispirited passages of a writer, so with these friends, some of many years' standing, he treated himself to a garland culled from the shining aspects of their lives and characters.

We live, each of us, in a world of our own making. Logan's, apart from the world of books, was somewhat gimcrack, and largely a second-hand one. He would often regale me with stories and principles of life which seemed to me very doubtful; when I questioned them he would say, completely unshaken, 'That's what So-and-so tells me.' He once related to me, about a friend of mine, a mildly scandalous story which I happened to know to be not only untrue, but impossible. I told him this, with my evidence, upon which he retorted, 'That's what—— tells me.' The story was fixed and he couldn't be troubled to unbelieve it. More than once after my refutation he told me the same story again. This little weakness was harmless enough, though I sometimes shudder to think how my authority may have been used, from a misremembering of some remark, to support opinions I never held or facts I had never asserted. (That it sometimes happened, I know.) Had he not written, 'People say life is the thing, but I prefer reading'? There was a darker truth behind it. He shrunk, shudderingly from the fullness of life, and didn't care to question overmuch convenient, carelessly accepted, and comfortable assertions.

Often enough, too, he would twist his encounters into a likeness of something he had read. Once he wrote to me, after visiting a clerical household, 'It was a scene from the Barchester novels. Mrs —— was Mrs Proudie in person.' To make a good story, that household *ought* to have been pure Trollope; therefore he reported it as such. Now, I was in a position to know, from my own experience, that it was nothing of the kind; the lady in question, with whom I, too, was acquainted, bore neither in behaviour nor character or appearance the remotest likeness to Mrs Proudie.

In the *tête-à-tête* privacy of a familiar friendship, he was free from all exigent etiquette of the dinner table. He was then even less reluctant to dominate the conversation, and was liable to set forth on long, often-repeated monologues, which became, in the end, more than a little wearisome. On the other hand, laying aside the playful and even face-tious note with which he lightly regaled his guests, he could, if he put his mind on a subject, bring a wit and a sensibility into his talk, an exposition of honest scholarship and fine discrimination, such as I have never heard before, and scarcely hope to hear again.

There are aspects and attributes of a friendship which cannot be communicated. If these cannot be experienced, they are incompre-hensible, for in such matters we can only come down to Montaigne's 'It was he; it was I'. There are also intellectual and social qualities in a friendship which may be shared and communicated. Something of these, as I discovered them in Logan, I can make an attempt at recording.

His ordinary talk, both gay and serious, had, like the prose of any master, its peculiar curve and break and flow—its own phrasing and rhythm, all of which made his casual remarks easy to recall, even though it might be over many years. His more solemn enunciations would have required learning by heart. I once asked him casually about Buddhism. He said —— I cannot, alas, write down his answer as he gave it me. Brushing aside its myths, he presented the teach-ing of Buddhism as a stark and godless and inspiriting philosophy, a rational belief that consoled by the very frigidness of its austerity. 'It is,' he said, 'the only one of the great religions which, if one leaves aside its myths, appeals directly to the reason. Santayana has a great deal of Buddhism in his temperament, though not, of course, in his philosophy.'

On this occasion he revealed a depth of intellectual feeling which only at the rarest of heaven-sent moments glimmers up from translu-cent depths through the glassy surface of his prose. The effect on me was that I read, under his remembered guidance, a number of books on the subject, and even bought some coins bearing the portrait of a Graeco-Indian prince, whose conversion, in the third century before Christ, gave rise to one of the classics of Buddhism.

These aspects in Logan of public and private intercourse were sub-ject to his mild depressive mania, with its cyclical moods of elevation and depression. Before these moods had developed excessively, the light exuberance of his euphoria added a tang to his more public conversation, which was none the less enjoyable for being a little alarming. In private this fever of the mind led, it is true, to the planning of extravagant practical jokes; but it also brought an alertness of spirit, and a heightening of sensibility, which made him at times the best company in the world.

His attitude to affection and friendship was unusual, and brought a problem into his life which he never solved—never, I think, attempted to solve—for the simple reason that he was never clearly aware of it. It was not possible to anthologize a close friend with whom he was often in company. He was not blessed with a capacity for balancing the faults and merits of a friend, and rejoicing when the sum was a creditable one. In consequence, even when his affections were humble, he might give way to unseemly complaints and expostulations. It was perhaps remotely symptomatic of his attitude to personal relations that one of his favourite sayings was 'The only true happiness is a rush of thought'.

His chief faults—I mean the faults of his proper self, and not those inspired by the possession of his demon—were two. The first and worst, indeed his only fault that was absolutely vicious, was that implacability which he ranked as a merit, the fact that he considered it might be at times wrong to forgive. To balance the wickedness of this principle I must add that I hardly know of more than one case in which he really indulged it. (One or two others I suspect.) The other fault was his innate suffusion of selfishness. It was not the common sort of selfishness which leads a man to take the last cake on a plate or the best seat by the fire; I mean the sense, which almost unaware he possessed, that the world of his own life was a world where everything should go on for his benefit and comfort. In his best years, this fault was under good control, and not often, until his mind began to give way, did he surrender himself to it.

Of his minor faults almost all of them arose from a capacity for self-deception which I have rarely seen paralleled, and never in persons of comparable intellect. I once noticed in a Chelsea antique shop, a pretty pottery figure, Italian, of a cupid playing on a guitar. It was, I thought, too large for my house, and, as it had greatly taken my fancy, I pointed it out to Logan; he immediately succumbed to its charms and, after making quite certain that I wasn't intending to acquire it, he bought it for himself.

A few days later, when some people had come to tea, he called attention to the figure. The guests properly admired it, and one lady asked him how he had got hold of it.

'I was passing a shop,' he answered, 'and it caught my eye. I fell in love with it at once, and went in and bought it.'

I said nothing at the time, but afterwards, feeling that this was a fair occasion for teasing him, I said: 'How *could* you tell such preposterous lies about the figure? Saying that *you* had discovered it!'

'Did I say that?' he responded, with an expression of puzzled interest. 'Why so I did! Now I wonder what in the world made me do that!'

If he had thought that I really wanted the figure for myself, he would quite certainly have given it to me, for he was very generous, with a generosity that was even more of the heart than of the purse. He enjoyed giving presents, and did so with a peculiar grace, as though the recipient were granting him a favour. When he was staying at my mother's, in Suffolk, we all went, with my sister-in-law, to a miraculous junk-shop in a village, where one could then buy beautiful old chairs, for instance, more cheaply than ugly modern ones. My sister-in-law was spending money that had been given to her as wedding presents.

She wavered for a long time between two chairs. When, at last, she had made her choice, Logan said, low and pleadingly, 'May I buy the other one for you? I should be very grateful if you would let me.' I have told how, when Kyrle Leng and I bought some Italian iron gates for our garden, Logan begged that he might pay for them, and that when we consented he was deeply and feelingly grateful.

Indeed, his attitude to money in general was curiously unworldly. He regarded five hundred a year as poverty, and two thousand, or a little over, as really great opulence. He was not quite happy about it when his income was at its largest. When the slump of 1929 and the following years noticeably diminished his American dividends, he said to me, 'A very curious thing has been happening to me. When I was really rich, I found all my desire for possessions fading away. Whereas before I used always to be peering into antique shops, and falling in love with things, and wondering if I could afford to buy them—I felt nothing of that. I began to think my brain was getting dull from old age. And then when my income dropped I discovered all the old desires suddenly coming back again.'

It may be imagined, then, that his little faults were so easy to forgive as hardly to require such a process. When his grave ones had displayed their uglier heads, as once or twice happened, he was afterwards, I noticed, unexpressively and rather pathetically ashamed. This was revealed—and only to people who knew him well—by an expression that seemed almost more puzzled than penitent. Though he rarely made any form of apology, I found these exhibitions rather touching, and the pity I felt always dispelled my resentment and stirred my affections.

He liked luxury and required comfort. The former he could do without; absence of the latter made him querulous. When he went to a hotel, whatever its pretensions, he always tried to engage a room with a private bath; but he never minded if, as usually happened, this was not available. But when he had to put up with a lesser standard of comfort than he was used to, he would often vent such petty complaints as did not enhance, in a companion's eyes, the dignity of his character. I was once staying abroad with him at an hotel where we had boiled potatoes at every meal. He always demanded butter to eat with them, and would be quiet, almost sullen, with impatience until it arrived. He evidently felt that some excuse was required, and accomplished this by saying, deprecatingly, 'I'm too old to be asked to eat plain boiled potatoes.'

In matters of health, he had a superstitious fear of undefined germs. In Teneriffe, I noticed that he never ate the inviting salads put before us. When I asked him why, he said, 'They say you're liable to catch infections from salads.' Since, as I believe, the chief danger attributed to such indulgence is the danger of typhoid, and we had both been inoculated against this, I felt that he was being a little over-cautious. At one time of his life he avoided theatres and buses, for fear that their occupants might infect him (at the same time he had no fear about entering the more confined space of a taxi). Yet he endured the risk and discomfort of several grave illnesses with great courage and cheerfulness.

His politics, so far as they were fixed, were a kindly, moderate Fabian Socialism. In a model of brevity and irony he has expressed his feelings about property.[1] He used to say that all morality was in favour of Socialism. This opinion, however, he would qualify with the observation that only under capitalism could those circumstances arise which

---

[1] 'It's endorsed by Society, defended by the Church, maintained by the Law, and the slightest tamperings with private property are severely punished by elderly Judges in large horsehair wigs. Oh, certainly, it must be all right; *I have a feeling that it is all right;* and one of these days I shall get someone to explain why the world keeps on putting adequate sums of its currency into my pocket.

'But of course it's all right——'

All Trivia

made possible the fruition of artistic talent; and that fruition he valued above all other harvests of human endeavour. And it should be added that his political feelings—they hardly amounted to anything so sturdy as opinions—did not deter him, if he was in a malicious mood, from trouncing those who strongly maintained them.

It could not be said of him with truth that he was charming, or entrancing (or, still less, glamorous); and yet there was that about him which requires to describe it some other, still unemasculated adjectives from the vocabulary of sorcery or enchantment. There's no word that will exactly do, for there was never anybody else exactly like Logan. At his best he inspired, without causing terror, apprehension, and, without pomposity, respectfulness. He has declared that his family was liable at any time to throw up an ogress; and he was not himself without a touch of the ogre. When he had died, I was aware, amid a myriad tumultuous feelings, of a sense as though a manacle had been broken or a prohibition removed. (This was altogether apart from the circumstances of his last days.) A little reflection showed me the prohibition—one that I hadn't any desire to be free from; but I had been as it were within sound of a voice saying, 'You can try to write for money now, as often as you want to, and whenever you like.' It was, fortunately, even if I ever had this capacity, too late; nearly eighteen years of Logan's tutorship had planted his principles too firmly in me.

His intimates well knew such prohibitions, which, if they were flouted, left the perpetrator a little hang-dog in Logan's company, and uneasy in his own heart.

He had three rules which he imposed as essential on all aspiring writers. Carry a notebook, and write down any striking words or phrases which you hear, or which come into your mind: mark the passages in your reading which take your fancy, and make an index of them (if he lent me a book of his own, he asked me to mark and note such passages in it): read the dictionary. To fall short in any of these rules implied a lack of seriousness and a distaste for proper application.

He was as generous with critical assistance as he was with material gifts. He would devote much time, and the most passionate attention, to picking fleas out of the work of a friend. On these occasions, when all reasons for formality had gone, he would praise or blame with the utmost candour. The blame was salutary and helpful; it had this advantage too, that, purging away all flattery, it made the praise especially welcome. Sometimes, in a most magnanimous way, he would, on thinking it over, retract a criticism. Once he made me cut out a phrase that I had thought rather pretty. Next morning he said to me, with an expression of extreme gravity, 'I committed a dreadful crime yesterday. I murdered a beautiful phrase.' It was the phrase I had crossed out. 'Put it back at once,' he said, 'all night long I seemed to be hearing a voice, "I'm a beautiful phrase, and you murdered me".'

He was just as ruthless with himself. No serious criticism of his work disturbed his temper. He had written, in his early middle-age, a number of quite accomplished, but dead poems. To these, wistfully, and even a little guiltily, he was forever harking back. On one appropriate occasion I called his attention to a theme which he had treated both in verse and in a *Trivia*; the prose was opalescent with an exquisite myriad-hued polish, and all alight with irony and alertness; the poem was dull and flat as a nicely cut paving stone. As I have said, he cherished his verses with a sort of illicit passion; for all that, he accepted the truth of my contention with a complacence that was altogether happy.

For the complete man appeared in the writer, and only there. He had lost his religious faith early in life; but the moral structure or pattern of his character remained still as it had been shaped by his puritanical and peculiar religion. His passionate and exacting devotion to art could hardly be paralleled save in the life of a religious devotee. To write and polish and re-write—this was the ecstasy and divine exasperation of his life. 'How lucky we are,' he once said to a friend who was a painter, 'how lucky we are to have each a delightful talent which we can tend and nourish and indulge!'

In the world of art, his only social faults were a mild and amiable vanity, and a tendency to be sometimes over-severe towards those who sold their talent in the form of journalism, or who sought for a cheap fame.

As to his vanity, when he was reading out a new work, he could not refrain, at times, from calling attention to a felicitous phrase, or the successful use of an idiom, or some other device. 'You see how effective that is,' he would say. And sometimes if a problem in writing cropped up during conversation, he would illustrate a happy solution of it from his own work, reading out the passage with evident satisfaction.

In many cases the necessity of writing for money has, it is true, a devastating effect on fine talents; more damaging in its consequences may be the desire for immediate acclamation. Have we not all of us seen young writers of promise surrendering, on the impulse of a too

EPILOGUE

early success, to work which turns into a parody of their own immature but marketable productions? This second falling off from integrity is to my mind more reprehensible than the first, as to which Logan was, I think, too intolerant. He would justify his castigations by saying that he himself had lived obscure and in poverty for over twenty years; but since his poverty consisted of five hundred pounds a year during Edwardian and late Victorian years, he was not in a position to judge a man who is short of money. He was, however, eminent among those who have despised unworthy fame for the sake of perfecting their art.

His rejection of such fame was a fine sacrifice, for he did not accept initial obscurity without any reluctant flinching. He once said to me, 'If *Trivia* had succeeded when I first printed it, in 1902, the encouragement would have made a big difference to me.' He implied that he might have become more of a creative, and less of a linguistic and critical writer. In this, I think, he misjudged himself. Apart from *Trivia* his little creative writings—*The Youth of Parnassus*, and *Stories from the Old Testament,* and his poems—were not outstanding; his critical writings, his one biography (Sir Henry Wotton), and the few more general essays which he wrote are of a much higher order. The stimulus of original neglect impelled him to polish and perfect and limit *All Trivia* to the brief and irreplaceable little masterpiece which it is; nor can we regret the apparent failure which led to the composition of his reminiscences, portraits, criticism and studies of language.

The reception of Sir Henry Wotton had not been all that he hoped; he once, in a moment of weakness, said to me, 'I ought to have been given an honorary degree for the work I did on it.' This may have been true; yet, again, one such work was enough. He himself declared what excellent and enlightening discipline it proved; but a series of such books must have deprived us of others more worth having.

Some rare and fortunate men have been granted a birth towards the upper slopes of Parnassus; to most artists the ascent is a matter of infinite toil and a deliberate choice. If we judge such a man by the distance he has traversed as much as by the altitude achieved, Logan Pearsall Smith deserves all but the highest praise. He started with little talent, and less promise. I have seen a schoolboy essay of his, a discourse on Carlyle, composed when he was about sixteen; it is entirely undistinguished, and I should never have prognosticated for its author the least eminence or accomplishment in literature. His mother, who at first had small hopes for him in that respect, encouraged him in the pursuit of letters. His association with Walt Whitman, as he himself has told, provided an inspiration of inestimable force. In his early years at Oxford, he had made friends with members of that 'Great World' to which he always gave too much importance. Some quarrel, or gradual estrangement, separated him from these friends, and he started afresh with associates of a finer stamp and infinitely more befitting. This 'fortunate misfortune' confirmed his destiny. He settled down to a hard-worked, scrupulous, and never to be concluded apprenticeship in the life of letters.

It was a favourite joke of his to speak of himself, up to his latest years, as a young writer, who had almost learnt his job, and was just embarking upon a career of the greatest promise. He was always learning; when he was 79, he contracted from Flaubert (such fads are as catching as a cold), a dislike for the double genitive, for instance 'the decay of the love of letters'. About the same time, he made his discovery—for it almost amounted to that—of adverbs. A year or two before he had almost come to the conclusion that no words or constructions should be used in writing which would seem uncouth or unnatural in common speech.

His continued re-writing of *Trivia* was not just a polishing indefinitely prolonged. Double genitives? He must cut them all out; or rather not all, but most of them, for there must be no pedantic surrender to such rules, any more than to the rules of grammar ('Idiom before Grammar' was one of his regular apophthegms). Adverbs? He looked at his book. His introduction of these was not a cosmetic titivation; it was as though, before his eyes, gaps had suddenly opened in his text, gaps that could only be filled up with these particular parts of speech.

His path had been like that straight way of the Gospels. After a false start, in imitation of Maupassant, he had modelled himself upon Pater; he even, as I have said, wrote of himself in a journal as though he were a new 'Imaginary Portrait'. Meantime his own private, crisp, ironic voice crept in, and he had found himself. Very few and slight were his subsequent lapses into forms and themes unfitting to his talent. Owing to some occult torment of the spirit, he could rarely or never face in composition the greater depths of feelings. In almost every other such case, a writer would have made up for the deficiency by the uncritical insertion of slipshod or false emotion; Logan, although I believe he never faced or defined this incapacity, composed as though he had considered and allowed for it with the coldest and most pedantic precision. His only lapses on this account were into a sometimes unhappy facetiousness (and this facetiousness, I believe, time will happily sere away). In such circumstances to write so meticulously within limitations which he could not have defined, appears to me as one of the more noticeable miracles of art. Very few have equalled his particular accomplishments—the resolute eschewing of all that was outside his powers—together with the culture and perfection within them, of a very considerable talent out of the very smallest of insignificant beginnings.

It was a favourite saying of his that anybody can learn to write good prose. He was speaking from the evidence of his own case. In making so wide a generalization, he was forgetting that, in one quality requisite to artists, he was more than richly endowed.

Art is an aesthetic activity; I should not have considered this truism worth writing down, were it not so often and so strangely ignored. An artist must have experienced something in the nature of ecstasy before he can make aesthetically effective the baldest drawn line, the severest harmony and sequence of notes in music, or the quietest of sentences.

As I have already told, Logan exhibited towards literature an angelic, an almost miraculous sensibility. Being, even in this matter, human, he did reveal gaps in his powers of literary appreciation; like every ageing man he was deaf at times to the song and message of younger contemporaries; and he was apt, I think, to over-value work by some men of his own generation (their names are not mentioned in this book).

In other arts, his taste was less finished. Of music, he was largely ignorant. As a young man he had followed the crowd to Wagner's operas; but his later taste was more for composers of the eighteenth century, Bach, Handel, Mozart and Haydn. Among those of our own days, he would hardly acknowledge any except Van Dieren, although he did allow, grudgingly, that he received pleasure from some works by Mr Benjamin Britten.

When I had known him for a few years, he bought a gramophone. He wanted, he said, to make an anthology of music, as might be done with literature. But he complained that all experts, when he consulted them, gave him to understand that it was wrong to cut up big works, and that he ought to listen to them in their long entirety. With my slight knowledge, which, however, was larger than his, I helped him to make his selection. I cannot remember all we got. He had already decided on the dance of the blessed spirits, from Gluck's *Orpheus*, and the slow movement from Beethoven's Ninth Symphony; to these he rather strangely added the *Blue Danube Waltz*. Of my own suggestions which, when he heard them, he enthusiastically accepted, I recall only the slow movements from Bach's Concerto for two violins in D minor, and from Schubert's piano trio in B flat. Just before we made the purchases, he had heard on the wireless a work by the obscure eighteenth century Mozartian composer, Stamitz. He was very disappointed at not being able to get hold of a record of this.

He had a fixed idea that almost all English music was intolerable. It used to vex him when I suggested that Byrd, and even more Purcell, might be looked on as great composers; like Roger Fry with St Paul's Cathedral, he was apt to forget that they were English, and he would evade the subject by saying, 'Do you like So-and-so?' mentioning some contemporary composer whose work he knew I disliked as much as he did.

In matters of the stage—as opposed to the drama as it can be read—he was remarkably ignorant and inexperienced. As I have already stated, it has been suggested, and I believe with some truth, that he never altogether sloughed off his Quaker disapproval of the stage (curiously enough, in spite of this, he had, as an undergraduate composed some facetious dramas; but since there was no merit in them, it may perhaps be casuistically held that there was no sinfulness either). I believe that during the period of our friendship he did not go more than about once or twice to the theatre. I am under the impression that he was once persuaded into witnessing some performance of Shakespeare, from which he returned with dismay. Once, and once only, on a strange aberrant impulse, did he ask me to go to the theatre with him. He had decided—heaven knows why!—that he would like to see Mr Noel Coward's *Cavalcade*. He bore up as best he could; towards the close of one scene of more than usually revolting sentimentality, he murmured to me, with the air of a man jesting in the face of disaster, 'I really must wipe my eyes'; he was actually doing so, with mock pathos, when the lights went up, and the audience around us saw in Logan, no doubt, a soft-hearted, elderly gentleman, overcome by the tenderness of a sickly little incident. Harmoniously, and with no reluctance, we left before the end. The impact on his sensibility was such that he retired to bed for several days, groaning, when I saw him, with reminiscent horror.

I have never understood what made him go to this vastly successful piece, for he altogether ignored the finer spectacles to be seen on the stage. I was surprised one day to learn that he had never been to the Russian Ballet; he had never seen even Pavlova or Nijinski. 'Why, Logan,' I expostulated, 'you profess to live for art; and here was an art coming to its finest and greatest flower, right under your nose! And you did nothing about it.'

'My trouble is,' he said, 'that I'm an anti-snob snob. When I found that everybody was going, I had to keep away.'

Indeed, through all regions of art, his taste was fastidious, and his dislikes innumerable: in all regions, that is, but one. In the world of radio, curiously, he displayed a more catholic susceptibility. Once, in the early days of our friendship, when he was staying with me, I risked —later on, I think, I wouldn't have dared it—I risked making him listen on the Children's Hour to one of the Toy Town plays, from the miniature saga of Larry the Lamb.

'I shan't like it,' he said imploringly. But when I suggested leaving the room, where we had just finished our tea, he said, 'But I want to hear the end of this.'

After that he used to make a point of saying that the best things on the wireless were to be heard in the Children's Hour. For all that, however—and a larger effort could hardly have been asked of him—he diatribed against many things on the wireless programme; in particular, as I have said, he would object to English music, and, above all, to what he called English clean fun.

Over pictures he was more knowledgeable, though less than one might have expected from the intimate brother-in-law of Bernard Berenson. He became doubtful of works dating from about the mid-nineteenth century onwards. In Paris once we went to the Louvre. We looked at Manet's *Olympia*; expressionless he gazed; 'Do you really feel that that's a picture by a great artist?' he dubiously asked me. I doubt if he ever much enjoyed a work by Cézanne. Sickert he admired, and many pictures by Mr Duncan Grant; almost at the very end of his life he became fascinated by the work of Mr John Piper. I think his favourite among all paintings was a picture in the National Gallery, the little St Dorothy, by Francesco di Giorgio.

Even with this endowment of sensibility, the technical labour of perfecting his style was a huge one. His life and all around him were, if necessary, to be sacrificed for its accomplishment. I do not think that he ever formulated this principle as a definable rule; he was probably not aware that he held it; but his sense of values was thus founded, and thus were his aberrations intensified. In the innermost core of his intellectual being he was a substance which wrote and which read.

From this it does not, of course, follow that he was a man without passion, or not subject to strong affections. It did follow, however, that when he began to suffer from a mental disintegration, his strongest powers were not those most requisite to combat a moral decline. Nevertheless he had, for a large part of his life, mastered a strange and unruly spirit. He had made himself into the man and the friend and the artist, whose intimate friendship it was, for many years, my pride and happiness to enjoy. If an athlete becomes lame, or if age makes him decrepit, we do not therefore expunge the memories and record of his triumphs; still less should we do so when the mind of a fine artist becomes afflicted. Logan remains privately for me the friend I knew so long, and have rediscovered in these backward explorations; and to the books of the artist I would allot a place on the shelves of literature close to those writers he so greatly admired, close to Halifax, and Addison and Chesterfield, and others who from inconsiderable beginnings have perfected a fluid and evasive talent into something as bright and lasting as crystal.

A month of two after his death I came across a small work by that patron of Jeremy Taylor's, Lord Carberry, whose ghost we had deferentially visited together, some seventeen years before, at Golden Grove. The wounds in my spirit were aching still, worse perhaps than when I first received them; I had lost that 'most precious of the gifts of heaven, hope'; the incidents and feelings of recent months had become, by his death, unalterable. At this small discovery my interest freshened, and I caught myself saying 'How excited Logan would have been!' A resurrection was taking place within my spirit. I was beginning—salutary grief!—to miss him. Indeed in the composition of this book I have seemed to be writing, strangely enough, as though for his eyes and appreciation and criticism. 'What would Logan say to this epithet?'— the query would often surprise me—'or to the run of this sentence?' The tormenting madness, dead already in the flesh, was dying away in my memory, and there was beginning to be restored to me the incomparable artist, the strict and beneficent mentor, together with the friend, close and cherished, of so many years' standing.